REAL STORIES, REAL WOMEN

Women Who Win

Inspiration, Resilience, and Ambition from Women Around the World

SHALEEN SHETH

DR. DEEPA JHAVERI

DR. MANJU SHETH

CONTENTS

Foreword

By Shabana Azmi

Actress of Film, Television and Theater

My favorite stories are those that not only entertain but also inspire and ignite change in our society.

This book is an inspiring collection from remarkable women who have defied expectations, broken barriers, and are trailblazers in every walk of life, whether they come from the business world, technology, healthcare, arts, culture, or social impact. Each of these stories deserve to be heard, celebrated, and shared. In a world where gender inequity continues to persist, we need to remind ourselves of the boundless potential that lies within us.

When women are empowered, society as a whole benefits and barriers crumble. I hope these stories will inspire you to rise above limitations and challenge you to achieve your dreams.

I commend the women in this book for sharing their empowering stories and amplifying the voices of women. They help us celebrate their achievements and pave the way for future generations of women to dream without boundaries.

We are all Women Who Win.

Introduction

Welcome to *Women Who Win*. We're thrilled to take you on a journey through these pages, where you'll meet women from every corner of the globe, each with a story that will inspire, uplift, and empower you.

Think of our collection as a gathering of friends, swapping tales over a cozy cup of coffee. These aren't your typical stories. These are the stories that don't always make headlines, but they're the ones that matter – stories of courage, pushing boundaries, innovation, creativity, leadership, and taking life head-on. Relatable, real stories from real women, whether it be your neighbor, colleague, friend's mom, doctor, a local business owner, mentor, or your child's teacher.

In these pages, you'll be introduced to women trailblazers coming from all walks of life, such as a heart-wrenching mother-daughter story of resilience and overcoming trauma, a woman's journey battling breast cancer as a technology executive, a mom's relatable experience with starting her first podcast, and an inspiring journey with embracing one's facial disfigurement and empowering women through it.

You'll be inspired by women with a mission to change the world, such as a dedicated human rights lawyer from Trinidad fighting for refugees, a changemaker's powerful fight to end gender-based violence, women philanthropists at the world's largest NGO serving midday meals in schools, and grassroots nonprofit leaders empathetically supporting domestic violence survivors in navigating cultural taboos.

You'll follow one woman's path in leaving the corporate world to empower people through yoga, meditation and mindfulness and learn from women breaking barriers and paving the way for others, including an international female commercial pilot bringing gender equality to the world of flying, a Kashmiri poet preserving her heritage through the arts, a charter school executive director advocating for DEI in the classroom, and the first black woman to chair the Massachusetts Commission on the Status of Women.

You'll experience a day in the life of a New York City fashion editor and one of London's youngest city councilors. You'll gain insights from a senior entertainment news editor on the future of media and technology. Step into the lives of women working on Wall Street at 21 years old. Get inspired by two entrepreneurs who started a Malaysian food business to celebrate their culture and a Great British Bake-Off contestant's sweet journey as a global pastry chef.

You'll learn the success secrets of women in business and how kind-heartedness and giving back was integral in who they are today, including a pharmaceutical CEO's dedication to philanthropy and what a motivational speaker learned from growing up in one of the world's largest family businesses. You'll hear a museum board member's perspective on how art can be used as a tool for activism and be inspired by one woman's journey to educate thousands of young girls across Asia. You'll read about a couple who had significant impact in their communities by starting a cultural center and art school. You'll meet the women behind Akshaya Patra, one of the world's largest NGOs, empowering children through food and education.

As you flip through these stories, you're not just reading words on paper. You're stepping into lives, feeling their struggles, connecting with their dreams and motivations, and celebrating their triumphs. With this culmination of our stories since the launch of our website, www.WomenWhoWin100.com, we would like to thank all of the remarkable women who've trusted us with their personal stories. To our readers, we hope you will share your journey with us.

Sangeeta Moorjani

Life As a Balance Sheet

What has your journey been like as a woman in finance?

My journey started from a little town in Gujarat, India. From there it has been a tour around the world. I did all my schooling in Dubai, went to college in India, then lived for several years in Toronto and have now lived in the Boston area for two decades. I feel fortunate that life's journey has taken me to new places, new experiences, and new relationships. In many ways, this journey has shaped my approach to life, teaching me that change is inevitable, and reminding me to always give new things a try. Now coming to financial services, one could easily say my career choice was a mere coincidence. I started as a summer intern in Citibank, in Dubai during my MBA. It was a beautiful new building and I was drooling at the chance to work there! Fast forward a few decades and I've stayed in finance. After 25 years in the industry, I can say it's more than a mere coincidence. I've always gravitated toward facts, figures, data, statistics. I anchor decisions by rolling through them head first and bringing my heart in next, so it's no surprise I was drawn to financial services even though it's not an industry that a lot of other women from my graduating class were drawn to. Personally, I've been committed to changing the narrative around the need for women in finance. Women make strong leaders and great decision makers. We need more of them in every industry, and finance is definitely one of them.

I've always thought of life as a balance sheet. For those of you who are accounting or finance geeks, assets and liabilities have to be in balance. Similar to finance, life is seldom a bed of roses or just thorns. It's about taking the positive with negatives. That has always been one of my life mantras. I am fortunate to be able to combine my life values and work interests and merge them into one in finance.

You are currently at Fidelity, working primarily in the retirement business. During the pandemic, people had new challenges with savings and retirement planning. What is your perspective or any trends you have noticed? And what is your top advice for retirement planning and saving this year?

It's very natural to worry about money and finances. As women, we are innately caregivers and worriers. We want to make sure that everyone is taken care of. And as a result, we can put ourselves and often our finances on the back burner.

To top that, we have just gone through a global pandemic. There are lots of trade-offs women are facing. The number one reason women state for not taking care of their finances is lack of time. Responsibilities at work and at home are just too great and we are pushing things to the bottom of the to do list. Another phrase I hear too often from women is, "Finances are complicated; I let my male partner, father, or someone else do it for me." I've always been surprised by that response. There's no secret that money helps us live the life we want. So how can you ignore spending time on your finances? Spending time on one's personal finances is simply about being smart when it comes to one's life. A question every woman (and man) should ask: What happens when we don't prioritize our money and finances?

You are also passionate about a service-driven mindset, embracing service and helping others in every aspect of life, and you bring this to the businesses you run at Fidelity. Tell us more about this. What inspires you to encompass service into your life?

> "Spending time on one's personal finances is simply about being smart when it comes to one's life. A question every woman (and man) should ask: What happens when we don't prioritize our money and finances?"

One value my grandfather and my father lived by is the belief that service of the poor is worship of God. There are two key words here: First, "poor" is not just poor in money. I had to stop thinking narrowly. Look around and we see people who are poor or lacking in money, confidence, friendships, relationships, courage. Second is "service." Once you understand what someone is lacking, you ask yourself: How can I serve, how can I help, what can I do to ease the burden for someone, to bring a smile to someone's face? Service doesn't have to be complex or require a lot of planning. Just be you – a note of encouragement, listening to someone who is looking for advice, giving money to a cause you are passionate for. A few years ago I went through my cancer journey and some of the most meaningful things that helped me were sweet notes of encouragement left at my door, in my email, in my mailbox, or through texts. How simple, and yet tremendously powerful! Service can and should be a joyful experience for the giver and receiver.

Anusha Nanavati

Passionate About Sustainable Architecture

When did you realize you were interested in architecture and design, and how does that relate to your family's experience in healthcare and schools?

Though I come from a family background that runs healthcare and schools, honestly, it was all right with my parents that I pursued my interest in architecture. Luckily, my parents were very open and left my career choices up to me. It wasn't particularly difficult for me to take up a creative field for myself because when I was in school I had a very strong imagination. I loved drawing, painting and anything to do with design. Every time we would travel, I would explore the art, culture and design that cities offered. Following my interests and my creative nature, I decided to take up architecture.

You are a "sustainable architect." Can you tell us more about what that means? How have architecture and infrastructure changed and become more sustainable over the years?

David Attenborough mentions in his beautiful documentary *A Life On Our Planet* that using anything that cannot be used forever is not sustainable. Sustainable architects apply a similar principle in which we use local and renewable materials that are eco-friendly and have low carbon dioxide emissions. We create systems that reduce the energy consumption of spaces by using renewable energy sources such as solar, wind, hydro, etc. Ultimately, we try to work in harmony with the environment to create green or ecological architecture.

Over the years, most countries have developed a strong sustainability agenda for their nations. This includes giving a LEED certificate to buildings that are highly sustainable, making city centers completely automobile-free on certain days or even months, and using sensor and other data-driven technologies to optimize the use of energy. Within the United Nations 2030 Sustainable Development Goals, Goal 11 aims to make cities inclusive, safe, resilient and sustainable, and outlines key metrics to make cities sustainable. There is a lot that is being done to make Earth sustainable, but to be honest, we have a long way to go.

We have the work of certain architects like Jeffrey Bawa to look up to for his sustainable designs. His use of natural elements like light, wind, and materials that perfectly suit the tropical climate that he designed for are marvelous and still so relevant, enhancing natural ventilation and getting more of the outdoors indoors.

Of all the projects you've worked on, which has been your favorite?

For a designer, every project is like their own baby; each is highly cherished. And yet, I feel biased toward my project called Edible Cityscapes. It grew from my architectural thesis and was based on the idea of sustainable, urban farming. This is especially special because I love food and I wanted to explore the food chain through my designs. I wanted to provide a self-sustained system where the user experiences the entire process, from growing vegetables to cooking them to finally eating them, in engaging spaces. Unfortunately, our vegetables go through considerable processing before they reach our homes. What we finally receive are vegetables highly depleted in nutrients. Edible Cityscapes utilizes the dead spaces of homes to help people grow their own fresh stock of vegetables.

I feel so grateful for the opportunity I received to do something similar in a squatter settlement in Mumbai. We were a team of four, and we managed to work on prototypes that would help the people of the settlement grow fresh vegetables on their roofs and verandas. We conducted workshops to educate them about the process, which was a great learning experience for them and for us, too. We also managed to put these prototypes in pre-primary schools of the settlement where kids would learn how to grow and appreciate their own vegetables.

What are some of your hobbies? What do you do for fun?

> "Ultimately, we try to work in harmony with the environment to create green or ecological architecture."

My biggest hobby is to bake! It's something that I am also growing as a business. The best feeling is to wake up to something you love doing, and this is one of the things I love most. I have always enjoyed learning and exploring new things. I recycle candles, learn classical music, and have tried my hand at pottery, and have totally loved all of it.

Being an architect, I am also passionate about changing the spaces in my own house. You will see me playing around with artifacts, planters or adding new art and colors, which will completely change the look of any room.

Sonica & Rayna Arya

Relying Upon the Existence of Hope

You wrote a book entitled "Hope Exists" about a personal experience that changed your life. Tell us about the experience, and what you learned from it.

Rayna: I was just 12 years old, on a school hike, when I was hit by a car that sped away after flinging me onto the highway. I suffered a traumatic brain injury (TBI) and lost a lot of time before I reached hospital and got the appropriate medical care. It changed my world in a split second. I went into a coma for almost five months, and when I woke up I didn't speak or eat for almost a year. I was in a hospital for over three months, and then under 24-hour medical care for almost a year at home. I couldn't walk or do anything by myself. It was as though I was living a horrible nightmare. I used to listen to music and communicate via a PROLOQ app that

would speak for me. I would practice art therapy to vent my feelings. I had a lot of thoughts running through my mind, and it all got stored to be given expression later in my writings of prose and poetry that I started doing after I came back from my rehabilitation at Spaulding Rehabilitation Hospital in Boston. When I returned to school, I was grappling with an alternative reality. I used to go to school in a wheelchair, and I couldn't do a lot of the things I used to be able to do before, physically and otherwise.

There was a lot of grief at the loss I felt and bitterness and anger at the unfairness of it all. I needed to channel it and be able to get it out of my system. My art and writing helped me do that. My book, *Hope Exists*, became a compilation of all that I wrote in the seven years after my accident. There are a lot of emotions that I describe, as well as some surreal experiences of my conversations with God. My young mind questioned him – *Why me?* All the artwork in the book represents the paintings done by me over the years.

What does "Hope Exists" mean to you, and how do you embody that in your daily life?

Rayna: I believe in the motto "Never give up – your time will come." I did not speak or eat for a year after my accident, and only when I returned from Spaulding did I learn to do both. I did not walk for three years, but now I can walk by myself. Playing the piano, riding a bicycle, riding my favorite horse, painting, singing, dancing on stage. I achieved all of this after coming out of a coma. It involved countless hours of relentless therapies: physio, speech and language, occupational therapy, music therapy, art, cognitive therapy and counseling. I never said no to anything as I wanted to get well and I knew that I had to work very hard in order to get back to who the old Rayna was.

I may not ever become the old Rayna again, but I want to enable myself to do everything I love in the best way I can. I want to become independent and lead my own life. My parents have been standing like rocks beside me every step of the way, and I want them to be able to get back to a life of their own. I believe that hope truly exists, and that's what keeps one going through the most challenging times.

> "Passion becomes soul food that is so essential for our emotional needs and keeps us afloat in the most trying times. So please always follow the things you love and invest time and effort into them."

You have been achieving so many of your dreams at your young age: pottery, interning for a vet, writing a book, music and more. What is your advice to other people looking to pursue their dreams and stay motivated during adversity?

Rayna: My family and I believed that in my recovery period I should continue to do all the things that I felt passionate about. It motivated me to give it my best shot, no matter what. I love animals, and started interning with a vet for a few hours every week. I also love art, music and writing, and have been doing all

three vociferously. I started taking singing lessons over Zoom during the pandemic lockdown. I feel all these outlets help me reconnect with myself. They help me heal and make me realize that life is beautiful as long as you are passionate and you are pursuing your interests and loves. Passion becomes soul food that is so essential for our emotional needs and keeps us afloat in the most trying times. So please always follow the things you love and invest time and effort into them. These become your strength. They help you through adversity and the unpredictability of life.

Sonica, as a mother and a caretaker, how did you stay grounded and positive during this experience? What is your advice to other moms?

Sonica: As the primary caregiver, one is living the trauma with one's child. Sleepless nights and hours by her bedside praying for her to heal and wake up from her coma were the norm. Over the years, I have started keeping some time to myself and doing things I enjoy, from taking a short weekend trip with my girlfriends to cooking lessons to studying Shakespeare again and being part of a book club. Studying our ancient Vedic scriptures, which are fountainheads of knowledge, also gave me solace. I visit a lot of the ancient architectural sites – that is very satisfying for me. Having trusting and meaningful relationships and reaching out and helping people in a similar situation fulfills me, too.

Kathleen Walsh

Fostering Equity and Building Community at the Y

You are the president and CEO of the YMCA of Boston Metro North. Tell us your background and how your career led you to work with the YMCA.

At a young age, my mother mentioned to me that I might not want to consider a traditional desk job; that was her way of telling me that I could not sit still. She encouraged me to look at roles that allow for creativity, flexibility, impact, and fun. As luck would have it, a job opened up at a local YMCA. Then, I started to see that as a young manager, I could make decisions that literally changed people's lives for the better. Whether giving someone a job, a program scholarship, or even an opportunity to get fit with a membership, the feeling of being at the Y and doing something for the greater good is so rewarding.

You also have expertise in team building. What do you think are some of the bigger challenges women leaders face in building teams?

Despite the forward progress in gender equity, women are still forced to "prove" themselves. One of the biggest challenges that I think all leaders have when building a team is being consistent in expectations. Whatever the team member brings to the table with regard to their skillset and talents, expectations should be high and managed accordingly. That is not saying everyone's success is measured at the same ability. It is saying success is being measured equally by potential. Consistency is critical. Once you deviate from that, you become ineffective.

What are your top three tips to building an effective team, perhaps for female leaders in particular?

Team building is more of an art than a science. I believe in organic team building by getting your hands dirty, being accessible, and establishing a relationship that weaves in both personal and professional goals.

Let me give you an example. At the Y, we have a 5k road race series. As an incentive to have staff participate, any employee who runs and beats me gets two hours of my vacation time. It is a great way to get to know staff, encourage them to be healthy, and show them that you support their race series. And, well, a lot of them earn my vacation time! Ask your team members questions – not just about work, but about their children, their vacation plans, or even their new car. Get to know them; it will help you be a better leader.

What is the most rewarding part of your work with the YMCA? What were some programs you got to be a part of or helped initiate?

I am in a forward-facing service job, with a twist of fun! We listen to what our community needs, and then have a chance to build a program to support them. For example, our Y has successfully launched the Partnership Program, designed for folks with balance or spinal cord injuries. Our Y Academy focuses on early learning and better educational outcomes for children. We designed the classrooms and curriculum to let their imaginations merge with academic

> "Ask your team members questions – not just about work, but about their children, their vacation plans, or even their new car. Get to know them; it will help you be a better leader."

learning. Most recently, we launched a food program including a refrigerated van for neighborhood deliveries. If there is a need, we try to create a solution.

What is your long-term dream under your leadership for the Boston Metro North region?

Health and wellness equity and accessibility is a long-term and short-term dream. We just opened up a $31 million facility in Lynn, Massachusetts, and we now serve four times the number of people expanding our impact in the city and region. We found partners that believed the city needed a new Y and were dedicated to helping me raise the money to build it.

A pandemic proved again that people and communities are not treated equally. I want our Y to continue to level the playing field for everyone through a thoughtful menu of affordable access to fully funded services. The bottom line: we need to be the health equity solution in all of the cities and towns we serve.

11

Kavita Navani

A Doctor, Businesswoman, and Advocate for the Underserved

Tell us about your journey from India to Boston, how you knew you wanted to be a doctor, and your leadership at eClinicalWorks, bringing technology and healthcare together.

When my father fell seriously ill in a village in India with limited access to treatment, I was heartbroken. Though he recovered, the feeling of needing help that wasn't available stayed with me. He taught us the value of education in shaping people's lives and helping others. So, at a young age, I made up my mind to pursue medicine and provide healthcare to those who could not access it. I pursued my dream in medical school and residency, eventually coming to the U.S. for further education as a resident at UMass Memorial Health Care.

While practicing in Clinton, Massachusetts for 20 years as an internist, I was able to see the struggles many families went through to get medical care and was able to help them. Those first few years of residency and practice were a blur, but were all worth it in the end. eClinicalWorks Electronic Health Record allowed me to make a larger-scale impact in addition to the daily medical care I provided to my patient population as a physician. As I started to use eClinicalWorks in my own practice, I began to see the power of using technology to solve problems at a larger scale, locally or even nationally. Seeing the company grow and seeing its impact has been one of the most fulfilling parts of my career.

You are also passionate about multiple social causes. What causes are closest to your heart?

I am most passionate about being an advocate for the underserved, as well as women's empowerment. My mother always taught me that a woman should stand on her own two feet and have a career that allows her to support herself and find fulfillment. I have focused my work and philanthropy on how we can make this a reality for women. With the power of education and a support system, we can truly achieve anything.

Tell us about Sankalp and your passion for philanthropy.

At Sankalp, we have a mission to empower rural India. Many farmers struggle with storage for their crops, and as a result, have to sell them at a loss before it's too late. Sankalp provides solar-powered electricity and cold storage to the farmers so that they can sell their crops at a fair price using an environmentally sustainable solution. This economic support coupled with environmental sustainability has long-term benefits for the health and vitality of this region.

We are proud to collaborate with Ekal Vidyalaya, as they have a strong foundation in promoting literacy through schools and mobile digital labs. Working with Ekal, we have had the opportunity to provide funding to rural primary schools, as we firmly believe that empowerment starts with education. For example, the Sankalp team successfully raised funds to support 620+ Ekal schools through its events based in the United States and India.

> "My mother always taught me that a woman should stand on her own two feet and have a career that allows her to support herself and find fulfillment. I have focused my work and philanthropy on how we can make this a reality for women."

Who is your biggest role model, and what is a lesson they taught you?

I have always gone with what my heart says to do. I always dealt with myself and the world with my conscience. I learned this, as well as the value of hard work, from my father. I miss him.

Rollie Lal

Reflections on Security Challenges in the World Today

When we look at the major security challenges that we face in the world today, the same themes come to the surface again and again. And most of them – war, poverty, religious violence, health insecurity – have deep connections to the role of women in society.

The way we conceive of war and conflict is tied tightly to how women are excluded from the conversation. In decisions on whether to engage or bomb societies, women on both sides of the conflict are seldom consulted. Even in the U.S., fewer than 20% of senior positions in the Department of Defense are held by women. Believing that women's absence makes no difference is naïve. Even for rebuilding societies, studies show the impact of education of mothers is far more significant than that of fathers in determining family health and children's education outcomes.

And this brings us to the well-hidden issue of the double minority: It is critical to bring the voice of the minority woman to the table in global security. This individual is more likely to bring to the table the effects of military action on vulnerable communities. Rather than simply perceiving Yemen or Iraq as an "enemy" that needs to be bombed, a minority woman in the U.S. can call out the effect on the women and children who will inordinately bear the brunt of our actions. The perspective of a Muslim woman on girls' rights to education or against child marriage in Afghanistan is fundamentally different than that of the male Taliban negotiator. And yet, when dealing with these issues, we set a few white men at the table with Afghan men and believe that the situation is resolved.

> "It is critical to bring the voice of the minority woman to the table in global security."

When minority women are absent, there is literally no one to speak out against the exceedingly white male-biased security policies that we choose. Raising awareness of the absence of women in these spheres is central to dealing with human security. For each of us in every field, calling attention to the absence of women at the table is at the heart of the fight.

Ami Ambani

Running For the Victory Line

When I wake up to the ear-splitting sound of my alarm clock and blindly search for the snooze button, a sudden thought dawns: *What am I doing?*

Marathon running, a sport that requires a fusion of the body and mind, strives to maximize your physical ability by testing your mental tenacity. Every day represents a new struggle to beat yesterday's maximum output, sometimes simply an issue of mind over matter.

As convincing as my morning doubts are, I do not heed them. Through pains and sprains and through adverse weather and unfavorable conditions, I run because I made up my mind to run marathons and it is now my passion.

And these grueling runs differ from a relaxing jog to a coffee shop. I am pushing myself constantly to run faster and farther, for my team as well as for personal satisfaction. Somehow, with tireless effort and unflagging commitment, I run through the sleeping streets of my neighborhood, with the awareness that I am steadily reaching my goal: maintaining the discipline that running long distance demands. In my mind I see a victory line that symbolizes the results of my perseverance and hard work. This victory line makes me realize that ambition and tenacity do not go in vain. It

The time is 5:30 a.m., all is dark and hushed. My weary body feels completely drained of energy. While straining to open my eyes, still warm and snug in my comfortable bed, I am

> "Every day represents a new struggle to beat yesterday's maximum output, sometimes simply an issue of mind over matter."

overcome with a feeling of lethargy: *Perhaps I should call in sick,* I think. Despite all my musings, and my bed's magnetic pull, I still manage to rise each morning, at this ungodly hour, to join the cross-country running team in rigorous training.

constantly reminds me that all those mornings in which I struggled to leave my cozy cocoon are what have allowed me to fly. While the world slept, I was and am awake and working hard to attain my goal.

Brenda Thompson Stuckey

Bringing the Power of God's Word to All

In January of 2002, I created Auntie Brenda's Cards. The name came from my two cousins, Taylor and Amani Haynes, who were brought up calling me their Auntie Brenda. The concept was inspired when my close friend, Barbara (Johnson) Thomas, lost her mother, Mrs. Hazel Johnson. I was there when Mrs. Johnson took her last breath and went from this earth to her place in heaven. This was my first experience seeing a transition from earth to glory. The experience was overwhelming. It led me to think about my purpose for living and I asked God what He would have me do with the talent(s) He has given me.

I believe that God whispered a message to me and I eventually began to express myself through art, creating a line of greeting cards.

The first generation of cards had very spiritual undertones. I met someone who enjoyed the cards and said that I should really add Bible verses to the cards. I believed this message may have been the voice of God. I heard it, but I was not moved. Putting Bible verses on cards seemed too commercial then. While the cards were well liked, my momentum for continuing waned and I stopped working on the cards.

In September of 2007, I received news that I had breast cancer. Again, my search to define purpose for living and God's calling on my life appeared. During that illness, I received prayers, cards, visits, and calls from friends, family, acquaintances and even strangers. I found solace in God's word. Each Bible verse that was read, each prayer that was spoken on my behalf, each sermon preached, strengthened me. This time God's whisper and voice became a shout. From this adversity, I was able to experience the power of God's Word in my life and drew strength from the Word. I knew I had to share His word with others. I knew then that I had to add Bible verses to the cards. From there I developed a vision statement which is "to teach God's word, one Bible verse at a time." I don't profess to know God's word in its entirety, but I know the Bible verses that are special in my life. If I can share those verses with others and have them share their favorites with me, together I believe we can learn God's word and follow His direction.

Initially, I wanted people to draw their own conclusions about the meaning of the cards and use them to express themselves as they were led to feel. In 2012, the next generation of cards developed would have words on the inside of the cards. I learned through this experience that not all of us know what to say or how to say it, and sometimes, a little help is all that is needed. I created a Thanksgiving card complete with a verse on the inside of the card.

Again, life happened, and I put my talent to rest. In 2023, I resumed my

> "I believe that God whispered a message to me and I eventually began to express myself through art, creating a line of greeting cards."

work with the cards. I don't know what this generation of cards will look like yet, all I know is that God is not through with me yet. I think God wants me to send a message to the world reminding us how to treat one another with kindness. We are one race, the human race. We are one family and I believe God strengthens us all through His word. May God bless you and keep you.

Kay Khan

At the Intersection of Nursing and Public Service

You initially started your career in nursing, and then moved into state government. You have been dedicated to public service for approximately 30 years. Tell us about your journey.

After graduating from Boston University School of Nursing, I began my career as a pediatric nurse at Boston Children's Hospital. When my three children were young, I earned a master's degree in psychiatric mental health nursing at Boston University and worked in a private psychiatric group practice. While raising my three children, I became interested in politics and started helping local candidates run for elected office. With an interest in giving back to my community in some way, I began thinking that my health care background could be helpful in public service. With the support and encouragement of family, friends, and community leaders, I

was elected state representative. I have represented the city of Newton in the Massachusetts House of Representatives since 1994 – almost 30 years. I was introduced to the Indian community in Massachusetts through my husband, Nasir A. Khan, MD. He was a member of the Indian Medical Association and later its president. I am currently on the advisory board of Women Who Win.

What are some issues you are particularly passionate about? What are the key initiatives you are most proud of?

With my background in health care, it seemed important to serve on legislative committees related to health and human services. In 2009, the speaker of the House appointed me as chair of the Joint Committee on Children, Families and Persons with Disabilities, and I continued as chair of this committee for 12 years. I also founded a legislative mental health caucus and, through the Caucus of Women Legislators, organized a task force with a focus on women in the criminal justice system. I am proud of many successes over the years. A recent piece of legislation signed into law in 2022 will end child marriage in Massachusetts for all those under the age of 18, no exceptions. Addressing the needs of many in our Commonwealth is one of the great honors of my legislative career.

What is your advice to women looking to run for public office?

Women interested in running for office can reach out to organizations that offer training, and we are always looking for more women to step up. Once elected, it is important that legislators stay connected with constituents in the district one represents. As an elected official, it is a privilege to work with others on the local, state, and federal levels. We sometimes work internationally as well. It's helpful if one is a leader, a mentor, and a helper who

values making our world a better place for future generations.

How do you relax and unwind? How do you find your work life balance?

During my downtime, I spend time with friends, family, and especially my seven beautiful grandchildren. I try to introduce them to my passions: the arts, culture, travel, learning, and actively supporting organizations that enrich our communities – these are my pleasures in life and have always provided a balance with the work that I also love.

> "As an elected official, it is a privilege to work with others on the local, state, and federal levels. We sometimes work internationally as well. It's helpful if one is a leader, a mentor, and a helper who values making our world a better place for future generations."

Krupa Sheth

Representing Her Community: London's Youngest Asian City Councilor

London is more than just a city; it is a powerhouse of history, culture, commerce and fashion. A city that has inspired many others across the world. A city full of hopes and dreams… The city I have proudly called home for all my life!

My journey in politics began back in 2010. I was a law student with little interest in politics at that time. My uncle was running for a seat in the 2010 elections in the London Borough of Brent, and much to my dismay, I was forced to go out and help him. I came home that evening very surprised! I really enjoyed talking to local residents and the community, learning more about the area and what the local issues were. I also found myself questioning: why hadn't the Council already done this and what we could do for these people and the community? The more I helped, the more involved I got and the more thoughts, ideas and questions ran through my mind. Shortly after, I joined the Labour Party, and in October 2011 a by-election was announced. I took the courage and put in an

application form to become the party candidate, but being a young Asian woman up against older more experienced people, I did not have much hope. I was rather shocked to have been selected as a candidate at the end of the process. Others were more shocked and questioned the organizer of the selection process with "How did she get selected as our candidate?" That was the first hurdle I passed and also the first lesson I learned: it was not going to be easy for a young British Indian woman in politics, I had to have thick skin, I had to have faith in myself, and I had to keep dreaming big and working hard to accomplish my goals.

In December 2011, at the age of 20, I was the youngest British Asian to ever be elected. I became a councilor in the London Borough of Brent, the home of Wembley Stadium. Local government is complex enough without the politics, and being the youngest in the Council by a mile made it harder. However, I threw myself into it and soaked it all up. I learned that fear will only hold you back and confidence is something that you have to dig deep for, but once you take that first step, you will surprise yourself, and confidence grows with experience and knowledge. You have to be patient. I learned to make sure my voice was heard, to fight for the vision and ideas I believed in and to never stop challenging myself to DO better and BE better.

After winning my third consecutive election in May 2018, I was appointed Cabinet member for environment, infrastructure, climate action, leisure and sports. I am currently in my fourth consecutive term in the Council and have been in my Cabinet post for five years now. As a local councilor, I represent my local ward, Tokyngton. I take on their issues and support them. In my Cabinet role, I oversee the entire Council department for environment, leisure and sports, managing the policies and the budget. Also sitting on the Cabinet means discussing our borough plan, scrutinizing policies, drawing up visions and ensuring our borough and our residents, businesses and communities continue to prosper and flourish. One of the roles my Cabinet portfolio involves is working with the world-famous Wembley Stadium and supporting them with their event days. It was an honor to be able to work on the Men's Euro2020 and Women's Euro2022 plans. For me, politics is not just about fighting elections and bashing the opposition party in the Council Chambers. It is about ensuring every individual is given the chance to thrive. Only then will our country thrive!

The work is tiring, but every bit of it is rewarding. It is always heartwarming to see communities coming together and supporting each other. If you ask me, this is what London reflects…the real London – a city full of love and compassion! In politics, you have to expect the unexpected! Each day is a new challenge, each day I get to do something good for the community and each day I learn something new. This is why I love what I do!

We all have goals and ambitions that we strive toward; I am not sure what the future has in store for me nor what I will be doing in 10 years' time. What I do know is that whatever I am doing, I always want to be giving back and helping those around me. Life is full of opportunities; sometimes you have to go looking for them and sometimes, if you are lucky, they land on your doorstep. Nothing is easy. If it was easy, it would not be worth it! You have to work hard, especially being a woman – a woman of color makes it even harder, but you have got to believe in yourself, you have to be brave, and you have to take the plunge!

We live in a world where work never stops. The one thing you will hear from any Londoner guaranteed is "I have been so busy!" But that work/life balance is more important than ever to ensure we keep healthy, mentally and physically, and if anything you will find with that balance your creativity and productivity levels are much better. It took me a while to find that balance, but it has taken me on a new adventure. I love trying new things, and of course, being in London, there is always something to do, somewhere new to explore, and gorgeous restaurants popping up. I am biased, but it doesn't get better than London!

> "I learned that fear will only hold you back and confidence is something that you have to dig deep for, but once you take that first step, you will surprise yourself and the confidence grows with experience and knowledge."

Archana Srivastava

Global Artist On a Mission To Improve Society

You are an artist deeply rooted in Indian history and tradition, and your work spans different mediums. You have had numerous solo art exhibitions as well and have had multiple recognitions for your work. What inspired you to become an artist? What inspires you creatively?

Since childhood I was passionate about art. It was like therapy to me. Born in a family that thrived on art and culture, it was an easy choice for me to draw, sketch, color and paint. In early childhood, I started drawing on slate, paper, walls, and floors as soon as I could hold crayon or chalk in my hands. My family saw great potential in me, and my parents would encourage me to draw and paint and to participate in school, district-level and regional competitions.

Winning in such competitions encouraged me to paint more. I was a sincere student and excelled in academics. Often my study hours would get stretched and I would get exhausted. I would then draw on my practice notebook a face, figure, landscape or still life. As a result, each of my practice notebooks would have multiple figures and forms drawn on the last many pages. Often, the pages with drawings would outnumber the pages with writings.

I was happy doing well in academics and pursuing art. My academic orientation helped me complete a Ph.D. in history and I started teaching graduate and post-graduate students as guest faculty in various colleges and universities off and on. As far as the art was concerned, formal training was never an issue. Over the years I have had the good fortune of learning from national and international-level award-winning artists, professors of reputed art schools, on a 1:1 basis informally. They did teach me technicalities of art, but asked me to remain original in my imagination. In fact, every one of them without exception encouraged me to have my own style. Thus I am one of those fortunate souls who learned everything about art without joining an art school full time. I took up art as my profession with great enthusiasm and gusto, becoming a full-time artist and a part-time academician.

Through art, intangible subjects can be made understandable. My art is mostly thematic and message-oriented. I enjoy portraying the complex messages contained in the verses of *Bhagavad Gita* and Sufi poetry. I try to depict the non-obvious metaphorically, thus making it understandable.

Your husband is also a highly respected bureaucrat in Mumbai, India. What does the life of a wife of a bureaucrat entail? What were some key lessons?

Being the wife of a senior and well-respected bureaucrat is both satisfying and challenging. Satisfying, as it gives you enormous opportunities to look at various problems and strengths of the country closely. It also gives you opportunities and roles to work for society directly or indirectly. Challenging, as it requires acting responsibly all the time. Bureaucrats are called the backbone of the nation. While you are supporting and informally advising the policymakers and law-enforcers, you can't afford to be anything but responsible.

Given the integral role the spouse plays in the future of an individual's life, career and field, it is important for a spouse of a bureaucrat to be level-headed, mature, dependable and conscientious. A supportive atmosphere at home can make one calm and stable to make positive and impactful decisions which can benefit society as well as one's city, state, and country. The key lesson from the experience has been that it is absolutely necessary for the wives of the bureaucrats to have their own

> "Through art, intangible subjects can be made understandable. I try to depict the non-obvious metaphorically, thus making it understandable."

identity. Bureaucrats and their families are closely observed and followed by many, especially at the district-level postings. You are always being looked at as a role model. It would be a failure to derive your identity just from your man. That's what women's empowerment is all about, and one can't just preach it. One has to practice it too.

You have recently started working on promoting the work of folk artists in India. Tell us more about that.

As CEO and founder of ArtSage Pvt. Ltd., I aim to safeguard the interests of the folk and tribal artists and artisans of India. Folk and tribal art of India is rich in tradition and heritage, and is celebrated throughout the world. But unfortunately, the condition of the artists and artisans is far from pleasant. They rarely get their due. Their art is bought for very low prices and sold at insanely high prices at regional, national, and international markets. Many of them quit their rich traditional or family art and opt for menial jobs in the villages. As far as some folk arts are concerned, there are only a few families left in the country who still pursue them.

ArtSage Pvt. Ltd. is committed to doing that. We help by providing resources and technology that improve their efficiency, assist them in honing their skills, provide platforms for them to sell their art, and try to create awareness about the value of their art in public through workshops and symposiums.

23

Yoshika Sherring

Developing Confidence in the Business World

Growing up, I was taught the traditional Indian values of respecting elders, respecting seniority, keeping your head down, and working hard. To add to this upbringing, I was shy, so didn't speak up much.

After receiving my undergraduate degree in biotechnology, working in a laboratory setting was a comfortable place for someone who was shy and inquisitive. However, after some time, I yearned for an opportunity where I could combine my science background with the business world, and pharmaceutical marketing seemed like the perfect merger and next step up in my career. I obtained my MBA while going to school at night and after graduating got my first role in marketing.

Upon entering the business world, I was naïve to the often assertive business environment, which is a less than ideal place for someone who is shy.

When I began my new role, I did not speak up much. I deferred to my seniors and always listened to what they said instead of being proactive. I thought if I kept my head down and just did my work to the best of my abilities, it would be recognized, and I would receive the accolades or the promotion I deserved. Unfortunately, this was not the case. My lack of confidence, my fears and my anxiety were all getting the best of me.

I remember the first time I was asked to give a big presentation to a room full of senior executives. After my boss and I discussed this, I went back to my desk and was feeling anxious, thinking, *Will I be able to do this?* I realized the responsibility I had to my boss and to the other members of my team who were counting on me to deliver a strong presentation. In addition, I was not given much time to prepare and the presentation was going to be at a meeting in California. Leading up to the meeting, I spent as much time as I could on preparing, including developing my slides and thinking through my story and how I was going to convey the information in an engaging and informative way. I reviewed my slides and talking points on the flight to California, and the day before the presentation, I practiced over and over in front of a mirror in my hotel room.

On the day of the presentation, I was so nervous. After introductions, I was first up. All I wanted to do was get through it and be done. I started speaking, and it was difficult in the beginning, but a few slides in, I gained my confidence and kept going. By the time I was done, it felt great and I knew I had nailed it. Afterwards, my boss and colleagues congratulated me. This was the first of many, many big presentations in my career. However, to this day, before any big presentation, my heart still races, and I still get very nervous. Luckily, there are a few lessons I've learned along the way, not just about becoming more comfortable presenting, but ultimately in how to navigate the business world with success.

> "For many years, I kept a professional persona at work. I rarely talked about my personal life, thinking it would be unprofessional to talk about my kids or share something fun I did over the weekend. After time, I realized, *Why hide this?*"

Above all, I have learned the importance of being myself. For many years, I kept a professional persona at work. I rarely talked about my personal life, thinking it would be unprofessional to talk about my kids or share something fun I did over the weekend. After time, I realized, *Why hide this?* Hiding myself wasn't getting me anywhere, so I embraced sharing myself. And the outcome has been that nothing has changed, except that I feel more connected by being myself and others respect my choices.

It took a long time for me to get comfortable adapting to the corporate culture, but the lessons I've learned along the way have been invaluable, helping me grow both personally and professionally.

Rita Advani

Solving Problems at the Community Level

You are a true business leader to know, with your extensive experience in leading teams and boards. Tell us more about your career journey and what made you who you are today.

I would not be where I am today without the active encouragement of my parents and my sister to get an MBA. In my class at the Indian Institute of Management in Calcutta, we were only 11 women in a class of 110! When we applied for jobs, one of the questions that was asked of all women applicants was, "What are you going to do when you get married?" The assumption was that we were going to quit working after we got married.

After I migrated to the U.S. in 1980, I started working in the industrial economy of Rhode Island and southeastern Massachusetts. Some years later, the economic landscape changed. Mergers, acquisitions, and a strong dollar made exports too expensive and imports cheaper. This changed the industrial landscape, and various industries and companies disappeared from the area. It was time for me to reinvent myself and to take my skills to different sectors of the economy. Years later, the 2008 financial crisis shook up the economy and millions of jobs disappeared. This time I made a radical change and chose to become an entrepreneur. I opted to work toward making kids better stewards of the environment through science education.

Along the way, I had put down roots in suburbia and found myself putting up my hand up to work toward solving a variety of local problems. My role models were neighbors who volunteered to oversee municipal functions and finances. I delighted in learning about aspects of the economy that were so different from the sectors in which I worked. I found I could utilize my business skills to make improvements in the community in which I lived. I served on a Commission for the Commonwealth on the formula used to fund local elementary and secondary education, the School Committee to work to improve the education provided and to increase funding for the schools, and chaired the Town Energy Committee to reduce energy consumption and bring a solar power project to the town.

When you volunteer, other organizations looking for board members find you! My husband Ramesh and I had been taking care of his mother in our home. This led to my engagement with healthcare delivery organizations. I served on the Board of Trustees of Atrius Health and am currently the chair of the Board of Directors of VNA Care, one of the largest providers of home health and hospice care in the state. I also serve as a trustee of the condo association in which I now live. I am engaged with the finances and operations of the association and in protecting the buildings from the impact of climate change.

How would you describe your leadership style? And what do you think is your biggest asset as a leader?

I lead by example. Treating others as you would have them treat you. Taking the time and putting in the effort to build consensus. Listening to diverse voices including those at the bottom of the ladder because they often have the best and freshest ideas. Speaking up instead of remaining one of the silent majority. Not being afraid to ask questions respectfully and in a constructive manner or raise concerns that others may not be willing to.

You mentioned that one big constant in your life is giving back to your community. Why is philanthropy and giving back important to you?

As Muhammad Ali said, service to others is the rent you pay for your room here on Earth. The inspiration for Seva also comes from our Sikh and ancient Hindu traditions. I need to give back to my community and the countries that gave me the skills and opportunities to succeed.

You are also interested in the art of reinventing oneself. This is something women in particular are becoming more focused on in their lives. Tell us more about this. Did you have a personal journey with reinvention?

My parents and extended family had to pick themselves up after the disruptions caused by the partition of India and losing their homeland. They restarted their lives from scratch. By comparison, mine was a much easier journey. For me, the key to reinvention was the joy of learning about the economic landscape, the ability to find my footing in diverse sectors, and utilizing my skills to benefit municipalities and nonprofit organizations. Along the way I realized that my strength was my ability to think differently and raise the kinds of issues that often only women seem to raise.

> "For me, the key to reinvention was the joy of learning about the economic landscape, the ability to find my footing in diverse sectors, and utilizing my skills to benefit municipalities and nonprofit organizations."

Reshma Kewalramani

CEO of Vertex Pharmaceuticals On Our Responsibility to Give Back

You are the CEO of Vertex Pharmaceuticals, making you the first female CEO of a large US biotech company. Tell us your journey and what inspired you to be the woman you are today.

I am a physician, executive, immigrant, wife, and mother. All of these roles – and the experiences I've had and the people I've met along the way – have helped shape the person and leader I am today. I grew up in Mumbai and came to the U.S. when I was 12. I often quip that in my family, the career choices were basically engineering, medicine, or priesthood – I chose medicine. I enrolled in the seven-year medicine program at Boston University and wanted to be a "triple threat," meaning that I'd conduct my own research, teach medical students and residents, and provide excellent patient care. During my medical training, I discovered a passion for clinical research and the opportunity it holds for advancing patient care.

Fast forward several years, and I realized that what inspired me most was seeing the impact of new medicines for patients, and I recognized that the front lines of this work were within the biotech industry. This is why I decided to move from academia to drug development. After spending 12+ years at Amgen, I came to Vertex in 2017 and after serving as chief medical officer, I became Vertex's CEO and president in April 2020. Our mission at Vertex is to invest in scientific innovation to create transformative medicines for people with serious diseases, and we have a unique corporate and R&D strategy that focuses on serious diseases where we understand the underlying cause of the disease in humans and where we have the potential to make a transformative impact, regardless of treatment modality. Our strategy and our success are exemplified by our long history in cystic fibrosis (CF) and the progress we've been making in many other serious diseases. In the last several years, we've expanded our leadership in CF, progressed our potential gene-editing therapy for sickle cell disease and beta thalassemia, and advanced multiple new programs into the clinic for diseases like type 1 diabetes, APOL1-mediated kidney disease and pain.

I have dedicated my career to improving the lives of patients; this has been a constant source of inspiration throughout my professional life. At Vertex, we have an uncompromising commitment to patients, and this commitment is what serves as my North Star when faced with challenging circumstances and decisions.

You are also a dedicated philanthropist, supporting causes such as Akshaya Patra. You were a past speaker at their Boston Gala. What inspired you to get involved with them, and what excites you about their mission?

> "Giving back is not just about money, it's also about giving your time, sharing your perspective and experiences, and opening doors for others whenever possible."

doors for others whenever possible. As a physician, I'm especially passionate about supporting the next generation of scientists and those interested in making a difference in healthcare. For that reason, I enjoy speaking with students or participating in events like the Akshaya Patra Boston Gala. My giving is focused on science and medicine, closing the opportunity gap, and bringing more women and underrepresented minorities into STEM fields.

What excites me about the organization's mission is how it is addressing a dual need in India – hunger and education. I understand the value of education, and have benefited greatly from my own, and I believe deeply that no child should be deprived of access to education for any reason. The foundation has set an ambitious goal of feeding five million children each day by 2025, and I am motivated by the opportunity to help them meet (and hopefully exceed) this goal.

Organizations like Akshaya Patra bring passionate and like-minded individuals together to give back for a powerful cause. Why is philanthropy important to you, and how do you find the time and opportunity to give back in your own life?

Philanthropy is an important part of my life, and I find the time because I make it a priority. Giving back is not just about money, it's also about giving your time, sharing your perspective and experiences, and opening

We also build philanthropy into the culture at Vertex through a variety of initiatives including corporate giving and the Vertex Foundation. In this way, we instill the value of giving back to our communities across all of our employees and offices around the world.

One of Akshaya Patra's new initiatives is the Young Professionals, and on Women Who Win, we also have a women's mentorship program. What is your top piece of advice to young women professionals and leaders?

I am the great beneficiary of outstanding mentoring, and it's important to remember that mentors don't have to be similar to you. Seek multiple mentors who come from different backgrounds and have different perspectives. Two of my most important mentors are men, and the diversity of thought, ideas, and life experiences is what helped these mentorships flourish.

Aleena Banerji

Making Inroads in Understanding Allergies

What is your background, and why did you decide to specialize in allergy and immunology?

I love the field of allergy/immunology because of the meaningful impact I can have on patients' lives, whether it is improving their seasonal allergy symptoms so they can enjoy time outside or helping a cancer patient receive lifesaving first-line therapy despite an allergic reaction.

My interests span patient care, training the next generation of doctors, and clinical research. I am an associate professor at Harvard Medical School as well as clinical director of the Allergy and Clinical Immunology Unit and director of the Drug Allergy Program at Mass General. I studied biomedical engineering and attended medical school at Northwestern University in Chicago, followed by an internal medicine residency and allergy/immunology fellowship. I have been on the faculty at MGH since 2005. I

have a special interest in drug allergy and angioedema, including patients with hereditary angioedema.

What are some common conditions you see in the office as an allergist/immunologist? How can some of these conditions be evaluated and managed in the office?

We evaluate and manage many different allergic issues, including hives, rashes, immune system problems, food allergies, and asthma, but my specific areas of research are drug allergies and angioedema (swelling). The first step with allergy skin testing involves pricking your skin with an allergen (food, drug, environmental, etc.) and then looking to see if you develop a local reaction in 15 minutes. We call this a "wheal and flare" reaction when the testing is positive. With certain drugs and environmental allergies, if the skin prick testing is negative, there is a second part called intradermal skin testing. This second step involves injecting a small amount of the allergen underneath the skin and monitoring for 15 minutes to see if a local reaction develops. We also perform oral challenges to foods and drugs to help people understand their allergies. Oral challenges are the gold standard to prove someone is not allergic and are usually done when there is a low likelihood of true allergy. Drug allergies that we can evaluate include antibiotics, aspirin, NSAIDs, insulin, local or general anesthesia, chemotherapeutic agents, monoclonal antibodies and checkpoint inhibitors. When we evaluate a patient with drug allergies, we review the clinical history and then decide if they would benefit from skin testing, a drug challenge, and/or desensitization.

We have heard a lot about desensitization. How and why do you use desensitization to help treat allergies in a patient?

Drug desensitization is a way of safely giving a medication to someone who is allergic to the medication. Desensitization temporarily allows someone to take the medication despite being allergic by tricking the immune system into tolerating it. Desensitization involves starting with an extremely small amount of the medication that someone is allergic to and then, over several hours, giving increasing amounts at regular intervals until the full dose of the medication is reached. Some common examples of where drug desensitization is really important is when it's not possible to avoid a specific medication despite an allergy. This can include situations like giving the best antibiotic to treat a life-threatening infection, using aspirin in a patient with heart disease, or using anesthesia in someone that needs to have surgery, and making sure that a cancer patient can receive first-line chemotherapy. We are able to evaluate drug allergies in many of these cases and help someone stay on this very important medication despite a prior possible allergic reaction.

> "Food allergies, including peanut and tree nut allergies, are increasing in the United States and are a major public health concern. The reasons for this are not completely clear yet."

With the exponential rise in food and nut allergies in children and adults, what advice do you have for prevention and for people suffering from these allergies?

Food allergies, including peanut and tree nut allergies, are increasing in the United States and are a major public health concern. The reasons for this are not completely clear yet. Food allergies can be very dangerous and cause anaphylaxis, so seeing an allergist can be very important. In terms of prevention, there is a lot of ongoing research and a few emerging key concepts. The most recent thinking is that early introduction of highly allergenic foods like milk, peanuts, eggs and tree nuts is very important, maybe even by 4-6 months of age. In fact, delayed introduction is thought to be associated with an increased risk of developed food allergies in certain cases. For people suffering from food allergies, we can evaluate the history and determine if skin testing, blood work or an oral challenge in the clinic would be helpful next steps. Additionally, there are emerging data and studies on the use of oral immunotherapy (similar to desensitization) in patients for food or nut allergies. However, this should be discussed with your allergist. While there is a good rate of success, not everyone is a good candidate, and food oral immunotherapy can be associated with allergic reactions. If appropriate, the allergist/immunologist will also prescribe an epinephrine auto-injector and instruct the individual on how and when to use it.

Renee Frohnert

Bringing Inclusion into Space

You are a space pioneer, with a passion for diversity and inclusion. Tell us your story, and what inspired your interest in space.

Since I was seven, I have been passionate about space with strong aspirations of becoming an astronaut. As a young girl, I watched *Toy Story* and fell in love with Buzz Lightyear. My dad, an electrical engineer, pushed me to pursue space and STEM by taking me to the NASA Kennedy Visitors Center to watch rocket launches. I followed in his footsteps by pursuing the same higher education program he completed, a bachelor's in electrical engineering from Penn State University.

My undergrad degree launched (no pun intended) my space career, as I accepted my first engineering position in the industry at Lockheed Martin Space following graduation. I continued to pursue a master's in engineering from Cornell University and an MBA from the University of Southern California while working full-time at Lockheed Martin and L3Harris Space. My space journey has provided me with incredible career opportunities, including participating in the Project PoSSUM Scientist-Astronaut program and the Lockheed Martin Engineering Leadership program.

Space technology tends to be a male-dominated field. Tell us more about how you navigated as a woman interested in space. Any challenges faced along the way?

My journey in space almost stopped just as soon as it started; as a woman in a male dominated field, I experienced challenges as a minority. In undergrad, I was one of only two women out of nearly 500 electrical engineering students. I had no women professors and did not know any women within the industry at the time. As a result, I faced severe imposter syndrome, feeling out of place and received a 1.5 GPA my first semester. Despite this setback, I overcame the odds against me and completed my degree with honors. My success can be attributed to support groups for people in similar situations, including the Society of Women Engineers.

As I transitioned from college to industry, the challenges continued, largely due to unconscious bias. I've been the only female on engineering teams of 30+ members. The first time I realized the impacts of unconscious bias was when I walked into a room as the lead spacecraft engineer and was assumed to be there to supply coffee rather than to discuss technical requirements for a project.

While experiencing unconscious biases at times was uncomfortable, these encounters have made me rapidly grow. I have navigated these challenges through the support of my mentors and champions within the industry. These experiences have shaped me to become a passionate advocate for diversity, equity, and inclusion (DEI) to overcome unconscious bias and create positive work environments. My DEI journey has led me to connect with people all over the world through various platforms, including public speaking engagements, nonprofits, events, and my social media (@ReneeFrohnert).

You have worked in the space industry at companies such as Lockheed Martin Space and L3Harris Space and Airborne Systems, and are an advisor to Women in Space. What was the most rewarding project you have been part of?

> "There is a saying I love: 'You can't be what you can't see.' I never want a person, no matter their background, to feel they must leave STEM and space because they don't belong."

It is hard to choose just one rewarding project because all of the space projects I have supported get me excited in different ways. If I had to choose one project, I would choose the NASA Artemis program, in which I had the opportunity to design electronics that will be sending the first woman and person of color to the moon around the 2025 timeframe. I was fortunate enough to watch a test flight at NASA Kennedy Space Center and was able to see my electronics perform as expected!

While designing the spacecraft is super exciting, traveling to space sounds like even more fun! I am fortunate enough to be scheduled to fly to the edge of space in 2024 with a new spacecraft program taking people into the stratosphere. Being in the space industry has opened doors like this for me to do things I never thought possible – even a few years ago.

What is your next big dream?

My overarching goal is to inspire young girls and women to pursue STEM and space. There is a saying I love: "You can't be what you can't see." I never want a person, no matter their background, to feel they must leave STEM and space because they don't belong. Space is a place for everyone.

Farida Kathawalla

Teaching, Learning and Exploring Through Philanthropy

You have a wide breadth of philanthropy experience, both in India and in the U.S. What inspired your interest in philanthropy and giving back?

"Be the change you want to see in the world," a quote by Mahatma Gandhi, has influenced me since I was a little girl. Having grown up in Mumbai, India, I have seen class differences very vividly, and I always wondered why these differences existed.

The foundation of my values comes from seeing my parents give support and resources to the underprivileged. I have been very

fortunate to have lived all over the world, and in 2010, I moved to Boston after spending four years in Paris, France as an expatriate. Having had such amazing life experiences, my need to find a way of giving back became even stronger. I started my nonprofit journey with World Boston, a nonprofit that fosters engagement in international affairs and cooperation with people of all nations, where I helped develop the international visitors program.

Currently I am a member of Global Women's Forum and the charter circle of The United Nations of Greater Boston, where I have focused on bringing attention to the Boston community, impacting women and girls via lectures, documentary films and conversations.

I am an active member with the New England International Donors (NEID), an organization that facilitates international philanthropy. I am on the program committee for NEID. I have been on the World Education Board for the last three years, which focuses on improving the quality of life through education for half a million children in 20 countries. I have also been involved as an advisory board member of the Bantwana initiative which improves the well-being of vulnerable children, their caregivers and families affected by HIV, AIDS and poverty.

Being on the advisory board of New Repertory theater, a theater based in Watertown, Massachusetts, was something I wanted to get involved in locally. While this is not in my normal realm, it has been extremely rewarding to learn as well help with strategic development.

I am also the chapter leader for Dining for Women, which educates and engages people to invest in grassroots programs that make a meaningful difference for women and girls in developing countries. This has been truly fulfilling since it is a small giving circle with my close-knit friends. My newest board position is with Woodlands, which is in the community I live in, Belmont, Massachusetts. This is truly an educational experience for me as I am learning about shingles, roofs, downspouts and gutters. This again is a need to give back locally to the community in which I live.

You are also a co-founder of Circle of Hope, under the umbrella of AIF, a group of women philanthropists. What inspired you to launch that, and what was that need you saw for something specific to women philanthropists?

I have been involved with the American India Foundation for the last nine years and I wanted to create something that would be innovative and aid my lifelong mission to empower women and girls. Hence, Circle of Hope was launched in 2017. My co-founder Nirmala Garimella and I spent nine months and many long hours at our kitchen table making this baby come to life. It is truly a labor of love, and it is incredibly satisfying to see it thrive. Most giving circles are groups of women who are grounded in a tradition of

volunteerism and sharing. At a time when individuals seem increasingly disconnected from each other, giving circles promote collective learning, decision-making and giving. They build community by rallying individuals who, over the course of their work together, have meaningful conversations and make real-world decisions. Through giving circles, donors learn about community issues and become deeply involved in nonprofit organizations they may never have known existed.

Since its founding, AIF's Circle of Hope has launched three chapters in New England, Chicago, and San Francisco. Collectively, the chapters have granted thousands of dollars and meaningfully impacted the lives of women and girls in India.

> "I wanted to create something that would be innovative and aid my lifelong mission to empower women and girls."

What is your next big dream?

There is so much more work needed to improve the lives of women and girls all over the world and I want to continue doing that. I would love to see Circle of Hope expand to the other AIF chapters so that we can empower and change the lives of many more women and girls in India. Post-Covid, I would like to do more field visits to all the different countries that I am involved in. I am also looking into different avenues locally as well as domestically to get involved with, especially causes like Black Lives Matter. Lastly, I never want to stop learning and keep my passion of empowering women and girls going.

Elvi Caperonis

Growing Up in the Dominican Republic and Being a Woman in Tech

You are a leader in business technology, with work experience at Amazon and Harvard. What are some challenges you faced along the way, and the mindset you adopted for success?

At an early age, I learned that life was not easy, but one had to keep fighting. I faced very tough odds of success. However, I always kept a positive mindset. Instead of feeling sorry for myself, I redoubled my efforts. My mom, with a meager salary as a nurse, managed to provide everything she could. My sisters and I did not have everything we needed.

I started to read books about successful people. I started imitating their thought process and attitudes. I studied hard to obtain good grades during high school. When many of my friends were having a good time going to parties, etc., I would be preparing assignments or studying for exams. As a result, I graduated from high school first in my class. The award received a scholarship to study computer science at Universidad APEC in Santo Domingo.

When I graduated from high school, my mom did not have enough funds to support my college education, so I looked for a job at a financial institution. It was hard to balance a full-time position with college. However, I still managed to maintain myself until graduation, finishing near the top of my class and earning a scholarship. The award was given for me to study for my master's degree in Madrid, Spain at Universidad Pontificia De Salamanca. I managed to work and study at the same time.

In 2011, I moved to the United States and continued working as a business analytics consultant. A few years later, I was contacted by Harvard University and had the honor to receive an employment opportunity as a techno-functional reporting analyst. At Harvard University, I was introduced to using advanced Agile methodologies and Scrum for project management. I managed and developed business analytics solutions with efficiency and cost-effective completion of many projects involving cross-functional teams. In 2016, I became a Certified

ScrumMaster® by the Scrum Alliance. During my tenure at Harvard, I enjoyed connecting with people, learning about American culture, and building relationships with positive, driven, and motivated people in the Harvard community.

Tell us about how your professional journey at Amazon started, and some of the diversity and inclusion efforts you have been involved in for women.

> "It's very empowering to know that I can inspire other Latinas to enter the Tech industry, and I embrace any opportunities to do so."

In 2017, I left Harvard University and joined the Alexa team at Amazon as a business intelligence engineer. My role involved developing BI solutions to support Alexa international expansion efforts. In 2018, I became an Amazon Scrum trainer and since then, I have been helping Amazonians to deepen their Scrum knowledge and assisting them as an Agile coach.

At Amazon, I have been given many opportunities to contribute to diversity and inclusion efforts. One example is partnering with Amazon Women in Engineering Boston to become an #iamRemarkable facilitator and help women and underrepresented minorities to boost their self-confidence and express themselves at the workplace and beyond.

What has your experience been like as a Latina woman working in a huge technology company like Amazon? How do you see the industry in general, and Amazon in particular, embracing diversity?

It's very empowering to know that I can inspire other Latinas to enter the tech industry, and I embrace any opportunities to do so. In my opinion, Amazon is by far the most diverse place in the world! Amazon provides employees with amazing opportunities to foster diversity and inclusion across all levels within the organization. Tech needs to foster more diversity and inclusion; however, I do see the trends going in the right direction. Companies like Amazon, Google, and Facebook are doing an excellent job at fostering diversity and inclusion. I see that as a positive sign.

What is your next big dream?

Recently, I got officially certified as a professional career coach. My main goal is to empower others with my life experiences, interpersonal skills, and education to discover their paths for life purpose, career, and happiness.

37

Chitra Banerjee Divakaruni

Crafting the Stories I Needed to Hear

You are an award-winning author, poet, activist and teacher, and have written 20 books including The Palace of Illusions. Your short stories have also been published in The New Yorker, Vogue, and Best American Short Stories, and your work has been translated across many languages. Tell us what inspired you to be a creative writer and what made you the woman you are today.

Immigration made me into a writer. I came to the U.S. at the age of 19 for further studies. Due to a family financial crisis, suddenly there was no money for me to go to college. I found myself in a strange country. All the things I had hoped for – higher studies and a career – seemed out of reach. I turned to writing as a solace, to remember my birth country which seemed so far away, and to make sense of the unfamiliar, exciting and scary country in which I found myself. I looked carefully at the women around me. Many were brave souls struggling against difficult circumstances. I started volunteering in the field of domestic violence. All of this inspired me to write my first books, and to become who I am today. I still do activist work in domestic violence. It has really shaped my life philosophy and led me to focus on strong heroines.

You have highlighted dynamic and strong female characters in your work. How do you believe writing and storytelling can empower women?

When we see ourselves and our communities portrayed in art and literature, it is a special feeling. We see that we are visible, that we are an important part of society, of the world we live in. We see that our joy and sorrows, our struggles and triumphs are meaningful. Our problems cease to be our individual problems – they become shared issues. In a strange, almost magical way, we draw strength from heroes and heroines who look and sound like us. When we cheer them on, we are cheering ourselves on, too. I have experienced this myself, when I read books with South Asian protagonists. I hope my books can do this for someone.

You were recently a keynote speaker at an Akshaya Patra gala. What inspires you about Akshaya Patra's mission? Why do you believe it is important to give back?

It is crucial to give back. That is how we express our gratitude to the universe for the blessings that enrich our lives. I think of it as a human duty. Also, it makes us happy – try it out and see for yourself!

Akshaya Patra's mission is particularly meaningful for me because, growing up in India, I saw a lot of hungry children, and a lot of children who had to start working at a very young age just so they could get enough to eat. Their parents made them drop out of school because they couldn't afford to feed them unless they were bringing in money, too. By feeding schoolchildren, Akshaya Patra enables them to remain in school and to do well in their studies. Who can study when they are hungry? The meals that Akshaya Patra provides for children change their lives, offer them a brighter future. Also, have you seen the Akshaya Patra

> "When we see ourselves and our communities portrayed in art and literature, it is a special feeling. We see we are visible, that we are an important part of society."

films, the faces of the children as they are eating? The simple joy. That itself makes it worthwhile for me.

What is your advice to budding young writers on getting started?

Read a lot! Unless you read, you cannot become a good writer. Books have been wonderful teachers for me. Also, make time in your day to write. Simplify your life so you have this writing time. Finally, find a group of writer friends you can share your work with. Feedback from other writers can really help you. It has certainly helped me.

What is your next big dream?

My next big dream is always the novel that's in my head, the one I'm writing, or planning to write! Right now, that is a book about India's independence movement, how this turbulent and exciting time affects a family of three sisters in Bengal. How they learn, through triumph and heartbreak, what freedom really means. I've titled it *Independence*.

Jaishree Deshpande

Finding Inspiration to Give Back

Tell us about your early years. Your parents put a lot of focus on education. What are some of the lessons you learned from your family that made you who you are today?

I grew up in a small town called Hubballi in Northern Karnataka. My father was a government doctor, and my mother was a homemaker. I have two older sisters and a younger brother. My mother always assigned each one of us a task. My elder sister Sunanda was in charge of putting the rangoli in the morning and braiding my hair. My other sister Sudha was in charge of vegetable shopping, and I was assigned to take care of my brother, as he and I used to go to school together. As each of us had responsibilities, we became responsible at an early age. Helping others was part of the culture of our family. My maternal grandmother was a very compassionate person. She would cook hot meals for students coming from nearby villages. She always lent a helping hand to people in need. My paternal grandmother was

a midwife (though not trained) and assisted pregnant women to deliver babies. She was fondly called "Mother of a hundred children." As my father was a doctor, we always had a houseful of patients. We learnt to adjust, share everything and help others.

We were told that no job was too small or too big. Whatever job we were given we were told to do it perfectly. My maternal grandfather was a simple man and a Gandhi follower. My family taught everything by example, and we absorbed that. As in any Indian home, education was given importance in our family too. My grandfather was a teacher, my mother was a teacher and my father was a professor. Our parents inspired us a lot and encouraged us to study well and to pursue our hobbies. My father was from a village, and he was very fond of animals. We had dogs, cats, and rabbits for pets. Taking care of the pets, we learned to understand the feelings of other living beings.

My maiden name was Kulkarni. Kulkarnis were the accountants for the village, so meticulousness and trustworthiness has always been the core value of our family. More than anything else, we learnt a lot from the actions of our parents and grandparents.

You have had amazing adventures throughout your life, including a trek to Mt. Everest Base Camp and Mt Kailash. How did you prepare yourself, and what did you learn on this journey?

When my husband Desh was recovering from back surgery, our friend Mahesh Ganmukhi came to see him and told us that he was going trekking to Mount Everest Base Camp with his daughter, Swati. Desh encouraged me to go. I was a bit nervous in the beginning, but I wanted to experience both the adventure and the spiritual aspect. I bought all the gear required for trekking. I boosted my daily walk to five miles every day. I started going up and down the staircase with a backpack on my back from the basement to the attic for an hour. As I started trekking, I soon realized that I couldn't talk to others as I was out of breath, and I couldn't keep up with others. I was the slowest of the lot. Being alone helped me to rewind my life and play it again. It was like going to Vipassana meditation camp.

Trekking to Mount Kailash, and then later to Gosaikund was easier as I knew what to expect. On my third trek my sciatica started acting up just before we were to start. I quickly consulted a doctor in Nepal and decided to trek anyway. I took the maximum amount of ibuprofen till the trek was over. Seeing how others live in a hostile environment made me feel very grateful and blessed. I stopped complaining of trivial things. Looking at the vastness of the environment, I felt how insignificant I was. Being with a group of friends, whom I did not know well, for three weeks and sharing the same room or tent expanded my ability to adapt. They became life-long friends.

"If you become self-centered, every problem takes on a magnitude of its own and life becomes overwhelming. But as you get involved with others, you will find that your problems tend to diminish."

Philanthropy has played a big role in your life, including your leadership with Akshaya Patra and Deshpande Foundation. Why is it so important to give back for you, and what are some causes close to your heart?

Desh and I feel lucky to have the opportunity to do what we are doing at this stage of our lives. We want everyone to have the same opportunity and that is the reason we give back. When I was in the working women's hostel in Bengaluru, I used to buy notebooks for the kid who used to deliver milk and take care of his breakfast. When I was at IITM I didn't have a room for the entire first term. Later when I started working for Indian Space Research Organization in Bengaluru, it took me a long time to get a room in a ladies' hostel. So, I always wanted to build a hostel for the ladies. When I got the opportunity to build one, we built the Sharvati hostel at IIT Madras. Desh and I like to help educational institutions as well.

What is your top advice to young women in their careers and personal lives?

Care for people and the environment around you. If you become self-centered, every problem takes on a magnitude of its own and life becomes overwhelming. But as you get involved with others, you will find that your problems tend to diminish. Life is beautiful and I hope all the young people find their own rhythm to enjoy it.

Shimna Sameer

Paying It Forward

You are a woman leader in the finance and business world, currently an executive at Bank of America. How did you find your passion?

I am of Indian origin and came to the U.S., specifically, Providence, Rhode Island, shortly after getting married almost 20 years ago now. I had just wrapped up my master's degree and I had a very active school life – extra classes, competitions, community events – you name it, I was there. After graduating, I felt unchallenged. So while I didn't yet have a driver's license or any work experience in the U.S., I decided to find myself a job.

The only place accessible to me at that point was a small café outside our apartment building. So, one morning I dressed up, picked up all my certificates and visited it looking for an opportunity. Although they thought I was overdressed and potentially overqualified, after some negotiation, the manager offered me a job – I would wash tables and pizza pans and also manage the cash register for $6 an hour.

My acquaintances in my short time in the U.S. all thought it was a bad idea, thinking it would be a "step down" to my family in India and their social status and that it would be unappealing to my techie husband. But to me, this was a way to learn and even earn a little money. Besides that, I sincerely believe there is no shame in any honest work.

That was my starting point. And through the many years that followed, while navigating through various unfamiliar cultures, learning to be a new mom, scaling new heights, managing my life as a daughter when my father got really sick, I persisted. I also since got another job – this time in the financial services industry with Bank of America – where I have spent the past 16 years growing in my career from starting out as a teller to now being a senior executive.

It's been an amazing journey, and I am so grateful to have found an employer that would let me be who I am and provide me with a strong support system to help me grow. All the while I haven't forgotten what it was like to earn $6 an hour, and that experience will always stay with me and keep pushing me forward. Now, I enjoy paying it forward by being a mentor for many and helping them find their dreams.

You are very passionate about women's empowerment. Please talk about why that is so important.

I passionately believe in parity. I like to say, "It's not a world for any, if it's not a world for all!" To me, empowering women has a domino effect – you empower families, you educate families, you shatter perceptions, and you move the world forward. I also believe that if we do not exponentially achieve parity in corporate workplaces, it will be really hard to just scratch the surface in even more complex environments where women are abused, neglected and consciously marginalized. So we have to move with speed and conviction.

> "I haven't forgotten what it was like to earn $6 an hour, and that experience will always stay with me and keep pushing me forward."

What are your top three tips for women looking for leadership roles in the finance or banking industries?

One: You may be the first, you may be the boldest, you may be the least experienced on every team. You also may be the most different – whatever that difference is, that's your strength; embrace it.

Two: Regardless of the industry you're working in, invest in people and invest in them unconditionally.

Three: Pursue excellence. I was the weakest at math in school. Thankfully, finance and banking involve much more than just math and numbers. It's about people and taking care of your clients and teammates. Pursue excellence in everything you do. Your clients and teammates deserve it!

What is your big personal or professional dream?

I would love to visit every country in the world, or at the least, visit countries impacted by war, and spend a few weeks every year living there, serving the people and helping with reformation and rebuilding.

I would like to build a small, nonprofit foundation that focuses on achieving economic equality at the grassroots level. I think social equality and economic equality are closely connected, and I want to put my energy in pursuit of this goal where it is going to matter the most for the most people.

I hope to continue to bring people along as I expand my horizons and eventually have the opportunity to lead a company. The best part of that vision is that I realize I have so much still to learn to get there. With so many people rooting for me and inspiring me, I am confident I will someday see this dream become reality.

43

Ritu Nadkarni

Bringing a Passion for Healthcare to a Wider Business Sphere

What inspired your interest in the healthcare industry?

Growing up in India during an era where she was opening her doors for the first time to global trade gave me a front row ticket to witness the impact of revolutionary medicine as I watched my father, in his entrepreneurial journey, provide life-altering therapies and medical devices. With each hospital bed and healthcare equipment his company manufactured, he enabled a healthier community and helped so many in need. I was fascinated by the ability of countries to use their unique strengths and saw firsthand the advantages of international trade.

Following the exposure I gained during my childhood, I went to a top-ranked college in Pune, India to pursue my master's in international trade. During graduate school, I interned at Dr. Reddy's, which is India's premium pharmaceutical company. After graduation, I moved to Germany to work for a medical device company in international marketing. As a young 20-year-old, I knew there was more than one way to help people via healthcare. I realized that my interests might not align with being a healthcare provider; however, they were a perfect match for bringing the best lifesaving, life-altering medicine and equipment to top providers and hospitals in the world.

After a very aggressive stint with the medical device company in Europe, I got married to my college sweetheart, who had just accepted a job with an oil and gas company in Texas. The European company asked me to continue working with them in the U.S. market. It seemed like a perfect solution, but the challenge became that their marketing functions were in their headquarters in California, and I was moving to Texas. And so the journey brought another opportunity to serve in the healthcare industry. They asked me to join their field sales team in the U.S. market as a sales rep and help launch a digital platform for their equipment that I worked on in Germany. That was one of the steepest learning curves for me: new country, new marriage, and a new job profile.

Those five years of medical device sales taught me so much about what it takes to launch and sell multi-million-dollar products. After learning the ropes and winning multiple sales awards, I went to business school at Thunderbird and was recruited by Merck for their flagship MBA leadership program. During my time at Merck, I gained exposure and experience to all aspects of commercialization, from market research to tender management to medical affairs. I grew in my leadership journey in sales, reimbursement and account management. I developed a passion for therapies that impact population health and became a strong proponent of health equity. Today, I am a commercial leader for Biogen's biosimilar business. It has been my privilege to serve the healthcare industry for the last 22 years on three different continents.

How would you describe your leadership style? What are the key characteristics of a good manager/leader in your experience?

I love this stage of my career because I get to share my learnings, mistakes, and growth with other women and young professionals as they look to make career choices. I have had an unusual career trajectory, and I am almost always the only immigrant commercial leader in a room. I don't take that responsibility nor reality lightly. Mentoring is one of the most satisfying parts of my job. Over the last five years, I have had opportunities to mentor young women through HBA, ERN, and other

formal programs. Here are the top three pieces of advice I share with them:

- **Run your own race.** Every person's journey is different. Focus on your strengths, continue building skill sets that complement your strengths, and never be afraid to take a chance and say yes to learn something new.
- **Surround yourself with people you want to grow up to be.** Even today, I am consistently seeking mentors and role models for various aspects of my life, whether it's building teams, developing business plans, navigating crises, or even parenting.
- **Invest in yourself.** Take time to get to know your authentic self and make decisions from that place. A ritual I do annually is a 3-day solo technology-free trip where I spend time in nature, disconnect, and make copious notes on how I want to grow and serve in the coming year.

Is there a particular empowered woman you admire?

Empowered women surround me, be it my mom, my nine-year-old daughter, my current boss, my kickass colleagues, women on my team or the boards I serve on, my career coach, or my mastermind friends. I have developed a personal "board" of empowered women, and I seek their expertise as I make various personal and professional choices. I am so fortunate to be surrounded by women who make a conscious effort to lift each other up.

> "Empowered women surround me, be it my mom, my nine-year-old daughter, my current boss, my kickass colleagues, women on my team or the boards I serve on, my career coach, or my mastermind friends."

Kimberly Perkins

Clearing the Runway for Women in Aviation

What inspired you to become a pilot?

When I was in high school, I used to spend a lot of time in the science lab. I loved science classes. I dreamed of doing a variety of science-type jobs, but never aviation. While touring universities, I came across a college with a flight program.

While on a campus tour, I became interested in the flight program and got excited about the idea of flying. I inquired about the program to the student giving the tour. He was quick to compliment the program, but followed up with, "It's very competitive; most people drop out; and you probably wouldn't make it." Without hesitation I thought, *That sounds perfect.* I enrolled in the program that fall, completed it three semesters early, and went on to have a career at the airlines and within business aviation. Sometimes an adversary's

doubt is just an invitation to be more tenacious.

What is it like being a female pilot? Were there any challenges or adversities you faced along the way?

I've been fortunate enough to pilot jet aircrafts on six continents, and live on three. Piloting has allowed me to see the world in an extraordinary way, and for that, I'm so very grateful. Seeing the uniqueness of different cultures and the similarities in us all formed a deeper appreciation of humanity. I used my experiences overseas to create the nonprofit Aviation for Humanity, which engages the traveling public to bring school supplies to underfunded schools, shelters, and orphanages around the world.

While aviation has been great in so many ways, it can sometimes feel isolating, and this is one of the many challenges female pilots face. Female career pilots make up just 5% of all pilots in the United States. And, as captains, we make up only 3.6%. After decades of recruiting, these numbers have barely budged. Traditional explanations, such as high training costs and rigorous schedules, have been named as probable causes, but these hurdles are nongendered, and disregard the unique challenges that women and minorities have to overcome.

What are the barriers women face in aviation that you observed? How do you seek to support other women pilots?

Women face invisible barriers, making a challenging career even more rigorous. There are five major barriers that I've experienced in my 18 years within aviation: the double bind, myth of the meritocracy, conformity for social capital, tokenism, and the ideal worker default. Women make up 14% of student pilots but only 5% of career pilots, so we lose women somewhere along the career path. A survey of 100 career women pilots revealed that bias and discrimination show up as dissuading factors in both the recruitment and retention of women. Overt discrimination and explicit bias are usually easy to recognize, but biases can show up in subtle ways, creating invisible challenges that disproportionately affect women, caregivers, and minorities.

> "Women make up 14% of student pilots but only 5% of career pilots, so we lose women somewhere along the career path."

In order to find solutions to these challenges, it's important to label and define them: the double bind (femininity requires a softness but leaders require strength, so as women become more successful, there's a there's-just-something-I-don't-like-about-her factor to overcome); the myth of the meritocracy (a false belief that everyone has an equal opportunity to success, which negates the advantages bestowed on the majority and masks the rampant gender stereotyping holding women back); conformity for social capital (the more a woman can blend in, the larger her network becomes); tokenism (having to prove your worth because people think you didn't get your position on merit); and the ideal worker default (a structure that benefits those free from caregiving responsibilities, which don't tend to be women).

These challenges are not unique to aviation, but they are persistent here. I feel so fortunate to be in the position I am in, and I feel an overwhelming desire and sense of responsibility to give back to and help others access the industry that I love. For the last few years, I channeled this desire toward supporting women in aviation. I began researching, writing and speaking about gender parity and the invisible barriers that are creating challenges for women in the field. While there is energy and encouragement from many allies, the discussions are sometimes met with resistance and hostility, creating a strong "us versus them" posture, which makes it very difficult to effect change. To this end, recently I co-founded Third Wave Aviation. At Third Wave, we are committed to reframing the emphasis from "difference" to "shared purpose" of ensuring an integrated approach to aviation safety that honors the individual while supporting the collective. We aim to include broader definitions of personal and physical safety and give professionals tools that will empower them to create safety for themselves, their colleagues, and the collective people and companies they serve. Everyone will benefit from a fresh approach that transcends blame, judgment and categorization, and promotes whole-system wellness.

Gouri Banerjee

Always Dream of Doing Something Good

While some women dream of fame, wealth, and amazing professional success, I always dreamt of doing something "good." The desire to do good was inspired by my father, an extraordinary scholar and a devout, loving, religious man. It also came from my strong mother, a patient, tolerant, and calm woman, always staying in the background.

Growing up in New Delhi in a large Bengali household in the 1960s, I was inspired by the strength of families and the love and sacrifice of parents. India was under rapid change then; traditional and modern values clashed ceaselessly, and I was often not quite sure of my own place. On the one hand, I witnessed male privilege, misogyny, the preference for male children, and the shaming of women who challenged traditional values. I saw women – some relatives – so miserable in their marriages that they put an end to their own lives, or lived in the midst of great sadness, male dominance and divorce. Yet, I

also saw successful female prime ministers and legislators, professors, doctors and scientists. I saw how much marriage was valued above all else for Indian women, and I wondered why that was the case. These contradictions in modern India inspired me deeply to do something.

At Boston University, working toward a Ph.D. degree, I studied developmental economics and geography, capitalism and European colonialism, xenophobia, Islamophobia, patriarchy and homophobia. I read feminist literature, and witnessed huge gaps between the lives of educated South Asian professional women in the U.S. and the not-so-well-educated. I witnessed the persistent struggle of American women to be safe, to obtain a fair wage and security in employment. As I mulled over these issues in an academic setting, I was drawn toward doing good by volunteering. I volunteered in numerous organizations – the Winchester Multicultural Network, four Parent-Teacher Associations, a peace and anti-nuclear movement, three political campaigns, and several local Indian clubs and ethnic groups. My husband and my children, Rajat and Joya, were eager participants in volunteerism as well; it became a "family thing." For all of us, doing something to improve the lives of others was deeply inspiring.

The opportunity to do more significant "good" came when Mrs. Kamal Misra, a senior member of the India Association of Greater Boston, invited me to join her to create a group to work on behalf of abused Indian women. I was excited to be asked; it was the start of my journey with Saheli, both as a co-founder and as a volunteer board member.

Every weekend for over a decade, my fellow Sahelis and I attended events organized by South Asian ethnic groups in Massachusetts, New Hampshire, and Rhode Island. We raised awareness about domestic abuse in our own communities and met inspiring leaders in other agencies: lawyers, doctors, funders, and state representatives. We collaborated with men and youth, attended South Asian gatherings, organized walks against violence, and held discussions about the broken immigration system in the U.S.

Being a grassroots organization, Saheli gave me the opportunity to combine my education, aspirations, and the desire to do good, and use these strengths to work on a grand project that lasted for twenty-five years. At Saheli, I led the domestic violence program and I navigated my way around the social, economic and family injustices stacked against Asian women. We focused upon timely interventions, prevention of abuse, and empowerment. I established a legal program at Saheli for women's safety and protection, and a funding program for the sustainability of the future of Saheli. I brought our survivor-centered social justice lens to the task of improving the lives of survivors of violence, their families, and to South Asian communities. Finally, I had found a cause close to my heart, in my own community, and a good use for my knowledge of South Asian culture and language.

> "I saw women – some relatives – so miserable in their marriages that they put an end to their own lives, or lived in the midst of great sadness, male dominance and divorce. Yet, I also saw successful female prime ministers and legislators, professors, doctors and scientists. I saw how much marriage was valued above all else for Indian women, and I wondered why that was the case."

I retired from teaching at Emmanuel College as an associate professor emerita, and I retired from the Saheli Board in December 2020. In doing so, I believe that I was passing the baton of leadership on so that younger, talented women would have the same opportunities that I had. Looking ahead to the future, I see Saheli being run by committed professional women, ready to face the challenges of the changing demographics of Massachusetts and the U.S.

Priyamvada Natarajan

An Astronomy and Physics Professor Reflects on Life and the Universe

You are a leading professor in the departments of astronomy and physics at Yale University, noted for your work in mapping dark matter and black holes. You have received numerous awards for your work, including recently being elected to the American Academy of Arts and Sciences. What inspired your interest in physics, and what have been the key lessons you have learned along the way?

I was very curious as a young child (and this is not a euphemism for being naughty!) and was an early, avid reader. I devoured all manner of books, and after looking through a telescope and a microscope as a kid, it was clear to me that it was the night sky that fascinated me more than anything else. The fact that stars were distant, mysterious and unreachable made me want to understand them. Their existence was an inviting challenge. I was also very interested in mathematics and in maps from a young age. I knew that I wanted to be a scientist fairly early on.

I grew up in Delhi in an academic family – both parents are professors, my father is a civil engineer and my mother is a sociologist. I am lucky and won the birth lottery, as it were, to have extremely supportive parents, who led a life of the mind, and who indulged my various interests and allowed me to explore anything that took my fancy. I had a wonderful childhood, filled with simple joys, the most vivid of them being the kind of elation one feels when one figures things out by oneself. I am fortunate to have that still with my research work. Even now, I savor the moment when I finish a calculation, or have pushed my understanding even a little bit further.

My father bought me a Commodore 64 and a Sinclair ZX Spectrum when I was in school. This is before anyone else really had access to these early computers. I learned to program, and my first foray into research was when I was in high school under the guidance of Dr. Nirupama Raghavan, who was then the director of the Nehru Planetarium. With this first taste of research, I was hooked. I was fortunate to get a full scholarship to go for my undergraduate studies to MIT – one key attraction being their Undergraduate Research Opportunities Program. My academic journey began there and took me to Trinity College and Cambridge University and then to Yale, where I currently am – it continues to be exciting and fulfilling to this day. I really learned how to learn at MIT – something that I am super grateful for. Being always open to new ideas, taking intellectual risks and not giving up easily when obstacles have come my way have been key lessons. But most of all, I feel deeply grateful for the abundance of opportunities that have come my way. I continue to be a dreamer, in search of a deeper understanding of the incredible universe that we happen to inhabit.

> "I continue to be a dreamer, in search of a deeper understanding of the incredible universe that we happen to inhabit."

This space has traditionally been male-dominated. Did you face any challenges or obstacles as a woman in the industry, and how did you navigate those?

My area of research has been male-dominated, and that is slowly changing. I faced many challenges along the way and continue to do so. To navigate them, I have been inspired by Mahatma Gandhi, and I try to be an agent of the change I wish to see in the field. I am deeply committed to making science equitable. I want every kid who dreams of being a scientist – no matter what they look like or what they are born into – to have the opportunity to explore and chase that dream.

Who is an empowered woman in your life that you admire?

My mother is the woman in my life whom I admire the most. I feel so lucky to be her daughter. She is wise, brilliant and compassionate. Amma has been my guiding compass, by my side always, through all the ups and downs of life and career – with unwavering, unconditional love, support and belief in my capacities.

What is your next big dream?

Dreams of exciting new intellectual breakthroughs in science with my work; dreams of a more equitable world; dreams of a more sustainable and a peaceful world. On a personal and more immediate level, I am currently working on a book in which I present my vision for science, a complete re-thinking of the process of science and offer a brand-new understanding, demystifying how radical new scientific ideas are accepted, and how advances are made. While every aspect of our lives is suffused with science and technology, there is rampant denialism of reason and science, especially in the United States. I fervently believe that a deeper understanding of what science is and what scientists really do will permit the public to interrogate the information ecosystem, develop discernment and appreciate the beauty of science and the powerful nature of scientific explanation. My immediate dream is to provide this new intellectual toolkit and see it used by the public to understand both the power and the limits of science.

Dahlia Mahmood

On Designing Your Dream Home

What inspired your passion for interior design and entrepreneurship? How did you build your interior design platform to where it is today?

I was born and raised in sunny California, literally next to Disneyland. Growing up, it was my playground. I was so mesmerized by the magic detail and enchanting environments Walt Disney created. At the age of five, a spark was lit and I knew I was destined to be a designer.

I was inspired by, "When you wish upon a star, it makes no difference who you are.

Anything your heart desires will come to you." Finding my path as a young Arab-American woman, especially as a designer and entrepreneur at 17, the obstacles and prejudices only fueled my desire to succeed. I'm very humbled, not hardened, by my journey. I have a sense of purpose and responsibility to help others, especially our next generation. When I was their age, I was met with much skepticism. I had to become self-reliant very quickly. I want to inspire and motivate our future dreamers, to give them the tools and encouragement to succeed. From the classroom to internships to speaking engagements, I tell these eager minds to embrace their authentic self, embrace their dreams… for their individual light shines as bright as their ambition.

In my career, I have been fortunate to experience groundbreaking opportunities and sit at the table where major decisions were made… but there has been a piece missing, another dream. I believe that mainstream design television needs more women of color… someone who looks like me. I hope to be a driving force for this, knowing millions of little girls and boys need to see this representation. The impact could be astronomical.

Post pandemic, more people started working remotely, leading to lots of home renovations, and often feel bored of their space. What are your top tips for sprucing up your living space?

The pandemic definitely impacted our industry in profound ways, from workforce shortages to supply chain delays. We are slowly achieving new normals. Despite the challenges, there has been a slight uptick in projects and developments, which is very exciting. As an influencer, I have observed not only our clients but the general public viewing their homes with a different post-pandemic lens. There is a conscious effort to make time for their living spaces. Investing in their homes can be a form of self-expression that has been bottled up for some time. From home offices, gyms to bedroom and bathroom sanctuaries, design has become the new comfort food.

> "Investing in homes can be a form of self-expression that has been bottled up for some time. From home offices, gyms to bedroom and bathroom sanctuaries. Design has become the new comfort food."

What is the most common stress you think people have when designing their space? And what is your tip for managing it?

Design and decor can be overwhelming and stressful when you view the bigger picture. Simplify the process, start with one element and build from there. It might be a piece of art or furniture you love, a paint color, or even a destination… start to build a story with your design concept and the pieces will fall into place.

You have a strong social media presence and post very inspiring content. You also started at a young age. How do you seek to empower the next generation? And what is your next big dream?

Social media can easily become a saturated outlet to try to gain notoriety; instead I've centered my profile around my day-to-day work life and the wonderful connections and experiences I've made along the way. I hope to share inspiration and motivation with my fellow women.

What is your next big dream?

As women, we have a lot on our shoulders. Always remember to give yourself grace. Take a moment for yourself, to connect, and find gratitude right where you are. And while you're at it, be glam; life's too short not to enjoy beautiful things. That includes you!

Sunayana Kachroo

Telling Stories Through Poetry, Prose and Film

You are an award-winning poet, film writer, producer, lyricist and columnist. What inspired your passion for the creative arts?

My parents, especially my father, nurtured my interest in literature, movies and music. We watched movies, listened to music and read books because there wasn't anything else to do. I remember getting Boney M's music cassette as a gift for getting good grades and topping the class. Even though the money was tight, I got the best of the best clothes and gadgets to use. We didn't do a lot of things, but whatever we wore or ate, it was the best in the town.

The story of my writing didn't just start with the first thing I wrote or achieved, it started much before that: the carefree childhood in the idyllic Kashmir valley shunted by terrorism, thrilling misadventures of hostel life in Pune, coming to New York on a software engineering job through H1, working in Manhattan, moving to Boston after marriage, making peace with the hyphenated dual identity, finding refuge in music and expression in words. My first book, *Waqt Se Pare – Beyond Time,* was published in 2013, and my second book, *Sunny Side Up: Poems and Short Stories,* in 2022. Meanwhile, films happened and I got an opportunity to collaborate with some renowned artists.

Life is the greatest inspiration. As cliché as it may sound, this is the only truth I know of. Most creative people have lived a colorful, adventurous life full of speed bumps, roller coasters and struggle. If you take the struggle away, there is no story to tell. Inspiration doesn't come only from what happens directly to you but also from what you hear, witness, or read. Sometimes your art is just your reaction or a reflection of your experiences. Ironically, the failure on page 41 in my life is connected to the success on page 78. I cannot tear one and spare the other, intertwined in destiny in such a way that what I understood at page 78 makes page 41 priceless. Anyone who can express without having to experience life is either a con or a highly spiritual being; poets, I think, are somewhere in between.

You are working on films currently. Tell us more about your current project. What is the story you aim to tell through this film?

My film writing and creative production work started in 2014 with *Half Widow to The Illegal,* which was released in 2021, as well as the beautiful short film *In Search of America* (selected for Cannes) and the recently released short film *The Good News.* I kept learning along the way. The process and the ecosystem of films is very different. Since I didn't have any formal education or direct association with the film industry, I had to learn everything on the job. Sometimes, the story is given to me and I have to develop the screenplay around that. Sometimes, the screenplay is ready and I have to write dialogue. In such cases, I may not have the liberty of saying exactly what I want because we have to stay honest to the world of the character. As a writer, I cannot force my morality on the characters. Yet, personal experiences do trickle in here and there.

> "I realized later that when I was writing biographical poems, I was also writing a history of Kashmir. My poems on my great-grandmother's death during Kabali raids is not only a simple story of my relative, but also a footnote in the history of Kashmir."

As you are Kashmiri, much of your work has Kashmiri influence. How do you aim to surface your cultural heritage in your work?

I see myself as a cultural activist. Kashmiri culture, especially language and music, is facing an extinction. One can either cry rivers over it or add a drop toward the preservation. I chose the latter. Through my work as a poet, filmmaker and a lyricist, I have tried to bring the Kashmiri language back into the mainstream music industry. We have used Kashmiri phrases, Kashmiri artists, poems of old forgotten poets and motifs through my work whenever possible.

I realized later that when I was writing biographical poems, I was also writing a history of Kashmir. My poems on my great-grandmother's death during Kabali raids is not only a simple story of my relative, but also a footnote in the history of Kashmir.

Who are some women artists you admire?

Kashmiri poetess Lal Ded for her mysticism, Lata Mangeshkar for her precision in perfection, the maverick Amrita Pritam for her I-don't-give-a-damn attitude in life and in her writing, Adele for having the courage to cancel her album the last minute and start again, Aynur Dogan for resistance poetry, Maya Angelou for her wisdom, Habba Khatoon for making melancholy so beautiful, Raj Begum for breaking the glass ceiling, Ishmat Chugtai for her realism, Sylvia Plath for her rebellion and Louise Gluck for every drop of word she wrote.

Sapna Shetty

When Everything Changes In an Instant

You have shown strength, resilience, and grace throughout your life. Describe the point at which your life pivoted.

I was stable and happy, and things were great until an unexpected tragedy changed my life. My husband passed away suddenly due to brain encephalitis, and overnight, my life was shattered. My two young kids and I were left shocked and not sure how we would continue.

Unfortunately, there was little time to mourn his loss, because I had a family to care for, and my husband's software company to manage. In the first few months everything felt alien to me because I had no knowledge of the business he ran so successfully. That, coupled with having to manage our

employees, in addition to the many consultants that his company employed, was an overwhelming task. I started by taking a few courses in computer science and business. As a beauty consultant, this work was uninteresting to me, but I did not want my late husband's legacy and hard work to go to waste. I overcame my fear and did my best to keep the business going for my family. Thankfully my hard work and blessings paid off, and we did really well for many years to come.

These hardships in my life have taught me to live life to the fullest. When tragedy struck, for my kids and myself I had to take on more responsibility. It was hard and at times, felt almost impossible to move forward, but I learned that it's up to oneself to be positive and learn new skills to focus on improving with the greater good of my family in the forefront. I appreciate and want to thank the friends and family who were always there to support us.

What was the biggest challenge when you took over your husband's business, and how did you overcome it?

The biggest challenge facing me when I took over my husband's company was my lack of formal education in computer software and business. I had no other choice but to learn everything on my own. I took a few courses in CS and business management which were very helpful. I thankfully had help from my employees and consultants who were always there for me when I needed technical help. The first year was the hardest, but after some experience, it became less stressful. I focused on adapting to the ups and downs in business, and in whole we were successful.

What were some challenges you faced as a single mother?

Being a single mother was extremely hard. My children's teen years were especially trying as I had the added stress of knowing that any decision I made would affect them for the rest of their lives. My love, care, and patience was what guided me to ensure the best for them. In the early stages of their father's passing, the grief and loss was really unbearable for the kids. Professional counselors helped ease their pain. I made sure that I always put my kids in the forefront of my decisions. We often traveled as a family, and I developed a deeper bond with my children. Gradually, this bond yielded to a wonderfully supportive attitude when I faced tough situations. When I look back on those tough years, I can see that we have come so far. My kids have risen past unimaginable pain to become strong and independent pursuers of their dreams.

> "When tragedy struck, for my kids and myself I had to take on more responsibility. It was hard and at times, felt almost impossible to move forward, but I learned that it's up to oneself to be positive and learn new skills to focus on improving with the greater good of my family in the forefront."

What is your best advice to people going through similar challenges in life, especially with the loss of loved ones?

My advice to people in similar situations is however hard life may be, it is best to be positive and look at the life ahead of you rather than looking back and living in the past. At the beginning of my loss, looking back at my pain would only cause me anxiety and depression, but I had my kids to think about. Managing my kids' lives, taking care of their needs, and making sure they were stable were my first concerns. I gave myself some care by enriching my life. I focused on learning new skills I had never thought of before. I took up dance lessons, which led to me performing on stage. I continued to pursue my passion for cosmetology by opening a beauty salon. All these endeavors helped me move forward and become not only a happier person, but a better one as well.

What was your biggest support system and how do you find that support system and resilience for yourself?

I had emotional and moral support from my immediate family, close friends, and our Bunt community. They all came together to stand with me and my kids. This is something we will never forget. We and are truly indebted to our community for their support.

Punita Kumar-Sinha

Bringing More Women to the Table

You were the chief investment officer and the head of Blackstone Asia Advisors, and you are also on the board of many organizations including the Chartered Financial Analyst Institute. What were some of the key moments in your life and in your career that define who you are?

When I reflect on the key moments in my career, getting admission into IIT Delhi was one of them. I was very fortunate to have studied with some very distinguished and bright people, and that really shaped my life in many, many ways to come. With only 1% to 3% of the students in the class women, one learned very early on how to cope in a male-dominated professional world.

Another defining moment in my career was stumbling upon the world of emerging markets investing. Being an early investor in emerging markets as well as in quantitative finance helped me rise in the corporate world

quite quickly. I am truly grateful that I was able to find a career that I am passionate about.

What defined my career in a very important way was when I started to manage NYSE listed funds which were run as investment companies. It gave me exposure to corporate governance and reporting to a board. That gave me the inspiration and experience to venture into becoming a board member myself. I am now on multiple boards, so this experience has been invaluable. Interestingly, I now chair the Investment Advisory Board of my alma mater, IIT Delhi. Who would have ever thought that one day, I would be invited to give back to an institution where there were so few women when I entered college!

What do you think was the key aspect in your personality that really drove your success and made you exceptional in some ways?

I think some of it, of course, is very intentional, and some of it is also destiny. I have been strategic about taking risks in my professional career by choosing to go into professions that were unconventional for women. Going to IIT to do engineering, doing a Ph.D. in finance at Wharton, were all very deliberate decisions. I am told that I was the first Indian woman to do a Ph.D. in finance from Wharton, and I was the second Indian woman to have gotten the CFA charter in the U.S. When I moved to Boston in 1990, I was one of the first few Indians in the investment profession in Boston's financial district!

I intuitively put into practice what I learned later in business school: it is much easier to succeed if one plays to one's competitive strengths. So, when you do something that is unique and different, you are able to excel, and if you execute well, you have tremendous opportunities ahead of you. There are challenges too when you do something new as you charter your own path and have to break many glass ceilings.

To a large extent, I attribute my drive to all the stories I heard in the family about Partition and how it impacted their lives. My father always said that one can lose everything but not one's education, so I ended up getting four degrees and a CFA! And of course, I saw how the Indians took pride in having sons but not daughters, so I wanted to prove that I too could accomplish all that the boys could.

Why do you think it's so important for companies to have women on their boards and in leadership positions?

It is well-known that diverse perspectives lead to better outcomes. I think when you have diverse perspectives, whether it is through gender or ethnic diversity or other forms of diversity, you come up with very creative solutions. So, thinking alike isn't always the best way to build a business. I think that's why everybody is now striving to have more

women on boards. Many, many companies in the U.S. now have 30% women on their boards. India actually took very progressive steps and instituted a law that required every company to have at least one independent woman director, and while I joined some of my boards before this law was instituted, I've seen how the law has enabled companies to get comfortable with first having one woman, and once they have seen the benefits of diverse thinking, more companies have voluntarily brought in more than one woman. Several of the boards I serve on now have two or three women on the board. Therefore, it was so critical to get that first board position for many women.

> "I think when you have diverse perspectives, whether it is through gender or ethnic diversity or other forms of diversity, you come up with very creative solutions."

In terms of gender diversity, the world is really progressing very well as compared to the times that I grew up in. Even when I look at institutions where I studied, in engineering at the IITs in India, we were four women out of a class of 250, but now the class is much larger, at least 20% women. Even at the entry level, all companies are trying to recruit almost 40% to 50% women, even in private equity. When I was at Blackstone, I was one of five women partners in the firm and I was the only one to head up a business unit, and one of the only women to be leading an investment team. There were very few women in that role, but now private equity firms are actually looking to bring in more women, so the pendulum has swung the other way. I think now it is up to the women to really stay in their careers.

Rachana Kulkarni

A Physician with Heart

Tell us about your background and the journey that led you to be a cardiologist.

I am from Nagpur and migrated to the U.S. after completing medical school at Government Medical College in Nagpur. When I was completing my residency at Robert Wood Johnson University Hospital, I realized the extent and severity of heart disease in South Asians. My natural thought process was to seek solutions for such an aggressive disease for my ethnicity.

In addition, I realized how heart disease in women is misunderstood and undertreated,

and that the lack of female cardiologists has compounded the problem. So, I definitely saw a gap in the treatment of heart disease in women. That was my inspiration to go into cardiology. It was a tough but very rewarding journey, and I would do it again in a heartbeat.

You are not only a cardiologist and a managing partner in your practice, but also the president of the American Heart Association in New Jersey. How do you make the time to balance all of these roles along with family life?

Passion! I love what I do as a cardiologist. It is extremely gratifying to see how your knowledge can make a difference in people's health and help them change the trajectory of their lives.

In addition, I strongly believe that most heart disease is preventable if we can identify and address the risk factors. I also believe in the American Heart Association's mission to raise awareness about heart disease in women. So it has been my honor to serve as their president in New Jersey. This is possible because of my passion for the cause and also because of the support of my husband and family.

You are on the board of the nonprofit Akshaya Patra. How long have you been involved with them, and what motivates you to be involved in a nonprofit? Also, why Akshaya Patra?

I have been involved with Akshaya Patra for probably a decade now. I came from a family that valued hard work and education, and I strongly believe that educating children – especially girls – is the most important intervention to change the world. Akshaya Patra's vision that no child in India should be deprived of education because of hunger was a very powerful vision to change the course of the country.

At Akshaya Patra, we dream of a world where families won't have to choose between food and education for their children. A wholesome meal prompts children to stay in school, thereby addressing both classroom hunger and education. So I feel that Akshaya Patra's vision and mission resonates with my desire to promote education and support women's empowerment through education. Akshaya Patra is the perfect vehicle to achieve that change in an entire generation of Indian kids. It's a way to give them real tools to break the cycle of poverty for them and their families.

You are invested in women's cardiac health. What are your top tips for women to maintain their best cardiac health?

Women need to know that cardiovascular disease is the number one killer for women, causing one in three deaths each year; that's approximately one woman per minute. Each year, more women die of heart disease than all cancers combined. But women can change this by adopting a heart-healthy lifestyle.

I suggest *Life's* simple seven steps for heart health: stop smoking, eat better, stay active, maintain a healthy weight, manage your blood pressure, control your blood sugars and cholesterol.

> "Women need to know that cardiovascular disease is the number one killer for women, causing one in three deaths each year; that's approximately one woman per minute."

We owe it to our loved ones to take better care of our heart health. Your "why" to take care of your heart is your mother, your daughter, your family.

What is your next big personal and/or professional dream?

I would love to see Akshaya Patra feed five million children in India each day by 2025, and for every Indian girl to be educated. My personal dream is to see the United States be a truly beautiful mosaic of ethnicities, where each piece contributes uniquely to make a beautiful end product. People of different beliefs, different hopes and dreams, and different talents coming together to pursue their dreams.

Ankita Narula

On the Power of Empowering Young Women

What has motivated you in your career journey?

I embarked on my career in the hospitality industry in India, dedicating about five years to corporate sales and marketing roles with renowned global hospitality brands. Although this period brought growth, it also presented an internal struggle as I sought to discern my true purpose in life. I found solace and a sense of purpose by devoting my weekends to engaging in nonprofit activities. Throughout this journey, my strong desire to study business, entrepreneurship, and strategy became evident. Equally compelling was my passion for working in the social sector, driving me to establish a club affiliated with nonprofits while pursuing a full-time MBA in Boston. A pivotal moment arose during a leadership class when I firmly committed to dedicating myself to the social sector in the long run. I have been deeply inspired by the remarkable individuals I encountered when I began working for Akshaya Patra, an esteemed and world-class organization, shortly after completing my MBA.

Witnessing their strong work ethics, discipline, and humble attitudes has been truly motivating. In my life, I hold on to the principle of focusing on the task at hand without becoming attached to the outcomes, embracing the theory of karma. Leveraging my strengths in my work is also of utmost importance to me. Moreover, I greatly value the guidance and mentorship I receive daily, recognizing the significance of continuous learning.

As the vice president of Akshaya Patra USA, one of the world's largest NGOs providing mid-day meals to millions of schoolchildren in India, what inspired you to work at AP and in the nonprofit sector?

I owe my inspiration to one of my esteemed professors, Mr. Mike Grandinetti, who taught a leadership module. It was during this time that I realized my calling to switch my career path and contribute to the social sector in order to help underprivileged individuals. After graduating, I found myself aligned with what I had envisioned in my mind and heart. Akshaya Patra is an exceptional organization that tackles a significant global issue by striving to alleviate malnutrition in children. Regrettably, India is home to 30% of malnourished children worldwide, making it a pressing concern. Dealing with food-related issues has been a part of my career journey, since I began working in the hospitality industry in India. Consequently, I have encountered numerous complexities associated with food. I am immensely grateful that an organization like Akshaya Patra has emerged to make a substantial impact, and I am privileged to be a part of it.

Akshaya Patra is committed to engaging the next generation. Why is it crucial to involve them, especially young women, in such causes?

I believe that any social cause, regardless of its location, requires the active participation of young voices, innovative thinking, ideas, and passion. The earlier young women get involved, the better, as it not only contributes to their personal development but also positively influences those around them. Women today play significant roles in society, whether it's at the board level, within their households, in their professions, or eventually as mothers and wives. By actively involving young women, we can make a significant impact on society as a whole.

What has been the most significant accomplishment of your career?

Every day is filled with excitement, and I feel a strong sense of entrepreneurship in what I do, thanks to the exceptional organizational culture and the tremendous support from management, staff, and our organization as a

whole. Another aspect of my role that I truly cherish is community building and interacting with passionate individuals on a daily basis. Nonprofits heavily rely on volunteers, donors, and the community. Everyone involved in the cause has a compelling reason, and their stories serve as a constant. The advice I'd offer to young women considering entering the nonprofit sector is to be deeply passionate about their chosen path and to cherish every moment of it. The key to excelling in this field is to have an unwavering passion that empowers us to consistently deliver our best, even during difficult times. Another essential factor is education and continuously honing the skills at which we excel. Nurturing our strengths is vital for personal growth and professional advancement.

Who are the women who have been role models and sources of inspiration for you?

One of my most significant female role models is my mother, who retired from one of the largest public sector undertakings in India, BHEL (Bharat Heavy Electricals Limited). Since my childhood, my mother has instilled in me the value of financial independence. Witnessing her dedication to her work and her commitment to providing for our family has been truly inspiring. Additionally, I hold great admiration for the board members and leaders within our organization. Each of them possesses unique qualities and expertise that I find inspiring. As I connect and engage with them, I continuously learn and grow from their experiences and insights.

> "By actively involving young women, we can make a significant impact on society as a whole."

63

Nithya Iyer Singh

Striving to Inspire Others By Example

Tell us about your journey as a woman in the biotechnology business world. What made you the woman you are today?

It started with a family member in the business. Believe it or not, I had always wanted to work in clinical drug development since childhood and develop new cures for patients. My journey was quite long-winded and convoluted in the sense that while I went to pharmacy school, I didn't start my career there. I worked in investing and various healthcare organizations before starting my career in biotech. What has carried me in my career is being passionate about my work, and I like work that is meaningful for humanity. Always follow your passion.

In addition to your healthcare work, you are dedicated to various philanthropies and are a big believer in giving back. You've also supported Akshaya Patra. Why is it important to you to give back, and what

inspires you about organizations like Akshaya Patra?

What I like about Akshaya Patra is their mission to enable people to get an education, which then allows them to get into the workplace. Getting an education enables them to eventually be financially independent as they grow up in life. I truly believe that this financial independence and self-sufficiency is key to the future of multitudes of communities and cohorts of people, whether it be women, people of different backgrounds, etc. I think that enabling and providing that opportunity is absolutely core. In terms of what inspires me to give back, I grew up in India, so I saw what these kids went through, and the inequality and lack of access. I always try to get behind good causes and organizations with good missions.

Volunteerism and the desire to give back often runs in the family. Does your family volunteer as well?

Yes. I teach my kids about the importance and power of giving back. With my volunteer work, I aim to set an example for them. I also think it is important to volunteer at the grassroots level. For example, I have volunteered with the STEM council at my school for the past several years to bring educational and enriching STEM opportunities to kids at an early age. I have also worked with organizations such as United Way, the Museum of Science and the Boy Scouts. I truly believe that if you start your life volunteering and end your life volunteering, that is a blessing. This is something I tell my kids, and I hope I am doing a good job leading by example, too.

One of Akshaya Patra's new initiatives is the Young Professionals, and at Women Who Win, one of our key focuses is mentoring young women. Reflecting on your own career, what is your top piece of advice for young women professionals as they navigate their careers?

My biggest advice is to follow your passion. I honestly think that as young professionals start their career journeys, it is important to get into an area that motivates and inspires you. When you do what you love, it is not just a job. It becomes a career and a way of life. Find something that is meaningful to you and where you have an opportunity to make a large impact on society. Focus on finding that industry you want to be in; you don't have to be stuck in a box. Painting, medicine, whatever it is that excites you and fuels your passion is what you should do.

> "When you do what you love, it is not just a job. It becomes a career and a way of life."

What is your next big personal and/or personal dream?

Professionally, I want to continue my journey in the oncology /drug development space. I've launched a drug already and would love to continue bringing medicines and cures to patients. One of the projects I am working on now is in the area of gynecologic oncology. I would love to develop something that helps women.

One of my personal dreams is to run a marathon in Antarctica. Running is a key part of my work-life balance. I started running approximately ten years ago. Running is time to myself. I love being outdoors and being in nature. Initially, I was just running a couple of miles here and there, but then I was inspired by a close friend who has run multiple marathons. She said, "You should consider running the Cape Cod Marathon." I was very hesitant at first, but within a year of that, I ran my first half marathon. I have run many marathons and half marathons since then, and hope to continue.

Gayatri Aryan

Lessons Learned at the Scariest of Times

2017

It was the week of Thanksgiving when the call came to confirm my appointment with the oncologist. This was after two weeks of what felt like an unending chain of screening tests: mammograms, ultrasounds, breast/bone biopsies followed by MRI-guided biopsies. *Another day off*, I had been thinking. It was just my third week at Virtustream as director of product development. With an organization distributed around the globe (Massachusetts, Georgia, Utah, California and Bangalore), my days were crazy as it was! All this in the midst of an Executive MBA program I was pursuing at MIT Sloan School of Management. More than halfway done with the program, I was super excited about next semester's Global Labs module, helping the

Puerto Rican government rebuild their power grids. I really didn't have time for this.

"It's Stage II. The tumors are very small," said my oncologist. "However, because there are multiple lesions in both breasts, we need to tag it as Stage III." I had had a mammogram just the year before, upon turning 40, per recommendation. I have no memory of the rest of the conversation. I just remember that I continued to look at Vikram. His eyes had welled up. "This is serious, Gayatri," I heard my oncologist say, rubbing my back.

How could this be? I was only 41. My kids were nine and 11. We started off in the first phase of grief: denial. I made an appointment at Dana Farber Cancer Institute (DFCI) to solicit a second opinion in the hopes that perhaps there was a way to turn the diagnosis back. *Au contraire*, it turned out that one of the lesions was very close to the rib cage. So, the oncologist at DFCI ordered a full body bone scan. For this I am eternally grateful, as it led to the final (and accurate!) diagnosis of my metastatic breast cancer (MBC).

2020

After almost three years of treatment, to say that life had changed would be such a cliché. And the dichotomy is stark. But that's not what this piece is about. This piece is about a few reflections on my journey so far, including the importance of:

Self awareness: You and only you are the best judge of changes in your body. Be aware and act on the changes observed!

Screening tests: Like all things in life, they are not perfect. This includes mammograms. Especially in younger women, dense breasts make screening mammograms less effective.

Getting a second opinion: Misdiagnosis seems rampant in the world of cancer. While there will be a strong urge to get going on the treatment as soon as possible, do take the time to get a second (or third) opinion.

Back office: As the patient journeys through the roller coaster ride of treatment options, insurance coverage gets super complicated super quickly. If the hospital's billing department is well structured, it will literally improve your quality of life, no kidding, as you will spend less time understanding and negotiating every invoice.

> "As Morgan Harper Nichols said, 'Tell the story of the mountain you climbed. Your words could become a page in someone else's survival guide.'"

Self-advocacy: What can I say about this, it's more important than ever to advocate for your situation.

Community: I cannot insist on joining a community enough. With candor I'll confess that cancer treatment is an extremely personal journey. However, there is so much strength in knowing that you are not alone. For all you know, you may end up lending a hand to a fellow cancer patient and that is powerful.

Mental game: It may sound ironic, but MBC has been liberating for me. It has encouraged me to shed the unwarranted obligations and inhibitions. I believe that I've been able to achieve this mindset because I try to stay away from the question of "Why me?"

Share your ride: As Morgan Harper Nichols said, "Tell the story of the mountain you climbed. Your words could become a page in someone else's survival guide."

Danielle Naer

A Leading New York City Fashion Editor's Journey

You've had a dream career in the fashion industry. What inspired you to pursue this career in fashion?

I kind of circuitously wound up working in fashion. I always had a strong passion to write. When I graduated, it was about figuring out where I would plant that seed and eventually want to grow a full-fledged career. Condé Nast was always a dream company for me. I aspired to work at the World Trade Center office and have that glossy experience. I was so fortunate to get my first job there, working at *Vogue* on the sales team. From there, I just bugged a bunch of editors and asked them to take a chance on me.

And that's how my career in fashion started. I had very little fashion knowledge. I always cared a lot about clothing and found it to be an unparalleled means of self-expression. So when I finally had the opportunity to write about it and do it in a way that felt real to me, it was the best merger of all these different things I cared a lot about. I think working in fashion can feel alienating to people. I think the industry can be a little exclusionary. My favorite part of having this kind of a career is being able to give people the opportunity to see that fashion is really just a way of feeling good.

To me, I think a lot gets lost in translation, and it can feel really isolating, or commercial and capitalistic. I think the biggest thing we should all remember is that whatever you put on your body is supposed to make you feel amazing; my job is really just showing people that and giving them the tools they need to have that experience with clothing. I've been in the fashion journalism world for quite a long time. And now I'm with the *Editorialist*. We are trying to give people that kind of luxury lifestyle and that aspirational experience. Wherever they are in the world or whatever their salaries are, we want it to be something aspirational and exciting for everyone.

What is your advice to young women interested in fashion?

I think within fashion and media worlds, a lot of it is connected to the schools you went to. I went to Rutgers; I didn't go to a fancy private or Ivy League school, which is totally OK. I think it goes to show that it doesn't matter what your background is. What's really important is to know the value you bring, to carry your head high, and be proud of where you came from. That impresses people; when they see that confidence in your background and your upbringing and the context of where you're coming from, it resonates with them. It's really important that I uplift other creatives and people who are just getting their start, because it can feel lonely when you are first trying to get that foot in the door.

Did you face any challenges or obstacles in your personal or professional journey? How did you overcome them?

Fashion is famously cutthroat, and just competitive in general. It's important to have integrity whenever you're at work or in a situation whether you're leading a team, or if you're trying to make a decision about something you're writing about. You have to stay true to who you are and really stick with your guns on things. I always try to have a strong center of gravity and to be vocal about things that matter to me.

Also, I try not to lose myself. When you are in a quick environment and everything is "go go go" all the time, it can be easy to forget to prioritize yourself and your well-being. So taking that time out, to be present with yourself and make sure that you're taking care

> "I think the biggest thing we should all remember is that whatever you put on your body is supposed to make you feel amazing; my job is really just showing people that and giving them the tools they need to have that experience with clothing."

of you is crucial and vital to everything else that you'll accomplish. If you're doing that, then you'll be far more successful.

What inspires you to give back and uplift people in your community?

It's been something that's been pretty important to me for most of my life. I had toyed with what kind of organization I'd want to work with for a while. I recently began volunteering for Safe Horizon, which is New York's leading domestic violence shelter. They support victims from all different walks of life. It's a wonderful organization, and they do a great job of helping these families and women transition out of their homes and get back on their feet and get jobs again. I am really passionate about using the fashion connections and knowledge I have to help women who are having to leave home and make really hard choices for themselves and their children by giving something less to worry about, by providing a good high quality clothing element that will stick with them throughout this hard time and make them feel good because so much of it is confidence related. I think that what I set out to do originally was to give back once I had that chance, and looking now at my career, I'm able to do it in such a more profound way because I've given that time to think and see what was going to be right for me and what I could give. I'm really proud of it. And I can't wait to see how it blossoms.

Poonam Kamdar

Practicing Charitable Outreach Since Childhood

You were a Youth Ambassador and founder of the Coin Jar Program at Akshaya Patra, one of the largest organizations serving nutritious lunches to millions of kids daily across schools in India. What inspired you to give back at a young age?

Throughout my childhood, my parents always taught me the importance of helping others. No matter how big or small the task, helping others and giving back has become an integral value for me to this day.

I was first introduced to Akshaya Patra (AP) in 2010 by my father, who had attended an annual gala and was deeply moved by the cause. He thought that AP's mission would strongly resonate with me too, and was he right! Akshaya Patra's midday meals are solving three different causes at once: education, hunger, and equality. As a young student at the time, I could not imagine going a school day without eating. AP's amazing work inspired me to get more involved.

With my parents' support and guidance, in 2011, I started the Akshaya Patra Coin Jar Program, a grassroots fundraising initiative. Over time, I have continued supporting Akshaya Patra in a variety of ways and am still very active in the Tristate chapter. I am continuously inspired by Akshaya Patra's accomplishments to keep helping others.

It is challenging to balance giving back and service with day-to-day work and school. How did you strike this balance against the backdrop of your college education and early career?

Establishing priorities, along with good time management and organizational skills, allows me to successfully balance my philanthropic goals with educational and career goals. I made helping others a top priority in my life once I started college. Similar to my childhood days, this meant everything from mentoring an intern at work to volunteering with my sorority in college to helping Akshaya Patra. Helping others and giving back was often integrated into my college experience and early career responsibilities, giving me even more opportunities to do everything I love.

Backtrack to your freshman year of college. What is the biggest piece of advice you would give yourself and to young women on networking and building your career?

Don't be afraid to put yourself out there. Early in my college career, I had a good idea about what I wanted to do with my life, but it wasn't until I did my research through networking that I found the perfect career path for me. Part of getting yourself out there is having the

confidence to do so, and the other half is really just "faking it till you make it." Having an open mind, along with a positive attitude and curiosity, will help you differentiate yourself from your peers early in your career.

What is your next big dream?

In all honesty, I'm not sure! What I do know is that no matter what I end up doing, both personally and professionally, I want to be able to look back proudly on my legacy. One of the ways that I know I can accomplish this is by continuing to help others and giving back.

"Helping others and giving back was often integrated into my college experience and early career responsibilities, giving me even more opportunities to do everything I love."

Sumaira Ahmed

Making the Best of a Bad Situation

How did your own experience with Neuromyelitis optica (NMOSD) lead to your decision to create the Sumaira Foundation?

I was diagnosed with Neuromyelitis optica when I was 25. It started with vision loss and it escalated to other symptoms pretty quickly. When I was first diagnosed and then discharged, I was given medical instructions, but no one really told me, "This is what you do now when you have a rare disease; these are the people to connect with, etc." And I felt that's so important. If you have a rare disease that nobody knows about, you need to feel some sense of belonging.

So I took the liberty of Googling NMO in 2014, and it was not good. Basically Google told anyone who Googled NMO at that time that they didn't have more than five years to live. It was a very bleak future for us, if there was any future at all, and that didn't sit well with me; I had just turned 25. My life was supposed to be just starting. I got diagnosed

with this crazy rare disease, and was taking treatment, but what about my heart? What about my head? What about my soul? I didn't find what I was looking for. So that's kind of when I decided I would just start one myself, and see what happened.

The possibility of helping even one person was enough for me. So that's why I started the Sumaira Foundation. I was two months into my diagnosis when we launched. So very, very new still to the illness, to the experience, to the community, but it's been eight years, so I think we've been doing something right.

Would you say that the foundation focuses more on helping people mentally and giving them support that way, or on research and development in the disease itself?

All of the above. We pride ourselves on supporting or trying to support every stakeholder involved in this disease. So of course, patients first, right? I'm a patient myself. We're patient-led, we're patient-powered, we're patient-centered.

What can we do for patients? There's a whole slew of things that the foundation does to support patients, to provide patient education, and build that sense of community, but we also support researchers. We support doctors, we support our industry partners. TSF is what we call it for short. We have four pillars: awareness, community, advocacy, and research, and all four pillars support virtually every stakeholder in this.

Prior to the foundation, you were an actress and a proficient kathak dancer. Was it difficult to transition to the new career, or did it come easily to you? Do you still harbor those earlier interests in your daily life today?

"I got diagnosed with this crazy rare disease, and was taking treatment, but what about my heart? What about my head? What about my soul?

My parents did a really nice job of introducing us to aspects of our culture. And for me, it was like love at first sight. I loved all of that and then at a very young age, I decided I wanted to be a Bollywood actress and my parents were crazy enough to support me. My childhood was very colorful, very adventurous and very different for an American born in New Jersey. But I definitely don't dance anymore. It's very painful for my body to dance. And it's something that I grieve kind of every day; I love dance.

I think once you're a dancer, you're always a dancer, but the pain is so bad and it's just something I've had to part ways with. It's interesting because I think somehow my life has come full circle through the foundation and all of this work that we're doing. I am back to filming. I am back to taking pictures all the time. I'm not dancing anymore, but I'm on stage. I'm giving talks and presentations and things that I like. I like having an audience. It's just kind of who I've been since I was a kid. In a way, this advocacy work, this illness has brought me back to my roots, which is being on stage.

What is your current favorite venture or project done through your foundation?

At the moment we are filming a docu-series on all these patients and vignettes around the world. I get to meet so many amazing, inspiring people all over the world through this project. It also fulfills some kind of a personal thing too, because I'm filming. I'm back in front of the screen, but I'm also behind the screens, strategizing, helping the director, helping the producers and all of that. I'm really excited about this project. It's going to take a long time, but I think when it finishes, it's going to have a great impact and raise a lot of awareness to hopefully millions of people across the world.

What would you say to people struggling with neuroimmune conditions?

This is not ideal, but there is a light at the end of the tunnel. You have to work hard for it and you need to keep your chin up, and positivity goes a long way. Our minds are so powerful, and these are things I told myself and I'm glad I had that mental wherewithal to do that. But I do wish I heard it from other people. I would tell others that if you want something to happen for whatever situation you're in, and it's not happening, make it happen. You have no idea what you can accomplish, what you can do, whose life you can influence or inspire or who you can motivate just by trying.

Linda Mason

Finding a Need and Meeting It

You have had a remarkable journey in both the business world and nonprofit space, from Bright Horizons to The Boston Foundation. Tell us more about your journey, and what made you the woman you are today.

I grew up in a small farming village in the Finger Lakes region of central New York. My father was a small-town and country doctor. My mother was an active civic volunteer and served as mayor of our village for a time – all while raising five children! Although my world was small growing up, my parents instilled in me a sense of adventure and a sense of responsibility in giving back. I had a very happy and secure childhood foundation, which gave me the strength to spread my wings as an adult.

I was a serious student of classical piano growing up and throughout college. Upon graduation, I moved to Paris, France to study piano at the Rachmaninoff Conservatory. After a few years there, I realized that I wanted to branch out from piano. I went back to the States to get a management degree at the Yale School of Management.

My father took off from his medical practice every couple of years to volunteer as a doctor in Africa and Central America, so that kind of work was in my bones. Upon graduation from Yale, I moved to the border of Cambodia/Thailand to work in the refugee camps after the Khmer Rouge crisis. That started a path of humanitarian work that carried me to the Middle East, Southeast Asia, and finally to Africa, where I worked for a couple of years as co-country director, along with my husband, Roger Brown, for Save the Children in Sudan.

Save the Children had never operated in Sudan before, so it turned out to be an entrepreneurial effort. We started the program from scratch, raised money, and built it into a large national program, running two Eritrean refugee camps and serving a large province, Kordofan, in Sudan that was suffering from drought and famine.

We were bitten by the entrepreneurial bug, and upon returning to the U.S., my husband and I decided we wanted to start an organization of our own that served a societal need in our country. Thus, Bright Horizons was born. We ran it as a team for 17 years.

We now have 1,200 childcare centers and 30,000 employees.

You are currently the chair of the Board of Directors at Boston Foundation, one of the nation's oldest and largest community nonprofits. Tell us what inspires you to give back. What is your advice to other women looking to give back to your community?

I have always felt a responsibility and a desire to give back where I can. It has, frankly, been what has fueled me throughout my life. There are so many people and communities that have so much to offer but are held back by societal barriers and discrimination. I have no illusions that I am truly making a difference,

> "I admire women who are able to be intentional in their choices in life – whether they want to stay home and be full-time mothers or whether they want a demanding career."

but this is where I want to concentrate my time and efforts.

How do you define women's empowerment in your own life, and who is an empowered woman that you admire?

I admire women who are able to be intentional in their choices in life – whether they want to stay home and be a full-time mother or if they want a demanding career. I hope that all people can be empowered to follow the path they want and to be the fullest version of themselves. My mother was a great role model. She made a difference in so many people's lives by being authentic, supportive, inspirational, and humble.

Rosemarie Day

Rethinking Healthcare for the Good of Society

Photo by Sheridan Kahmann Photography

What are the different types of activists you've encountered, and what kind of role does each one play in healthcare reform advocacy?

I group the activists into four main categories: those who are aware, those who share, those who participate, and those who lead. The roles each play in healthcare reform advocacy are along a spectrum of engagement. By writing *Marching Toward Coverage*, my level of activism has moved from "participator" to "leader." My book's mission is to inspire a movement for universal healthcare coverage. I believe that we don't have to agree on our specific path to get there, but we all need to be working in that direction and women should lead the way.

What inspired you to pursue this? When in your life did you become passionate about healthcare reform?

I started my career working on inequality and social justice issues, which led me to the Harvard Kennedy School to study public policy. This program made me excited to work in government, especially in an innovative state like Massachusetts, which exemplifies the idea that states can be the laboratories of democracy. I've worked on different initiatives, from welfare reform to health reform.

When I worked on welfare reform, the pressure was always to get people employed. However, once they were employed, they tended to get low wage jobs with no benefits. I saw that there was a huge gap in the provision of healthcare for the people who were working but did not receive health insurance through their employer. I wanted to work on health reform to fill those gaps.

During my tenure, the Health Connector became a model for national health reform. I went on to serve as the chief operating officer for the Massachusetts Medicaid program. I then became the founding deputy director and COO of the Massachusetts Health Connector, where I helped to launch the nation's first state-run health insurance exchange. Because I had the experience of launching the first exchange, once the Affordable Care Act (ACA) was passed, I founded Day Health Strategies to help other states implement national health reform. I began working with insurers and providers as well and found that I loved consulting. Day Health Strategies is now serving organizations that want to transform their approach to offering or delivering health care.

Over the course of my career, I have gone from focusing on filling coverage gaps to believing that health care should be a right and should not be tied to other factors, such as employment. I am now focused on improving our health care system and achieving universal health care coverage.

What are the biggest flaws in the current healthcare system?

First, the U.S. does not have universal healthcare. We do not treat healthcare as a right, which is leading to people getting sicker than they should and dying unnecessarily. Second, when you look at overall population health, we spend too much to get too little. As a country, our system does not focus or invest enough in prevention. If we redeployed some dollars from high-end specialty care to prevention and public health, we would get to better overall population health. Third, we do not spend enough on social safety net services. Compared to peer countries, the U.S. government spends much less on social services and we have worse health outcomes. As a country, we tend to over-medicalize and under-support people. Generally, our investment strategy is off – we spend a lot of money in the wrong places. Fourth is price. Compared to other countries, we have far higher prices for the exact same healthcare service, whether it's pharmaceuticals or procedures. There is a lot embedded in what goes into these high prices, some of which is legitimate, but other aspects are wasteful, including excessive profits. Capitalism is not working in the health care industry because it's full of market failures. Other countries successfully have government intervention in their healthcare industries, but we have been squeamish to do so, and we pay a high price for that.

> "The gender bias has only been heighted further by the pandemic. The COVID-19 crisis has shown everyone that we are essential – women make up over half of the workforce deemed "essential," including 77% of healthcare workers."

Does gender bias play a role in healthcare/ healthcare reform?

Yes, absolutely. The gender bias has only been heighted further by the pandemic. The COVID-19 crisis has shown everyone that we are essential – women make up over half of the workforce deemed "essential," including 77% of healthcare workers. Our lives are on the line as front-line healthcare workers: the CDC reports that 73% of healthcare workers who have contracted coronavirus are women.

Parul Sharma

Beauty Is for Everyone

Currently, you are the associate creative director at Sephora and have previously served as a creative/arts director at various leading businesses. What inspired your passion for creativity?

I remember drawing nonstop in the back of my school notebooks ever since elementary school. My teachers were exasperated with me! I grew up in small-town India, where the trope of the starving artist was well-established. I was a good student and ended up studying economics and doing an MBA. My first job was as an advertising account executive servicing FMCG clients at Publicis Mumbai. All through subsequent years at various agencies, I was more interested in the work my creative team did than my own role, but the barrier to entry was high given my lack of formal art training. I even did a copy internship at Ogilvy which didn't pan into a full-time gig. Fortunately, I relocated to the

U.S. after getting married, and realized that this was my chance to alter the course I was on. I took art classes at a local community college which allowed me to rustle up a portfolio good enough to transfer to a BFA design program at California College of the Arts in San Francisco.

By the time I started school, I had a three-month-old baby, so it was a rough start for sure. I had to lobby to have the school establish a breastfeeding room for students! However, I was motivated to do my best because any time spent at school was time borrowed from my infant.

Art school also immersed me in American culture, the understanding of which is critical to being a good designer. My skills improved with effort over time, and I was selected for an internship at CCA's prestigious in-house student-led agency Sputnik and even won a best thesis award. My tenacious efforts impressed my professors, who eventually referred me to my first job opportunity at Levi's.

Tell us what a day in your life looks like as a creative director. What excites you most about the work you do?

This varies greatly depending on the type of company, the industry, and even the team one is on. In my previous role at Meta as a creative director, I was working with large global cross-functional teams, collaborating with designers and marketers and working with multiple agencies.

At Sephora, creative directors need to bring a fair amount of experience to the table, both in the beauty/fashion industry and in their design craft and team management skills. As a social creative, my day begins before I sit at my desk. I'll typically browse social apps to scan for emerging trends, to see what we posted on various platforms and what kind of engagement we're receiving. I spend a chunk of my day in meetings presenting work, reviewing work, facilitating group brainstorms, building consensus with XFN partners, and meeting my team one-to-one to coach and counsel them. My team is on set on many days and I check in from time to time.

The aspect that excites me the most is working on projects that invite a conversation with our audience or show our audience that we see and hear them and value their unique identities. This can range from cultural illustrations that celebrate various communities, to of-the-moment meme posts, to a really great tutorial that demystifies a beauty or skincare routine. I also love helping my team get unstuck when they are working on projects and encouraging collaboration between them.

The beauty space has been growing exponentially, and we've seen some exciting trends in diversity, representation, etc. What are some beauty/makeup industry trends you think every woman should know about? What are some of the key innovations you see in the beauty space?

The answer to this question is complex, and I can only represent my personal knowledge and experience here. The beauty industry is indeed constantly evolving. There are so many new brands emerging each year, and what I find fascinating are their origin stories, the founders and their reason to be. There's a trend of celebrity founders, but there's also founders from traditionally underrepresented communities, which is so exciting for consumers with unique needs and identities. And that is why representation is getting better. On the influencer side, the passion that people have for expressing themselves through makeup is like no other. I find that rigid beauty standards are being replaced with personal expression.

> "There is no one right way to do beauty anymore, which is incredible. There's a tutorial for everything! You can learn from an eight-year-old or an 80-year-old."

Sephora emphasizes the message that beauty is for everyone, and this message really resonates with me personally as well. There is no one right way to do beauty anymore, which is incredible. There's a tutorial for everything! You can learn from an eight-year-old or an 80-year-old. You can learn from a drag queen or a dermatologist. It's the ultimate "choose your own adventure." I am also encouraged by how many brands are rethinking social responsibility, while owning that producing anything inherently means borrowing from natural resources.

Swaroop Sampat

Renowned Indian Actress's Powerful Journey in Revitalizing Global Education

Transitioning from the world of acting to education has been a profound and life-changing experience for me. It has been driven by my unyielding belief in the transformative power of education, especially for those children who are vulnerable and marginalized. While my acting career brought me happiness and recognition, I felt a deep calling to make a meaningful difference in society through education, particularly for those who face adversity.

At the beginning of this transition, I encountered numerous challenges. The once-glamorous days were replaced by a new focus: creating a nurturing learning environment where every child feels valued and empowered. It demanded that I channel my creativity and passion from the performing arts into developing innovative teaching methods that catered to the diverse needs of my students. It has been an immense privilege to be part of this transformative journey and to contribute to the shaping of a more inclusive and equitable society through the extraordinary power of education.

Both acting and education have been fueled by my deep passion for positively impacting lives. From a young age, I discovered the power of storytelling in acting, evoking emotions and inspiring change. This led me to use my talents to bring joy and a sense of shared humanity. Similarly, I witnessed firsthand the life-changing effects of education, breaking barriers and empowering individuals. Education unlocks potential and creates better lives. Acting and education share a common thread of impacting lives and inspiring others through storytelling. They drive my dedication to making a positive difference.

Being selected as a finalist for the Global Teacher Prize was an incredibly exhilarating moment for me. It was a validation of the hard work and dedication I had put into my role as an educator, and it served as recognition of the impact I had made on my students and community. The honor of being among such exceptional educators from around the world filled me with a sense of pride and gratitude. It reinforced my belief in the power of education and further motivated me to continue making a difference in the lives of my students.

Being in between these two phases of my life, away from the limelight but growing and achieving in pursuit of a more purposeful life, was both challenging and rewarding. Embarking on a Ph.D. in education and drama in my forties brought a sense of

"Embarking on a Ph.D. in education and drama in my forties brought a sense of renewal and intellectual stimulation. It allowed me to delve deeper into my passion for education and leverage the power of drama in transformative learning."

renewal and intellectual stimulation. It allowed me to delve deeper into my passion for education and leverage the power of drama in transformative learning. While away from the public eye, I found fulfillment in contributing to the field of education, expanding my knowledge, and making a meaningful impact. It was a period of personal growth, self-discovery, and a renewed sense of purpose.

Shirley Graham

*Director of the Gender Equality Initiative in International Affairs
at George Washington Reflects on Her Journey*

It was a beautifully sunny day in Nepal, the lake sparkled with light, and the blue sky stretched overhead like a canvas beckoning me to paint the next chapter of my life. I was sitting in a small wooden rowing boat with my friend Jess, in the middle of lake Phewa in the foothills of the Himalayas. I had come to Nepal ostensibly to teach English in a primary school for underprivileged children, but privately it was an opportunity to review my life and figure out what I would do next. In the previous years, my long-term relationship had ended, I had worked through a series of promotions in my corporate job, been head-hunted by a tech start-up, traveled to exciting cities, taken on more and more professional challenges, and now I was burnt out and confused about my next steps.

Jess looked me in the eye and said, "Shirley, go back to school. Study what you are passionate about: women's rights and international affairs. That's all you ever talk about, so you might as well work at what you love." I was astonished. "Is my interest in the rights of women and girls so unusual?" I asked. "Yes," she said. "Now, go do it!"

This was the beginning of my journey into women's rights advocacy, research, writing and teaching. Previously, it had never occurred to me that I might follow such a path, but now when I look back and piece together the jigsaw puzzle of my life, it doesn't seem surprising at all. I had grown up in 1970s-80s Ireland, a place where girls were told to keep away from boys, not to have sex, and if you did have sex, to avoid getting pregnant at any cost. Conservative and religious values restricted many aspects of a young woman's life. It wasn't until 1985 that contraception was made legally available in Ireland. The Magdalene laundries, a church-run institution, operated until 1996. The laundries, led by nuns, took in women who were pregnant and unmarried or women who had been raped or were victims of incest, or were too flirtatious or otherwise considered problematic. The women worked for free, laundering, until their babies were born or such time as their families deemed they were ready to leave. Some women never left.

In Kathmandu, the school I was teaching in was in a poor district and the children were either orphans or had only one parent. The school was under-resourced and often children were left to their own devices without a teacher. As I walked by groups of younger children on my way to a class they would call out "teacher, teacher," waving their arms and urging me to join them, so eager were they for learning. It broke my heart that they had to beg to be given this time and attention.

The children I got to know as my students were some of the brightest, funniest, cleverest children I had ever met. But I was struck by how different the girls' and boys' behavior was in the classroom. The boys were typically talkative, noisy, playful, and having a lot of fun. The girls were quiet, silent, serious and anxious to please. I felt sad for the girls. So many hours of their day were spent at school, so many hours of self-regulation and self-control. It was this stark contrast between girls' and boys' behavior that got me thinking more deeply about the harm that is done to girls as a result of strict gender roles and norms in society.

It is estimated that 120 million women are missing worldwide due to sex-selective abortions, with a majority of these abortions taking place in India and China. One in three women globally will be a victim of sexual or physical violence by her intimate partner. Only 25% of parliamentarians are women, and 82% of them report experiencing harassment and threats of violence. In 72 countries, same-sex relationships are criminalized, and in eight of those, the punishment can be the death penalty. Two hundred million girls have undergone female genital mutilation (FGM), and three million are at risk each year. At least 60% of countries still discriminate against a daughter's right to inherit land in law or practice. No country in the world has full equality between women and men.

Fast forward, from that day in Nepal to today. I am now the director of a global gender policy program at the George Washington University's Elliott School of International Affairs in D.C. where we have hundreds of students taking courses on gender in international affairs each year. My students are passionate, articulate, driven young adults determined to create a more just, equal and safe world. They are powerful advocates for the rights of women, girls, and sexual and gender minorities. They understand that transnational feminist movements are key to bringing about women's rights, by advocating on behalf of women who cannot, by sharing best practices, and by lobbying governments and multilateral institutions. They know that how a country treats its women is an indicator of that country's stability, security and prosperity, as gender equality leads to better outcomes for everyone. And they are some of the brightest, funniest, and cleverest students I have ever had the pleasure to teach. When I think back to that day on the lake and how my friend Jess encouraged me to pursue my passions, it reminds me of how important it is for women to support each other to believe in ourselves and to dream big.

> "How a country treats its women is an indicator of that country's stability, security and prosperity, as gender equality leads to better outcomes for everyone."

Vaishnavi Kondapalli

Making Tech Careers More Accessible to Women

Tell us about your career path and your experience as the only woman on your team. How do you see gender balance and diversity on teams changing?

I started my career as an intern in Iperia back in 2001. I was writing code in C++ on Linux, and we had a very small team of six people. I was the only woman on the team. For that matter, most of the places I worked had very few women coders. It never bothered me much at all. Through the years, I have seen many women rise up and take on more responsible roles. I still don't find that many female coders, but there are women in HR, product teams, QA roles, and in management.

Many people dream of learning to code, and there are so many resources all over the

internet, yet often people give up. What is your advice to budding coders?

You need to be passionate about what you do for a living, whether it be coding, building things, writing, treating patients, singing, dancing or painting. There are a lot of resources online for free, and some with a very nominal fee to pick up any new technology. In the case of software, I believe that it is an art more than a science, and thus my advice would be, do as an artist would. Learn from a variety of sources (online tutorials, classes, videos free and commercial) and then try to apply it by getting an internship, work for free on small programming tasks, reach out to networks where small gigs are offered. Nothing beats actually building software for the real world. I think it's sort of like swimming: you need to jump in and likely flail a bit, but you get better with practice.

Between data science, AI, machine learning, etc., what trends in technology do you see having the biggest rise in the next few years?

Data science, AI, and machine learning all feed into each other. Cloud technology has enabled us access to petabytes of information. Life has to come to a full circle, right? It's the same with technology. Big data and machine learning technologies can be applied to so many fields: from medicine to finance to behavioral science to clean energy. The sky's the limit.

The big trend that we will see over the next five to ten years is the actual application of software that can make decisions and take actions autonomously to solve real world problems with minimal human intervention. The nirvana of technology is not about replacing humans, but leveraging software to have the ability to think and respond as humans would.

You are also a phenomenally talented musician. Tell us more about your music, and how you balance between music and work?

Music is my first love and I am not sure how I didn't end up being a full time musician. It is definitely a balancing act to be able to devote time to Riyaz and a full time job. Indian Classical Music demands time from me and Raag Riyaz takes a lot of focus, creative mind and being in the moment. I find it a bit difficult at times when I have used up my brain power for the day at work. As an artist I find myself trying to find that sweet spot where I feel accomplished at the end of the day.

> "The nirvana of technology is not about replacing humans, but leveraging software to have the ability to think and respond as humans would."

What are tech organizations doing to empower the women on their teams? Do you think there is room for more?

I get invitations to many conferences and meet-ups on women in tech. Facebook has an event almost every quarter inviting women to their campus and facilitating networking events. I think most companies have started paying attention to empowering women in tech.

The biggest challenge that nobody seems to actually address is work-life balance in the tech industry. This impacts men and women equally. I think one of the biggest issues, though, is that when it comes to part-time jobs, there are pretty much none in the tech industry. While tech provides flexible hours and work-from-home options, there isn't much being done by companies to enable part-time employment for folks who would love to remain in this industry but cannot devote 40 hours a week. This is something I would like to see change.

Pooja Ika

Navigating Healthcare As a Tool for Empowerment

You are the founder of eternalHealth and are one of the youngest healthcare entrepreneurs. What inspired your passion for entrepreneurship and healthcare, and what were some challenges you faced in your journey? How did you overcome them?

While I might not have 20 years of healthcare experience in a conventional sense, I have been surrounded by the healthcare space for as long as I can remember. I credit a lot of my passion for this space to both of my parents. I grew up watching my mother interact with her patients and I saw the close relationships she was able to build with them. She was not only their provider, she was also their friend and someone they really trusted. My mom would and still does share stories about me with her patients, and on the flip side, they would share stories about their own children and would

always make it a point to ask about me and all of the progress I had made since they last spoke. My mother's patients trusted her enough to never go to the ER without calling her first, and by building that unique relationship with her patients, my mother came home with an incredible sense of gratitude and thankfulness.

Meanwhile, I watched my father's dreams come to fruition as he built companies from scratch. I watched him go through the typical ups and downs that you face in a start-up environment and I saw him take on any and every task with a smile on his face. By always being optimistic, he was able to bring together a group of people who were equally passionate and shared the same mission and vision. My mother made me fall in love with healthcare, while my father helped me develop my business acumen and made me fall in love with the start-up environment.

As I started to think about my future and my career, I realized that given my specific skillset and strengths, starting a health insurance company was my calling. I knew that the space I was entering was dominated by older men, and I saw that in some of my very first interactions in the space. Not only am I a woman, I am a young, minority woman, in a space that was not used to seeing someone like me run a health plan. Some of the challenges include having to go against any stereotypes and biases that were already established about me prior to even having a conversation with me or being dismissed because of my age and "lack of experience." I knew I could either allow those comments to get to me, or I could brush them off and focus on the work. Someone told me a while ago that respect needs to be earned, and I am willing to put in the time and work to gain the respect of my peers.

You are also passionate about having diversity across the company, particularly having women and POC represented on the board and in director roles. Tell us more about this.

> "I want to foster diversity at all levels, so that our organization can represent the population we are serving, to allow for more comprehensive and inclusive decisions to be made around our members' care."

Fostering diversity at all levels and empowering women to step into leadership roles was always very important to me and something I was passionate about, but it was also the right business decision across the board. About 80% of healthcare decisions are made by women for themselves and their families. And while women are making 80% of the healthcare decisions, 58% of them do not feel confident in the decisions that they are making, yet they still continue to make them. At eternalHealth, we are committed to educating our members, because knowledge is power and we want to place the power back in our members' hands. I want to foster diversity at all levels, so that our organization can represent the population we are serving, to allow for more comprehensive and inclusive

decisions to be made around our members' care.

How do you define women's empowerment? Is there an empowered woman in your life that you admire?

One of my very first role models was my mother, and now with my career, she is the source of my inspiration because she has really shaped the way I approach healthcare and my job. One of the many reasons I admire my mother is because she has a big heart and is always committed to do right by her patients, which is now one of eternalHealth's core values. The first thing I always tell anyone who joins the eternalHealth team is that we must place the member at the center of everything we do, because every decision must be centered around our members' needs. In addition to that, the one thing I will always be grateful to my mother for is that she made me believe that nothing was impossible. She worked, took care of my grandparents, was always there for me whether it was at pickup/dropoff or cheering me on at soccer games, and was always there for my father. And most impressively, she did it all with a smile on her face. This encouraged me to have the same mentality, and made me want to empower other women. Over 50% of eternalHealth's workforce, executives, board of directors, and investors are women, and I'm very proud of that.

Dion Johnson

On Empowering Women to 'Unmask,' Lead, and Live their Best Lives

You are known as "The Womanologist." What does this name mean to you, and what inspired you to start this platform?

I was born with a pronounced facial disfigurement. When I was four, I was given an artificial eye and dark glasses to help me hide my facial flaws and blend in to look more "normal." I refer to the beginning of my life as being "behind the mask," and quite unconsciously, through that process, I was learning a powerful lesson: if something's not "right" or "normal" about you, then you should hide that thing, put it away so no one sees it.

Forty years later, in 2009, through a random series of events, life woke me up to the truth that I was hiding and petrified of being seen for real. I found myself being challenged by God to let people see the real me, and I was petrified. Back then, letting people see the real me was about no longer wearing an artificial eye and dark glasses, but as I prepared to show up maskless, I learned that my face wasn't the only thing I was masking. I learned

that I was hiding myself on a whole host of levels: trying to be a certain type of person for someone and another for someone else, always trying to fit in with what was expected of me and totally losing connection with the real me in the process. I realized if I was going to show up for real, I needed to know who I was for real. I've been on an incredible journey of self-discovery, and what I have learned about women and our masking and unmasking is profound and absolutely applicable to everyone I work with, women who want to show up powerfully and for real in the boardroom and c-suite.

One of the things I've learned about myself on this journey is that I was born to support women. My professional background is in midwifery, so I've been alongside thousands of women in pregnancy, childbirth, and the transition to motherhood, which I see as the ultimate leadership role. It's here that I discovered and developed a profound belief in womanity and the undeniable innate power of women. I believe this power will change our world. My job is all about getting women to show up for real in their professional positions and use that power to speak up, take an influential stand, and lead the important meaningful change the world needs so urgently right now.

You empower women who are looking to change their lives and become leaders. What are five things women need to do or think about in their leadership journey?

Womanity is innately powerful. She is gifted, strong, nurturing, intuitive, caring, compassionate, fierce and influential. I believe marketplace leadership needs authentic womanity now like never before if we are ever going to win the war against some of our most persistent global marketplace predicaments such as inequality, injustice, all the "isms," ill health, and indifference.

I also believe if we are going to answer the call to show up this way, we've got work to do. We must prepare. The pressure is real for women in marketplace leadership, and the reality is that we collectively are struggling under that pressure. We are caught up in power struggles, we are experiencing professional pushbacks, we are subject to genderisms and all the isms, our inner game is compromised by imposter thoughts, insecurities, excessive self-consciousness. Women are still the primary carers and cleaners in the home, and we are balancing family and professional lives in a way that our male counterparts simply aren't asked to do. If we are going to show up more authentically, speak up more powerfully, and shake things the hell up more confidently and influentially, we simply must be intentional about getting ourselves ready for this. Here are the three areas I help my clients work on:

HEAL: Women collectively and individually have been through a lot historically. I saw firsthand in my work behind the mask and woman to woman how that historical hurt and unaddressed issues from the past can affect the way we show up in leadership today in profound ways. We must heal.

HEAD: I've sat with hundreds of leaders, and one thing is for sure: it's noisy in our heads. We are entertaining thoughts about how "they" see us. We are all up in our heads about how we are coming across, our right to be in the room, game planning to manage the power struggle. The trouble is that this type of defensive thinking is a distraction and obstructive to the flow of our genuine authentic power; we must handle our heads and cultivate what I call HQT, Higher Quality Thinking, about who we are and what we are positioned in leadership to do.

HOOK: We must develop our ability to grab and keep hold of the attention of the people we want to influence with our ideas. This means developing our insights and ideas to sound a specific cause or mission and learning to deliver them in compelling and captivating ways to inspire buy-in from the people we need onboard to bring about the change we want to see. We must develop our influential hook.

> "My job is all about getting women to show up for real in their professional positions and use that power to speak up, take an influential stand, and lead the important meaningful change the world needs so urgently right now."

Make these your focus. Develop your networks to ensure you are connected with people who can support your intention around these key development areas. Invest in a coach, seek out mentors, read books, and join networks. It really is time for you to show up in all your authentic, powerful, influential glory, but you can't do it alone!

Mitzi Perdue

Learning Through the Lens of Family Businesses

You are a pioneer and thought leader in the family business world, drawing on experience from two successful family businesses: the Sheraton Hotels from your father's side and Perdue Farms from your late husband's side. What is your advice to women in particular when it comes to their family business? What role do they play and how can they establish themselves as leaders?

With family businesses, we put a lot of time into getting the business part right, but what often gets overlooked is getting the family part right. I grew up in the family business environment. My father is the co-founder of Sheraton Hotels, and the Perdue family has been in business for 102 years. The phrase that both our families use is "Happy family, happy business."

Seventy percent of family businesses don't make it to the next generation, and the odds of making it in the next 100 years are about 1 in 1,000. One of the areas I am focused on is understanding why this drop-off happens. The biggest proportion of this drop-off is actually due to family quarrels and conflict.

With family quarrels, we often have this rule to keep it in the family. We should get our grievances out early and often, not let them build up until they become catastrophes. Secondly, don't let the quarrels go public. The moment it reaches the public eye and necessitates lawyers, it is a bridge too far.

Women have room to make a profound impact here. Women, especially moms, have such strong authority and such stature in the family. They are also responsible for teaching the kids (i.e., the next generation of family business leaders) that they are a part of something bigger than themselves, and to leave the world in a better place than they received it. My tips for women are: Have a set of rules and a structure for handling issues. For example, what issues do you solve by consensus? By a two-thirds vote? By a majority? And everyone should know the rules ahead of time. There is no such thing as a family that doesn't quarrel. The biggest thing is how you handle it. Secondly, teach kids from a young age to be humble and open. One of the fun things about being 81 is you can tell people what to do (and you can get away with it!) I have such an array of experience and skills now that I can contribute more now than I could at 21. These life experiences and setbacks give you some humility that you don't have at 21.

You are a past speaker at the Akshaya Patra Boston Gala, and you truly inspired the AP community with your mindset and perspective. How did you find out about Akshaya Patra, and what resonates with you about the work that AP does?

Whoever had the idea of feeding people deserves all the credit and admiration in the world. Someone believed in it and made it happen. I give credit to AP for seeing things realistically and knowing how to get from point A to B, and taking the mission into action. In terms of how I found out about Akshaya Patra, it was a big coincidence. The Perdue family is in the food business, and we were trying to decide: where does our philanthropy go? We knew we wanted to combat hunger. We came across this organization in India (AP) doing this mission. We saw that Akshaya Patra has the same philosophy.

You cannot reach your potential if you are starving. They came to the same conclusion that we did that hunger is something we can and need to do something about. At Perdue, we work with a food bank, particularly from a refrigeration/infrastructure standpoint. We believe that there are whole classes of food that are nutritious that you can't have without access to proper infrastructure and refrigeration.

One of Akshaya Patra's new programs is the Young Professionals. What is your advice to young professionals in their careers?

I loved my career and the feeling of accomplishing things and getting things done. How I define success is using the abilities you have at your highest and best level for a cause you believe in. When I finished college at 21, I absolutely believed in something called the Alliance for Progress, which was an effort under President Kennedy in Latin America. I had all this idealism and was ready to work for the government. What I soon realized was that wanting something and having it be so are not the same thing. This was a big lesson for me: what you think is going to happen doesn't always happen. In this vein, a question I'd pose to AP Young Professionals is: You want to have an impact for good, but how do you make it happen without just dreaming about it?

> "The greatest gift is getting real-world feedback. Enjoy your praise, but be open to critical feedback and the chance to grow that comes with it."

Further, remember that you are going to make mistakes. The best way to make fewer mistakes is to get advice from lots of people. Cherish the people that tell you that you are wrong. My late husband had no use for "yes men." It is better to hear what's wrong and figure out a way to fix it, not to be flattered and be told you are right. The greatest gift is getting real-world feedback. Enjoy your praise, but be open to critical feedback and the chance to grow that comes with it. My motto is, "Nobody bats a 1,000." You can't always be right. Nobody wins every time.

Saumya Dave

The Roles That Culture and Family Play in Mental Health

You are a psychiatrist and a talented author who has published two books, What a Happy Family and Well-Behaved Indian Women. What inspired you?

My love for psychiatry and writing both stem from the same place: a curiosity for human nature. I've always been fascinated by what motivates, inspires, and dejects people, how relationships shape us, and how we can learn from our stories. For many years, I thought I had to pick one path and stick to it. But I realized with time that I could create my own rules and pursue my different passions. I had to be OK with things taking longer than I expected and to navigate a lot of uncertainty, but it was all worth it. I grew up craving fiction featuring strong South Asian women,

and at the end of college i decided to try writing my own. It's been a journey of learning, and I'm so grateful to be able to keep growing through both of my careers.

As a psychiatrist, how do you address mental health in your books?

The way mental health is addressed varies depending on the story and characters. In *Well-Behaved Indian Women*, a lot of the mental health struggles were depicted through Nandini, the mom in the story. In *What a Happy Family*, every member of the family is struggling with something they aren't sharing with everyone else. The stigma surrounding mental health is more directly explored. My third book addresses mental health in a different way, and I'm also working on a nonfiction project related to mental health.

What are some key lessons you want women to take away from your two books? What was your favorite line or passage in each book?

Well-Behaved Indian Women is about three generations of women navigating struggles in their careers and relationships. It explores the complicated bonds between mothers and daughters, what it means to live the lives we want instead of the ones that are expected of us.

Favorite line: "For years, we assumed ambition was a curse for us. Men could always wear it like a cape, while women were forced to tuck and hold it inside themselves."

What a Happy Family is about the seemingly perfect Joshi family and how they unravel after a public scandal. The book is about how family can hurt and heal us, what it means for us to show up authentically to those we are closest to. Favorite line: "By visiting their pasts, they were able to pave different futures together. She used to fantasize about what it would be like to have simple ties to her family tree instead of the twisted branches that are in theirs. But she knows now that she wouldn't want to be any other way. They still aren't always in perfect harmony with one another, but maybe that isn't the point. Maybe being whole and authentic with the people you love is the real victory."

> "Conversations lead to change. There can be so much pressure to present a strong appearance regardless of how we may be feeling. When we are open about our own struggles, we give permission for others to do the same."

found that the journey is about unlearning as much as it's about learning. Unlearning what makes you worthy. Unlearning what you're allowed to put up with. Unlearning unhealthy dynamics and creating new patterns.

Also, conversations lead to change. There can be so much pressure to present a strong appearance regardless of how we may be feeling. When we are open about our own struggles, we give permission for others to do the same. I have to say that I'm in awe of how so many people are advocating for their mental health. I've seen more and more talk about therapy, eradicating the stigma, embracing that it's OK to not be OK, etc. It's been incredible to see so much change in just the past several years and I can't wait to see how things continue to evolve.

What is your next big dream?

What are your top tips to women on their mental health? How do culture and family expectations tie into mental health?

If you're able to have access to a therapist, I highly recommend seeing one, even if it's for a few appointments. That relationship can be a source of support and growth. Speaking to the culture and family expectations, I've

My next big dream is to have complete agency over my time and be a part of helping other women have that as well. Being a new mom during the pandemic and publishing two books was quite an adventure. I hope that through my work as a psychiatrist and author, I'm able to play a tiny part in helping women avoid burnout, get the rest they deserve, and have time for themselves.

Rachna Hukmani

The First South Asian Woman to Start a Whiskey Company

You are the first South Asian woman to start a whiskey company. What is it like being a South Asian woman in the whiskey business?

I feel with anything that is unexpected or perhaps a bit niche, one has to create one's own path and finetune it as one goes along. This is my calling and my passion in life, so I always knew at that some point I would branch out on my own. My desire to be authentic has brought forth people who believe in me, who step up to help me succeed and spread the word about my business, my story and my reason for being. I hope to inspire anyone reading to know that if you pursue your passions, the right people, opportunities and moments will come. The universe has a way of paving the path for us when we are ready. All we have to do is step on it and watch that story unfold.

What brought you to the world of whiskey initially?

I had just moved to the U.S. from Cyprus on a work visa with a job in advertising but got laid off. I had a month to find another job or leave the country. But I refused to give up. I had been dreaming of moving to the U.S. since I was five years old. Literally a few days before my work visa expired, I found a job working at an agency with Johnny Walker as my client. It was at that job that something awoke in me. The intricate art form of whiskey, its versatile flavor profile, its history, and the people behind legendary whiskeys intrigued me. I was hooked. I started to dig deeper into the art form, and I loved it. I had found my calling. The rest is history.

That was more than a decade ago, and since then I've worked at Pernod Ricard, Edrington and with several whiskey makers to help market existing whiskeys and design new ones. I was part of the team that helped design and launch The Macallan 12 Double Cask, Highland Park Magnus, Noble Oak Bourbon, Relativity, and others.

What do you look for in a good whiskey and what's your advice to people just starting to appreciate its taste?

In a very simple way, I look for the story the whiskey has to tell. That first sip is always the strongest and I take my time with that whiskey, letting it breathe. Allowing your whiskey to sit brings out other flavors, and that is where the versatility of whiskey can be experienced. When a particular whiskey is new to me, I try it neat first, let it sit for a bit, then with a splash of water and an ice cube or two to see all the flavors that particular whiskey will impart so I can decide how I like that whiskey. This is also my advice to people just starting to appreciate whiskey. Spend some time with it, and you'll see the story it has to share.

What exactly is Whiskey Stories® and how did you come up with the idea?

Whiskey Stories® LLC is my Michelin Guide recommended luxury multisensory immersive whiskey tasting company, where premium/high end whiskeys are paired with music, comedy, storytelling, blindfolds, gourmet chef food courses, and more. No two experiences are alike, and we sell out months in advance.

I came up with the idea almost seven years ago at an entrepreneur brainstorming session. I had attended several whiskey tastings by then, and always felt there were elements missing to allow people to truly understand whiskey. When people attend a typical whiskey tasting, they do not actually get what it means to taste the grain of a whiskey, the different barrel notes and the impact a change in water source and temperature has on whiskey grain and flavor. So I decided to create just that: a way to truly help people understand whiskey via multisensory elements. At Whiskey Stories®

> "The universe has a way of paving the path for us when we are ready. All we have to do is step on it and watch that story unfold."

experiences, I use flavor, fragrance, sight, sound, emotion and more to open people's minds and palates, which allows them to tease apart flavors, aromas, and more in their whiskey. Even the entertainment, like our comedic performers, aims to incorporate multisensory elements to help people truly decipher whiskey. People are more likely to retain information this way, and also feel like they are part of something special. As a result, Whiskey Stories® is more than a company, it is a community.

What's your best advice to young female entrepreneurs?

Just go for it. There will be people who don't support you, but I believe one of the best things someone can do for us is underestimate us because that contrast sheds light on what we really want. As long as we continue to believe in ourselves, the rest falls into place, including the right company that helps us along the way rather than tell us we can't do something. So, keep at it and the right avenues of abundance will come along. And ask for help from the right people. I once heard someone say, "If you don't need help, your vision isn't big enough." So, don't be afraid to ask for help. Just be discerning about whom you ask.

Yasmin Padamsee Forbes

A Childhood Disability Yields a Powerful Professional Lesson

After graduating from Harvard, you went on to work in Myanmar for the U.N. You are currently the executive director of the Asian American Commission. Tell us more about your journey and what inspired your interest in global affairs and public service.

I am a proud alumna of the Harvard Kennedy School and graduated with a master's degree in public administration in 2008. My time at Harvard gave me the necessary skills and tools to boost my journey toward global affairs and public service.

After graduation, I was determined to apply my knowledge and skills to make a difference. I began working for the United Nations in Myanmar, where I was part of a team that helped assist and support communities affected by natural disasters and conflict. I joined the U.N. soon after Cyclone Nargis had decimated large parts of the Delta region in the country.

During my time at the U.N., I saw firsthand the impact of global events on the lives of ordinary people. This experience inspired me to continue being involved in public service, even after I moved back home to Massachusetts. Currently, I serve as the executive director of the Asian American and Pacific Islanders Commission, where I work to promote the concerns and interests of Asian Americans and Pacific Islanders in Massachusetts. In my role, I advocate for policies that address these communities' unique needs and challenges. I believe it is vital to use one's knowledge and skills to impact the world positively and to work to uplift marginalized communities.

You are known for your tenacity and determination. You struggled with dyslexia as a kid. Tell us more about your experience with dyslexia and how you navigated this challenge.

Dyslexia is a learning disability that affects reading, writing, and spelling. Growing up with dyslexia in India was a challenge, as people did not realize it was a learning disability; however, it made me even more determined to succeed. Dyslexia is unrelated to intelligence; many people with dyslexia are brilliant and successful.

To navigate some of my learning challenges, I used various strategies, including multisensory learning (using multiple senses such as hearing, seeing, and touching to learn and remember information), and self-advocacy (speaking up for oneself and asking for accommodations when needed). This helped me to be better able to navigate most challenges. Ultimately, I believe that as long as you have tenacity and determination, anyone can succeed despite dyslexia.

"I believe it is vital to use one's knowledge and skills to impact the world positively and to work to uplift marginalized communities."

You are certainly a busy woman. After a long day, how do you like to relax and unwind?

It is crucial to find time to relax and unwind. What I feel helps me is to go for a walk in a nearby park or natural area to get some fresh air and connect with nature. Also, to communicate with friends and family with a meal.

Amama Sadiq

Finding Your Voice

What led you on your career path in the healthcare industry?

Born and brought up in Dubai, an emirate of the U.A.E, I never really knew what it was like to not be an "outsider." My parents were South Asian immigrants, and despite it being my "home" – in fact, the only home I knew of – I was painfully aware that I was and will always be an expatriate in Dubai. Although we thrived on the buzz and excitement of the rapidly expanding metropolis, we also held onto to our culture and traditions. I was always passionate about public speaking and never let an opportunity go by to be on stage, using my voice to connect with and inspire an audience. Eventually, I won an award for a full scholarship to go to Oxford School of Drama for a summer, where I got formal training to advance my presentation skills.

Nevertheless, as with all "desis," my parents' dream of having their daughter be a doctor soon became my dream, and theater took a back seat. I moved to Pakistan (my parents' birth home) to complete my medical degree. I went to Aga Khan University (AKU), which has international acclaim; however, most of the students are actually from Pakistan, or have very close family living in Pakistan. This was my second foray into being an outsider: "the girl from Dooobai" trying to fit in.

By final year of medical school, I was yearning to find my passion again. I had been approached while acting in a self-directed play by George Bernard Shaw to host a TV show on Geo TV called Clinic Online. It was a health show where viewers could call in and get advice from an allopathic doctor, a homeopathic doctor and a faith healer and we would untangle important issues and connections between physical, mental, and spiritual health. I would go to the studio on a Saturday night, record shows for 24 hours and come back to my dorm to catch a few hours of sleep before class Monday morning. This side gig soon became my real-world education, my outlet, my way of connecting and helping the Pakistan that lived outside the bubble of AKU.

Soon, it came time for residency, and I moved to London, which became home for my early adult life. I worked as some would call it as a micro physician, seeing individual patients, but somehow knew I needed to hit a broader scale if I wanted to make an impact. My opportunity came in the form of a public health degree at Harvard University, and so I moved to Boston to study health policy and management while paying the bills with a clinical research fellowship at Beth Israel Deaconess Medical Center. The taste of broader public health decisions at school coupled with cutting-edge pharmaceutical funded research at work paved the way for me to think outside the traditional box of "practicing medicine," and I stayed in Boston, where I am settled today.

What is a challenge of being a doctor focused on women's sexual health?

By this time, I knew that I had a voice, and though it didn't fit with the masses, it helped others who needed it. Women's health, particularly sexual health, is an often taboo subject that no one particularly from my background wants to talk about, and between the women who suffer and the healthcare providers who aren't trained to ask, someone had to give it a voice. So, I took the stage once again and joined AMAG to lead the launch of a novel therapy to help women suffering from low sexual desire and associated distress. As a young brown woman in a leadership position, I knew I had one shot at the goal. The day our therapy was approved by the FDA, I came home late at night and found both my young daughters in bed asleep. I sobbed next to them silently, tears of joy. It had been 18 months of sheer perseverance, dedication, red-eye flights,

nonstop presentations to get there. But I could now tell them that finally Mommy and her team had made history for young women so that my girls could do the same. After the launch of the new therapy, I had letters from patients thanking us for allowing them to speak to their husbands, their significant others, their PCPs with confidence about a real issue and providing them with an option to save their relationships, their marriage, and their self-image.

"I found my way into women's health, particularly sexual health, an often taboo subject. It's a subject that no one particularly from my background wants to talk about, and between the women who suffer and the healthcare providers like myself who aren't trained to ask, someone had to give it a voice."

What are your thoughts on encouraging women to share their stories?

I was invited to the Mass Conference for Women in 2019 to give a talk on "Just Ask: Promoting open conversations about sexual health." This was really an honor for me to follow speakers such as Malala Yousufzai and Megan Rapinoe, who said "We are all more impactful than we think." I took those words back with me to share with my team at AMAG Pharmaceuticals. Every day, we have the power to initiate a small yet meaningful change, to help other women move forward. I am a member of the AMAG women's network, where we have unfiltered conversations about work, family, relationships – anything and everything that needs a tribe to help a woman succeed. I remind myself, my daughters, and other women around me every day to stop trying to fit in and just belong. It takes many baby steps, but we can get there eventually.

Smita Patel

Finding a Home Through Art

You have worked with many leading artistic organizations, including the Peabody Essex Museum and the Boston Museum of Science. What excites you about the art world?

The art world today has roles that are far-reaching. They are safe places where one can not only see art but can also examine, without rancor, different perspectives and points of view. Art has become a tool for activism.

All cultures and arts of the world, whether classical or folk, have value and a grammar all of their own. Folk art of the world used to get sidestepped often in favor of the "Classical," perhaps because the folk grammar involved was not properly understood. As the world becomes more connected, much is changing in the art world as well. There is more emphasis not just on the connections between color, motifs, and design but also the beliefs and philosophies of the cultural base of a particular art piece. There is so much to absorb and learn about cultural context before making value judgements on any piece of art.

My involvement with Peabody Essex Museum and the art world started many years ago. At that time, there were very few Indian cultural organizations, and performance offerings were limited. Furthermore, when we came to the North Shore area, the community we came in contact with were the patients and colleagues of my husband, a physician. I noted with interest the knowledge base and different points of view of those that we met, with those of the Indian community. One of the people we met at that time on the North Shore was Evelyn Bartlett; interestingly, she was the first wife of Eli Lilly. She made a great impression on me and was the catalyst for my first involvement with a museum in the U.S. Here was a person whose kindness and thoughtfulness was mind-boggling. An artist herself, her passion for art, culture, exotic fruits, flowers orchids, enriched me.

We met her due to a hospital assignment. When we first came to Beverly, we were living on the hospital grounds. One day the doorbell rang and when I opened the door, a huge bunch of peace lilies faced me. She had come to visit me, and from then on took me under her wing. Lively conversations at her dinner parties covered religions, world cultures, philosophies, arranged marriages in India and America, dress modes, playing tennis in a sari, even the different weaves and embellishments of saris, etc. all with the most wonderfully interesting and articulate people – artists, writers, individuals from the North Shore's first settler families – even museum directors such as that of Smithsonian.

I was fortunate that she exposed me to many interesting people and places on the North Shore, including the Peabody Essex Museum, one of the oldest museums in America. There used to be floor display cabinets in the East India Marine Hall, and while pointing to some beautiful Indian toys in one of them, she said, "India is here, take a look." This was how my association with PEM began. At that time not only did I still paint, but helping at the museum gave me an opportunity to be a cultural ambassador. I produced many Indian cultural projects and programs for them over the years covering Indian rituals, dance, costuming, cuisine, etc.

> "If you want to get involved in any art or cultural organization or institute, the first step is to volunteer there, study it, and absorb its philosophy."

What is your advice to young women looking to get more involved in the arts and culture in their communities?

If you want to get involved in any art or cultural organization or institute, the first step is to volunteer there, study it, and absorb its philosophy. You will come into contact with like-minded people who may not only broaden your horizon, but also help pinpoint a more precise role for yourself. Art platforms have such varied focuses. You won't know which area will excite you until you get involved and start exploring.

You have done so many amazing projects. What is one that is close to your heart?

I have to give two, for they both expanded my knowledge base and were very impactful. One of the projects was going to Kutch and Saurashtra in the late 1970s, and learning firsthand the culture and philosophies of the numerous communities there. It gave me the opportunity to evaluate, reason, and readjust my thoughts and values. Subsequently, it enabled me to share so many aspects of it through lectures, performances and discussions not just with the local American community of the Northeast but also with the Indian community throughout America.

The other project was the Brides of India Show for the Festival of India at the Boston Museum of Science. All the brides represented were young women from their respective Indian communities in the greater Boston area. Each bride was introduced with the background wedding music from her specific state while I gave my commentary on the finer points and meaning of their bridal attire, jewelry and significance of the rituals involved. The program received the Entertainment Critics' Choice in a Boston newspaper for two weeks in a row.

Meera Siddharth

A Dream, a Passion for Math, and a Vision

Tell us your personal and professional story. What were some challenges or interesting experiences you faced along the way?

Independent India created a lot of inner turmoil, especially for girls, who would wonder what roles were in store for them. Or were they limited to being a housewife? Indian parents should focus more on educating their girls, not on their weddings and dowries. My parents gave us a good education along with a deep sense of ethics and compassion. I was weak in many school subjects. I remember my father helping me with the multiplication tables of eight. Putting my pencil to draw the number eight, circling from the bottom going up, I felt a burning sensation as my father's heavy slap covered my cheek. Mom intervened as I felt

traumatized. I did learn to draw number 8 from the top right circling down but I avoided maths like a plague.

My father, an avid reader, read books about the World Wars and American writers James Hadley Chase, Louis L'Amour, and others. Our exposure to the Indian and English cinema was ample. Reading about Mars, Milky Ways, galaxies, black holes, Carl Sagan, JFK and the *Apollo* moon landing was synonymous to me with America. This was my exposure to "America," where freedom of thought, speech, opportunity existed.

As an idealist, I wanted my suitor to refrain from the dowry system, and my wish was granted. As a new bride, I left India, arriving in Toronto, Canada quickly after marriage. Both my children were born there. We eventually moved to Boston. After settling down I started my career, but what and where was a question.

My temp job as a filing clerk at State Street turned into a permanent position in its wire department. With no experience in the financial field, my work forced me to come out of my shell by finding courage, seeking help from anyone walking along the halls at State Street. Soon, every wire was properly identified by both sender and receiver. My next move was to troubleshoot the Claims Department. I learned many aspects of interest-based 30/360 or prime rate. I would pull out trashed calculated tapes of my manager and recalculate them for practice. Next, I targeted mutual funds. As I became more confident, my fear of math dissipated. In the years that followed, I targeted our Corporate Actions Department. As an administrator, I successfully trained others for the next ten years. In 2002 the financial market was going through its downward volatility and State Street consolidated. I was offered a generous severance package and retired.

Though I loved my work, I never missed it, as simultaneously I was working with my husband's business. My commitment to our real estate projects is still ongoing and we work as a team. I am usually the only female attending these work meetings. The men often do not make eye contact let alone listen to me. That challenge forced me to find my voice and show my knowledge in the field of construction and real estate development. I may not get accolades for my accomplishments or obstacles I face being a woman, juggling a career, business, and family life, but I am grateful to this country where women can work fearlessly and be who they want to be.

You do not have a formal business degree although you and your husband run a very successful real estate business. What are some advantages and disadvantages of not getting a formal business degree and education?

Education is the key to success and enlightenment. What type of education and

our access to it differs for many reasons. These days we have much freedom and have shed the cliché of a doctor, lawyer, or engineer. Because of my arranged marriage, having children young, and immigrating to the U.S., I plunged into work without a degree in finance and business consulting. But experience, common sense, and logic took over. Women have so many opportunities these days, and it is sad to see they still face challenges, such as having to choose between family and career. My advice to all young women is to face your fears by overcoming them. There is no such thing as a disadvantage for not having a formal degree if you work diligently and the output is sincere. Experience equates to a degree that surpasses any merits.

> "I may not get accolades for my accomplishments or obstacles I face being a woman, juggling a career, business, and family life, but I am grateful to this country where women can work fearlessly and be who they want to be."

You certainly have a head for math, and you are also known to be artistic in the fields of singing and writing. Do you believe there is a connection between the two?

Singing is a wonderful pastime for the community to connect. I write for myself. There is a connection between the intellect and what one creates. The best is if a person can find a happy medium by being an intellectual and at the same time your actions can showcase your productivity and progress in life! I do not like a passive intellectual, as it is a cheat and a burden on society when you are offering only 50% of your capabilities.

Sona Menon

Driving Change in the Workplace

You are the outsourced chief investment officer at Cambridge Associates, with over 25 years of experience and an alum of Harvard Business School. Tell us more about your journey. What were some key moments or lessons in your career that made you the woman you are today?

I have always believed that facing challenges along the path of life can serve as defining moments in making a person who they are. For me, this has certainly been the case. When I arrived in the U.S. at age eight as an immigrant, the transition proved to be challenging in many ways: socially, emotionally, and academically. But it also helped me learn to adapt and be more resilient. I attended college at Cornell University, where I studied government and international relations. My first job out of college was at JP Morgan, in a rotational program across different parts of the bank including sales, trading, and research. It was a fantastic opportunity to learn and develop a

broad set of financial skills, but particularly rigorous for someone who had a liberal arts education. I can recall having to work extra hard to keep up with my peers with finance degrees and more quantitative backgrounds, but once again, having to rise to the challenge helped me become better and more resilient.

After four years on Wall Street, I left to get an MBA at the Harvard Business School. This was another life-changing experience during which time I met some of the brightest, most interesting people from all over the world, and made some lifelong friendships. After my MBA, I was fortunate to find a job that combined my interests and skills in investments with my desire to do something with impact. In 2001, I joined Cambridge Associates, a global investment advisory firm that built institutional portfolios for endowments, foundations, hospitals, and a variety of large institutions.

I was deeply drawn by the opportunity to have a career in building successful investment portfolios that would further enable these institutions to realize their charitable missions. What I loved about the job was that I could use my investment acumen to have a positive impact on society by supporting the charitable missions of my clients. Twenty-one years later, I am still at this firm. I now serve as an outsourced chief investment officer for several institutions including endowments, pension plans, and healthcare institutions. I am a partner of the firm and the head of our pension practice in North America. As one of the leaders in my firm, I believe it's my responsibility to help pave the way for other female leaders and people of color in the investment space.

You are passionate about DEI in the workplace. What are some of the key initiatives and ideas you would like to see in the workplace in the next five years for DEI, particularly for women?

DEI – diversity, equity and inclusion – is indeed a very important topic for me, especially in the workplace. After all, in the world of investing, there continues to be a scarcity of female leaders and people of color. While this is gradually changing in numbers, I would still like to see more women of color in leadership roles and/or positions where they see an equal opportunity for career advancement.

How can I help drive this change? I have joined my company's Global DEI Council, where I have had the ability to influence the development of new policies and behaviors that enhance the firm's diversity through broadening the funnel of talent that we bring into the firm. I have also helped develop policies that will help improve the career advancement of diverse employees and impact their sense of belonging at the firm. And I will say that the proof is very much in the numbers. There is sufficient data available to demonstrate that increasing diversity, and in particular gender diversity,

> "There is sufficient data available to demonstrate that increasing diversity, and in particular, gender diversity, will improve financial outcomes for companies."

will improve financial outcomes for companies. So, it's not just the right thing to do, but it's the smart thing to do for a successful company. More informally, I continue to love mentoring younger women and supporting them in their professional and personal growth so that they can elevate their careers.

How do you unwind at the end of the day? How do you find a work-life balance?

Work-life balance is critical to enable me to do my job well and to help me reenergize and relax. I am a mother of two teenage boys, so life has a way of getting particularly hectic. A life coach once gave me this great advice: When it's very hard to take away the busy and stressful parts of life, try instead to layer in the things that bring you pleasure and peace. So, I have learned to do that in various ways, whether it means making time for a daily cup of morning tea with my husband before the day begins, going for long walks with friends, or traveling. Perhaps my most favorite hobby is travel. No matter how busy life gets for my family, we have made an intentional decision to travel the world, little by little. We have been fortunate to take trips to Tanzania, exploring the national parks of the U.S., and discovering other amazing places that remind us of just how big the world is. Travel is also an important way for my kids to see and learn about the world through different experiences. That's why we have also done several service trips over the years, individually and as a family.

Madhavi Reddy

A Global Ophthalmologist Shares Expertise on Eye Care and Work-Life Balance

Tell us what brought you to the field of global ophthalmology.

Growing up in little towns scattered across Andhra Pradesh, India, going to Telugu-language schools with tribal girls, and moving every couple of years prepared me well for a career in global ophthalmology. I switched to English language in eleventh grade, and at sixteen, I was the youngest in my medical school class. Medicine opened a door to an exciting world for me! I found the complexities of the human body, especially the brain and its related structures, fascinating. Eyes are amazing pieces of technology, converting light into chemical energy, then to electrical energy, then into a three-dimensional visual experience in the brain. To be able to fix when something goes wrong in this process was simply irresistible for me!

As a resident in ophthalmology in Hyderabad, I had the opportunity to assist American volunteer surgeons aboard a flying eye hospital, Orbis International. Their skill and commitment inspired me to seek further training in the United States. It took me years of research and postgraduate residency training to recertify as an ophthalmologist in the U.S. The challenges were formidable: I was a female, a foreign medical graduate, and a mother, looking to penetrate a white, American, male-dominated surgical specialty at that time. I was fortunate to find mentors, whose guidance was crucial to my success. Now, we have established a professional women's group that mentors disadvantaged schoolgirls. I am particularly proud of a sixteen-year-old high schooler who has developed a smartphone app that can be used to check vision, and another sixteen-year-old female medical student that I am guiding in Myanmar.

Why global ophthalmology?

Despite a full-time, busy private practice and a growing family, I kept remembering the reason I had chosen ophthalmology: the majority of the world's blind live in remote, rural areas. It was 2004 when I began working with SEE International, a global charity eye-care organization. My first trip was to Mexico, followed by Honduras, El Salvador, Ecuador, Peru, Vanuatu, Cambodia, Myanmar, Ghana, Ethiopia, Tanzania, and

India. All these surgical missions opened my eyes to how much more needs to be done! The key is not to do a few hundreds of surgeries but train and empower the local ophthalmologists to take care of their patients. My dream is to alternate working for six months in the U.S. and six months in Africa and Asia to train international residents in eye surgery to have more impact on blindness in the developing world.

There are many common questions that come to mind when it comes to eye care, such as screen time, sleep, how eye care varies in kids, etc. Can you share your expertise with us?

On increased screen time: All of us, children and adults included, are getting more screen time. The best way to rest your eyes is to follow the 20-20-20 rule. Every twenty minutes, take twenty seconds to look at something at least twenty feet away. It helps to have your chair face a window while working, so that you can look away periodically. Remind yourself to blink frequently as we don't blink often enough whenever we are reading or watching a screen. For older folks, dry eyes can cause tired eyes, burning, and watering. Over-the-counter artificial tears can be used to lubricate eyes, up to four times a day. Wearing up-to-date, prescribed glasses, when required, will also help reduce eye strain.

Sleep: It is advisable that children and adults take time off from bright screens at least two hours before bedtime to improve sleep quality.

Blue light from electronic devices: There has been much talk about blocking blue light from screens. In the evenings, and even throughout the day, it's good to switch to night settings on your screen.

How do you find work-life balance? How do you pursue your passions when you are busy?

> "I kept remembering the reason I had chosen ophthalmology: the majority of the world's blind live in remote, rural areas."

Sometimes my friends say, "You need to pull back and slow down. You are not getting any younger!" But we don't live forever. That's why I don't believe in having a bucket list. If you really want to do something, do it right away! My three children are seven years apart and when the youngest was three years old, I decided it was time to begin what I have always wanted to do, to go on surgical eye missions to developing countries. The first trip was such a life-changing experience that I made the trips a part of my to-do list for every year. I have worked as a volunteer surgeon in twelve countries so far. Seeing how a small act can change the life of not only one blind person but their whole family, is an indescribable feeling. I consider perseverance and fearlessness to be my strengths. My weakness is falling in love with too many people, too many places and too many activities.

Widline Pyrame

Creating Dolls That Look Like Us

What inspired you to launch your business? What was the need you saw?

As a young girl, I always wanted to be like my dolls. The problem was that my dolls' hair was always straight, unlike my hair. I am originally from Haiti and I struggled with embracing my hair texture. Because of these insecurities, I went through my hair journey. Perms, straight, braids, pretty much anything you can think of, I tried on my hair. One day, while watching something on the Doll Experiment, a psychological test designed in the 1940s to test children's racial biases, it became suddenly clear to me how having dolls that represent you at an early age has a great impact on who you will become.

There has been conversation about diversity in dolls and everyday children's toys, such as with Barbies and American Girl dolls. What

are your thoughts on this, and why do you think this is an important issue for parents?

This is a conversation (and implementation) that should have happened decades ago! Whatever nationality, parents should teach their kids about diversity. I strongly believe that it is important to teach our kids about race and expose them to diversity at an early age. Learning about different hair textures, skin tones, cultural backgrounds, languages, disabilities, and more is vital to a child's development. The toy industry is a little bit behind in this field. But I applaud all the efforts I have been seeing with the dollmakers you mentioned. This is a very important issue for women and parents as having diverse dolls can help facilitate and encourage discussion that leads to acceptance. Diversity in dolls, however, should not only be about skin color but should also be about culture and personality. It should feel authentic and not simply a way to "patch up" an issue. For us, at Fusion Dolls, we consider hair texture, skin tone, fashion, and more. Our mission is to teach self-love and acceptance.

What was the most rewarding moment behind your business? What is next for you and your business?

The most rewarding moment will always be seeing the child's face when they receive a Fusion Dolls doll. Attending vending events and fairs allowed me to experience this firsthand. I could see their expression and their excitement to finally own a doll that looks like them. It feels like THEIR doll. It reminds me of how I felt the first time I received a black doll from my uncle. At the Black Market, I remember a little girl who said excitedly, "They all look like me! I want all of them!" when she saw my booth. Also, it is very rewarding that our story has been told in various articles at many outlets.

How do you differentiate yourself from competitors and mass toy manufacturers?

What is unique about Fusion Dolls is that it came to fruition because of my personal story. I can relate to the young children (both boys and girls) that are excited to own my dolls. We capture different skin complexions. We are a local Boston business and have our clothing line for the dolls that can be personalized, as we have our seamstress. We bring clothes from all different cultures – Haitian, Jamaican, and many others. This is very important for the kids, as many of them grow up in a non-American household and yet have never stepped foot outside of the U.S. We create that connection for them. We create a unique and personal connection to our customers. As we expand, we hope to be able to bring more and more cultures. This is a huge difference from our competitors and manufacturers, and something that our customers value a lot.

When designing a new doll, how do you decide on the name and other characteristics? How do you draw inspiration?

The dolls are named after my nieces, and some are names that I hope to have for my kids one day. Kinara is named after my niece. Maliaka is a name I hope to use someday for my daughter. It means Angel in Swahili, and I just love that name. Angel is our main doll. When I designed her I considered her hair texture and clothes. I wanted hair that could be braided, washed, and styled, like mine and many of our customers. We are designing more dolls with much more diversity. Please stay tuned!

> "We create these dolls so little children have self-esteem and know they are beautiful or handsome as they grow up. We have to empower our young kids by giving back to the community."

Why is women's empowerment important to you, and how do you seek to empower women and girls through your business?

Well, I'm a woman. And I believe in women empowering each other. Without us, where would the world be? Often, men praise women for being the invisible and constant force behind their success. A mother is the one who keeps the family's strength, and we often hear about how powerful a woman's intuition is. As women, we have to empower each other and not compete with each other. We all bring our unique gifts to the table; there is room for all of us to shine. I use my platform to share the stories of women that inspire me. We create these dolls so little children have self-esteem and know they are beautiful or handsome as they grow up. We have to empower our young kids by giving back to the community.

Amrutha Ananth

Driving Success via Creativity in Marketing & Communications

What are you currently working on professionally?

In my current role at Dell Technologies, I proactively build and execute partner marketing approaches that involve evaluating, maintaining, and growing the loyalty and value of our partnerships through brand awareness and communication programs. The eventual goal is to translate these efforts into lead generation and sales, and ultimately into business growth. I also don another hat as the business operations and communications strategist for our family-owned business.

What draws you into your field? Any advice for those going into marketing and communications?

I have always enjoyed stitching consumer behavior with product innovation, developing creative campaigns to attract customers, and using the latest tools to translate raw data into insightful messages. The transformation that a good marketing campaign can bring about when multiple disciplines synergize is truly rewarding. What excites me about marketing and communications is its horizontal competency and the indispensable role it plays in any line of business. The field of marketing keeps evolving repeatedly. Yes, there are marketing principles that offer guidance, but there is no single formula that always works.

My suggestions for any aspirant would be:

- **The only way to learn is to dive deeper.** Develop a keen eye for branding, but also understand media production methods. Read up on old marketing case studies while being aware of the latest trends. Practice writing effective one-liners and equip yourself to write an elaborate technical brief.

- **Practice skills through volunteering or other avenues outside your day job.** For example, I translate my love for marketing communications in whatever way I can. At Dell Technologies, I am the co-lead for Cross-ERG liaison and facilitate collaboration. Through this, I flex my "brand-building" muscles. On the other hand, as the social media manager at Boston Content, I let my creative and analytical juices flow as I design campaigns for digital platforms. And while I was in India, I worked as a freelance journalist for leading newspapers and magazines which helped me expand my skill set in my day job.

You've been in the marketing and communications field for a decade now, in both India and the U.S. What are some trends you've noticed in the field, and how has the experience differed between the two countries?

I would like to approach this question in the context of "trend in the business" and "trend in the business setting" – and thereby bring out the differences I experienced between the two countries.

The trend in the business: I started my career in India as a creative strategist in an advertising firm and then shifted to a corporate setting. When it came to messaging for marketing materials, the mandate I received in India was predominantly focused on highlighting "product features." On the other hand, in the U.S., I have always been tasked with highlighting "product benefits."

The trend in the business setting: In India, I was required to be a specialist at being a generalist. Let me give you an example: I used to develop and execute campaigns end-to-end. This meant I needed to broadly understand the entire gamut of marketing, including product marketing, brand and creative, communications, digital, events, field, and channel marketing. When I moved to the U.S., I saw a different trend while giving interviews. Specialists who have deep expertise in a particular facet of marketing were preferred. But like any other industry, trends are changing here too, and in the last couple of years, the roles are expanding to T-shaped marketers. I opine that any upcoming marketer should first establish their base knowledge and build their marketing foundation before choosing their expertise areas.

We've read that in your past experiences, you express how "consistency and creativity" co-exist. Could you elaborate more on this concept and how you have come across it?

> "The transformation that a good marketing campaign can bring about when multiple disciplines synergize is truly rewarding."

Achieving creativity seems straightforward on the surface, but it's not always simple. Being consistently creative is a difficult feat, and to achieve a certain level of consistency, establishing a sound routine is important.

The key here is to settle on a realistic output for yourself – enough to sharpen your skills, but not so much that you feel burnt out. You start figuring out what works for you, improving your technique, and gaining the skills you need to streamline your process.

Solving problems creatively is about the systematic exploration of ideas, not about deriving solutions from thin air. And to know how to direct this, it is important to have consistently practiced your creative instincts.

Mandy Pant

Reflections on Family, Women in Tech, and the Future of AI

Originally from India, you studied at IIT Kharagpur and Georgia Tech, and are currently a technologist for Intel. Tell us about your personal and professional journey.

I strongly believe that my entire journey so far has been a magical ride intertwined with incredible challenges and amazing adventures and I have been thrilled to be able to share it with my family (in particular my parents, my spouse and my children) and close friends along the way. Whether in my professional or personal life, I have always been a strong advocate for gender equality. Throughout my formative years, I attended an all-girls school, which instilled in me the importance of equal opportunities for women. During my undergraduate studies at IIT Kharagpur, I found myself in a predominantly male environment, where I was one of the few women in the entire computer science and engineering department, including both students and professors. Through my subsequent higher studies at Georgia Tech and my current 20-year career at Intel, while there has been some progress toward achieving gender equality, the pace unfortunately has been disappointingly slow. On a personal level, I owe much of my success to the unwavering support of my parents, who played a pivotal role in nurturing my aspirations, never holding me back because of my gender. I have endeavored to provide similar support and encouragement to my two daughters, paying forward the huge support bestowed upon me.

What is your advice to women interested in pursuing tech careers?

With being on the threshold of the AI revolution, there has never been a better time to be part of the tech industry. Everyone's journey in the tech industry is unique, and perseverance, continuous learning, and support are key to your success. Here are a few things to bear in mind.

Be confident: It is important to have confidence in your abilities and believe that you can succeed in the tech industry.

Remember that your gender does not determine your skills or potential.

Seek mentors and role models: Look for successful women already working in the tech industry and connect with them. They can offer guidance, support, and valuable insights based on their experiences.

Be a lifelong learner: Technology is constantly evolving, so it's important to stay up to date with the latest trends and developments. Be proactive in learning new skills, taking courses, attending workshops, and participating in industry events.

Network and collaborate: Attend industry conferences, meetups, and networking events to connect with professionals in the tech field. Collaborate with peers to gain practical experience and expand your professional network.

Advocate for yourself: Take an active role in your career advancement. Promote your achievements, negotiate for fair compensation, and seek opportunities for growth and advancement within your organization.

Pay it forward: As you progress in your career, support and uplift other women interested in tech. Share your knowledge, provide guidance, and advocate for diversity and inclusion in the industry.

What is your next big dream?

Today we stand at the threshold of the AI revolution. The potential of AI to revolutionize various aspects of human life is indeed vast and exciting. In the field of healthcare, AI can help in early disease detection, personalized treatment plans, and drug discovery. It can contribute to enhancing transportation systems through autonomous vehicles and optimizing traffic flow. AI can revolutionize industries like agriculture, finance, education, and environmental conservation. Moreover, AI has the potential to bridge language barriers, improve accessibility, and foster global collaboration. It can assist in addressing complex societal challenges, such as climate change, poverty, and inequality, by providing valuable insights and solutions. However, it's important to recognize that with great power comes great responsibility. Ethical considerations, privacy protection, and ensuring that AI systems are fair and unbiased are crucial aspects that need to be carefully addressed. My big dream is realizing how AI can be harnessed through the collective abilities and efforts of all individuals irrespective of gender and race for the betterment of humanity. It is about leveraging the potential of AI in a responsible and inclusive manner to enhance human lives, foster innovation, and tackle pressing global issues.

> "As you progress in your career, support and uplift other women interested in tech. Share your knowledge, provide guidance, and advocate for diversity and inclusion in the industry."

Annette Philip

Creating a Global Community Through Music

What inspired your interest in music?

From a young age, I always felt that music gave a good visceral joy that no other pursuit gave me as a child. If I didn't do music in some form, I genuinely believed that I wouldn't make it. For me, music is a sensory thing, and an emotional energy. That is how my passion started evolving and I eventually started training (taught myself piano, took vocal lessons, etc.). That was just the beginning. It was a long journey of exploring and experimenting with different styles. The feeling I get from making music is something I can't get anywhere else.

How would you describe your music style in three words?

Intentional, borderless, and connecting. With the music I make, I aim to bring people around the world together.

Who are some female musicians that inspire you?

That is a tough one! Firstly, I would say Karen Carpenter of the band The Carpenters. Her vocal range was absolutely phenomenal, and I'd say she is the most influential on my own voice.

Secondly, there is a new artist that I've just gotten to know about named Raashi Kulkarni. She is a composer. She actually composed music for *Wedding Season* on Netflix. I'm excited to see more composers of Indian origin like Raashi.

Finally, Lenise Bent – she is a sound audio engineer. She is so cool. The stories she has are amazing. How she went about learning the craft of sound technology, as well as her unique openness to life, is inspiring.

The Berklee Indian Ensemble was nominated for a Grammy award. That is amazing. You must be on top of the world. Tell us about the category you are up for and how you felt upon nomination.

Thank you so much! We were nominated for Best Global Music Album, which is for albums containing greater than 50% of their playing time with new vocal or instrumental global music recordings.

This was actually our debut album for Berklee Indian Ensemble. This record has been years in the making. In fact, the past few years have been a logistical mountain, working all day with teams across the music industry (legal, marketing, branding, etc.). So many different things go into making a record, but ultimately, it's rewarding and enlightening.

The moment they made the announcement was unreal. In fact, John Legend was on screen announcing several categories. We did not know who would announce what, and it was so amazing to hear the announcement on the big screen. It was such a surreal moment (and his pronunciation of our album title *Shuruaat* was pretty good!). Many of us were on Zoom, but what a joyous moment of coming together virtually. We had people joining the call to partake in the excitement from around the world – Malaysia, Bangladesh, India, the East Coast. We were all watching in our own homes on YouTube. It was so funny because there was a lag in the video. You can see it in our faces! We stayed online for three hours just talking and celebrating. It was the best we could do as we were all spread all over the world.

I also want to say that getting a nomination on your first try is a huge deal, and we are very grateful. We are truly appreciative to all the members of the Recording Academy who supported us. We are in a category with some truly amazing artists. There are 98+ musicians (and over 200 people) involved behind the scenes in this, and we have 39 countries represented in this group of musicians. At this time, diversity in the music industry is needed more than ever. There is so much divisiveness in the world right now. This nomination is really a testament to how, despite having different beliefs and backgrounds, people in the world can come together to create something beautiful.

> "At this time, diversity in the music industry is needed more than ever. There is so much divisiveness in the world right now. This nomination is really a testament to how, despite having different beliefs and backgrounds, people in the world can come together to create something beautiful."

How do you think about gratitude in relation to your work?

I look at gratitude toward my work from multiple lenses. Firstly, I have gratitude for ideas. Secondly, I have gratitude for like-minded people, but also for "unlike-minded" people verging (i.e., coming together and co-creating). We've been a part of this music family since 2011.

I also have gratitude toward questions like, *What if?* and *Why not?* which is what spurred this whole movement and what we made possible.

Finally I would like to note that I have gratitude for our music community. People came to this group looking for connection and family, a community. It is a nurturing vibe that can never be taken for granted. I have gratitude for all of this and our craft, our community, and our imagination.

Shalini Ahlawat

Lessons from the Wife of a Diplomat

rewarding personal change. Now that my son is older, I can focus more on humanitarian and social work. I can truly say that despite all odds, all the negative circumstances, and a country still not having gained its full independence, I found Palestine to be one of the most intellectual, inspirational nations I've ever come across. The warmth and hospitality I received in Palestine are unmatched.

The similarities between our two societies stem from the cultures that are steeped in traditions, rituals, and obligations. We share parallel journeys as wives and mothers. Due to our common oriental customs and traditions, I was able to really relate to the women of Palestine. We are the backbone of our societies and are committed to moving our people forward. This binds me to these people, and the experience has truly enriched my life.

Your husband is currently serving as the representative of India to the State of Palestine. India just recently contributed $1 million USD for Palestinian refugees through his leadership, and has sent essential resources throughout the pandemic. What has the experience been like living in Palestine?

Moving to Palestine was a whole different game. I was nervous to leave the comfort and safety of London for a new city, especially one that is negatively portrayed on the news. Little did I know that moving to Ramallah was going to give me the greatest and most

What are the responsibilities of a diplomat's wife? What are some observations you have made about foreign policy and relations?

As the wife of a diplomat, I have many responsibilities. We dedicate our time and efforts to best represent our countries. Sometimes we have to set aside our own dreams and aspirations, as well as recognition of our own educational and professional accomplishments, in order to follow our husbands around the world. We may not have official acknowledged titles, but we always have the best intentions at heart and a desire to honor our origins and homeland. One aspect that we must hold onto is our own identity. Even if we travel from place to place, we have to remain proud of our heritage. As a wife of a diplomat, it is my job to nobly project my national image and to be humbled in the world of diplomacy.

What is a cause you are most passionate about, and what are some projects you have worked on that you are most proud of?

Social outreach to local communities has always been my focus. In Palestine, I have visited cities, towns, villages, refugee camps, and even remote hamlets. I am a firm believer that development should stem from the basis of any society with a clear focus on the less-fortunate individuals and marginalized areas. In this regard, my priority was, is, and will remain directed toward the less fortunate. The case in Palestine is quite unique. An observer can immediately witness the contradictions between areas and localities. For example, in a place like Ramallah, you get the sense of Western liberal society with all aspects of modernity, but just less than 5 km away, in a

place like Jalazoun Refugee Camp, you'll witness the hardships and difficulties of the conditions in which Palestinian refugees live under. Despite all the contradictions and differences, I was amazed to witness genuine equality in the roles of Palestinian women in all aspects of life and the responsibilities and duties they carry out in their society.

"It is a moral duty not just to extend help to others, but also to empower others to become capable of contributing to their societies and assisting others, too."

It is a moral duty not just to extend help to others, but also to empower others to become capable of contributing to their societies and assisting others, too. Women form the foundation of many societies due to the critical roles and duties they perform. We are the wives and the mothers that sow the seeds of the upbringing of future generations. We are the real architects that structure the futures of our nations. In other words, if women receive the proper opportunities in education, development and empowerment, then it's a guarantee that our societies, as a whole, will be healthy, prosperous, and progressive.

Anu Chitrapu

"You Can Be": Reflections on Women's Empowerment

Tell us about your personal journey and what made you the woman you are today.

My personal journey, like that of many others, was very much shaped by the family I come from and the experiences that I was very lucky to have as I was growing up. My dad grew up in a village, was home-schooled until college and then graduated at the top of his class from Banaras Hindu University. My mom did not attend college, but not having formal education did not stop her from learning how the stock market worked, and she traded stocks from home on a daily basis! I think who I am today reflects my parents – I chase my dreams and try my best.

You are a senior vice president at Bank of America. Tell us about your professional

journey and what impacted your career choices.

My first job was with a small analytics company in Cambridge. It was the first offer I received and one I accepted immediately. I was lucky it happened to be an amazing place to work and was founded by a visionary called David Friend, who went on to build several more companies. In the late 1990s, internet startups were the hot places to work at, so I moved to one founded by another visionary, Shikhar Ghosh. It was his encouragement that made me apply to business school. After completing my MBA at MIT Sloan School of Management, I wanted to work at a large company where I could put my newly learned skills to practice. I took a role at Bank of America in an MBA leadership program they had and there was no turning back. Eighteen years later I am still at the bank!

You have authored an inspiring book titled *You Can Be*, a book for little girls. What was your motivation behind this book? What is the message you are looking to send?

In February 2020, I visited a remote migrant settlement in Gujarat, India with the American India Foundation (AIF). I met little girls and boys in classrooms. When I asked them what they wanted to become when they grew up, the boys had many answers but the girls just smiled and said nothing. It struck me that they can't dream of things they are not even aware of! I realized they needed to see examples of

118

accomplished women who look like them and who have achieved success in professions that were considered unsuitable, or even impossible, for women and they needed to see them from a very young age. Growing up with the confidence that you can be whatever you choose to be increases the chances of that happening. That's why I created this book. I wanted all little girls around the world to know this: the glass ceiling has been shattered and even the sky is no longer a limit.

> "That's why I created this book. I wanted all little girls around the world to know this: the glass ceiling has been shattered and even the sky is no longer a limit."

You have been involved with several community and nonprofit organizations such as TiE (The Indus Entrepreneurs), Vision Aid, Co-founder of Nyrvaana, AIF (American India Foundation), among others. Tell us about your involvement with nonprofits and some of the achievements that you are most proud of.

Like with most nonprofits, accomplishments come not from a single person but from a team. As president of TiE Boston from 2020-2022 (the Covid years!), with a committed board, dedicated staff and a host of advisors and volunteers, I was able to grow our programs and create a women's pitch competition and a university student pitch competition. Our board was >50% women, we celebrated our founders at our 25th anniversary and the icing on the cake was TiE Boston receiving the "2022 Best Chapter" award! At Vision Aid, where I served as president for six years, I focused on building the brand and raising awareness. I am proud of the fact that during those years the organization went from a little known group with a large mission to a well recognized name! It is still early days for Nyrvaana but I am encouraged by the amount of fabric we are already saving from landfill and by the quality of upcycled products being made by our women.

What is your next big dream?

My dream is for a world where gender equality is a way of life and every woman has unfettered access to the opportunities she wants to pursue.

Sneh Jaisingh

A Nutritionist's Simple and Effective Guide to Healthy Living

Why are nutrition, health, and fitness so important to you?

Health and fitness are important to all, as they allow us to be able to live life to its fullest and achieve all the things we want to achieve. The role of nutrition in managing and improving one's health has gained more importance over time, especially as science has caught up with the age-old philosophy that you are what you eat. My interest in nutrition started very early in life: I would observe my dad, a physician, who, while prescribing medications, would stress eating right and exercising as his treatment plan. And my mom, who firmly believes that food can be medicine, always turned to her kitchen pantry for treating ailments. I started viewing food as a tool for healing ailments and nourishing the mind and soul. My parents saw this, and encouraged me to pursue my passion – and even to extend it to become my profession. I consider myself lucky to have been able to create a career living my passion.

When and how did you form the concept of NutriAge? What were some challenges you faced along the way?

My journey in the field of nutrition advanced after I got married, as my husband shared similar interests and values. In 2001, we came up with a concept to create an online platform to share our knowledge and also provide diet and nutrition consultation. It was first named PDC, Personal Diet Consultant, which in 2004 was rebranded to NutriAge: nutrition for all ages. For a number of years, the NutriAge website served the community via blog posts, nutrition calculators, one-on-one consultations, and more.

My personal journey shaped the evolution of NutriAge, motherhood being one of the biggest influencers. I started creating and sharing "SEAN" (Simple Easy And Nutritious) recipes that I would design for my family, especially for my son. The advent of social platforms like Facebook, Instagram, etc. greatly increased not only my ability to interact with people but also my outreach. Facebook allowed us to conduct virtual wellness workshops, which started out as simple group challenges and activities, to more intense detox workshops. That has also evolved with time, and we now provide hybrid (virtual and in-person) integrative workshops involving nutrition, yoga, and meditation. The biggest challenge of the 21st century is to have enough time to be able to do all that you have to and all that you want to. And that has been our biggest challenge as well, to be able to balance our duties with our passions.

As research continues, the nutrition industry is always changing and growing. How do you adjust what you tell your clients, based on these changes in the industry?

The field of nutrition sees new findings and discoveries almost on a daily basis. There are superfoods, fad diets, and new trends that crop up all the time. Some fade away as quickly as they gain popularity. And then there are companies marketing their "health" products and superfoods, leaving people overwhelmed and confused. My job as a nutrition and wellness expert is to not only keep abreast with the latest trends and data, but to filter out the noise and keep the small fraction that is actually useful. While evidence-based scientific research does contribute to clarifying nutrition information, when it comes to managing overall health the following basic framework applies to all: one,

> "I started viewing food as a tool for healing ailments and nourishing the mind and soul."

eat local, meaning food that is grown locally versus what is shipped from halfway across the world. And two, eat with the seasons, meaning eat in sync with Mother Nature's seasonal cycles and what's in season near where you live.

Please share some tenets that you follow in your daily life to help drop extra pounds and regain better health.

Honestly, there is no silver bullet; you have to put in the daily work to keep your mind and body conditioned, and this is what works for me and for most of my clients who now understand that there are no shortcuts and weight loss should always be the by-product, not the focus. Once we work toward creating a healthier lifestyle, weight loss will follow naturally. My favorite approaches to creating a healthier lifestyle include:

Plan and prep: These are my two most important tools. I pick one weekend day to create a menu for the upcoming week (sometimes it's two weeks to avoid frequent trips to the groceries). Once the list is ready and the pantry is stocked, I spend 2-3 additional hours on that weekend day to do some prep work: making the sauces, gravies, almond milk, soaking for sprouts, grinding idli/dosa batter, chopping vegetables, etc.

Set a positive tone to your day: Every morning I start my day by drinking one cup of lukewarm lemon water and spend 15-30 minutes doing some stretching and some mindfulness exercises like journaling, meditating, reading or listening to a motivational podcast or even listening to my favorite music.

Be consistent and follow a routine: Our body likes a routine, and I try to stick to a routine when it comes to mealtime, sleep, and exercise. I follow the 80-20 rule: 80% being wholesome, real, nutritious meals, and 20% being indulgent foods. Similarly, getting to bed early during weekdays (80%) and staying up late over the weekend (20%).

Nirva Patel

Crusading On Behalf of Animals

You are a former corporate lawyer and biomedical engineer, now a passionate advocate for animal welfare. How did you know you wanted to work in the legal sector?

Laws are legacies, and as someone who wanted to see lasting change and progress made in unfair systems, law school was the only real solution. On a day-to-day basis, you have a choice to live a very status quo life or lend a hand to those in need, whether people or animals, and I have always been the type to want to help those in need. It is also fascinating to understand that laws are not always set in stone; some work, and some need adaptation. The organic nature of lawmaking and policy appeals to me, whether in working with laws to protect inventions in biotech or toward the way society views and treats animals.

You are a global policy fellow at Brooks McCormick Jr. Animal Law & Policy Program at Harvard Law School. How did you get interested in animal welfare? And what are some of the pressing issues in animal welfare you've learned about?

Since I was a child, animals have always fascinated me. I grew up with two cats and a hamster, and later in life had a dog and now two rabbits. Animals have a fascinating relationship with nature; in fact, they are essential components of nature. Humans have taken them out of nature and commoditized them in such cruel ways. I grew up with Jain values which include the principles of ahimsa but also the notion that nature should be preserved and protected. There are so many pressing issues in animal welfare, but the most prominent of our time is the inevitable impact that the rise of animal agriculture in mega economies like India will have on our environment. As India's dairy industry moves from a co-op model to a more industrialized, centralized structure, the sheer number of processed animals will grow exponentially and become a solution to India's rapidly growing economy. I think India can do better, and this is the perfect time to take our dharmic principles and apply them to disrupt such solutions of scale.

In 2018-2019, you were an executive producer of The Game Changers (along with household names including Arnold Schwarzenegger, Jackie Chan, Chris Paul and many more). This influential documentary shows the power of a plant-based diet. Do

you follow a plant-based diet? What is your advice to others interested in shifting their diets to plant-based?

Yes, I am vegan and not only avoid animal ingredients, but also businesses that promote the exploitation of animals. So, no honey, no silk, no leather, no gelatin. My advice to others interested in shifting is to think long and hard about the suffering that goes into your food. Think about animals that are inherently designed to live out their lives, the animals who feel joy, have babies. Their desire to live is no different from our desire to live. Ask yourself what gives us the right to get in their way – for a chicken finger? If you can live a life on plants, why not? Let your conscience be your guide!

"There are so many pressing issues in animal welfare, but the most prominent of our time is the inevitable impact that the rise of animal agriculture in mega economies like India will have on our environment."

You are certainly a busy woman. How do you relax and unwind? How do you find your work/life balance?

I take each day at a time and try to be as present as possible. I also try to be forgiving of myself. If I haven't returned a phone call or prepared dinner, I keep things in perspective. My husband is very supportive, and I honestly could not attain my balance without him. I am very grateful. I love yoga, and have recently started up hot yoga again with a close friend. Your mind cannot drift in yoga; you need to be very present. Anything that allows you to be present is the key.

What is your next big dream?

I have enjoyed serving on several large animal protection boards, and truly enjoy my research at Harvard. I guess my next step would be to write a book or lead a nonprofit to create positive change for our precious planet. I love bringing people together and elevating voices. There are so many possibilities.

Ruthzee Louijeune

Creating Better Policies for Minorities in Boston

You made history as the first Haitian American woman to be a city councilor of Boston. Tell us about your journey in politics.

My journey to politics started with my upbringing because the personal is the political. I was born and raised in Mattapan and Hyde Park and am the daughter of Haitian working-class immigrants. I saw how my parents had to struggle with overtime and overnight shifts to provide for their loved ones, both here and in Haiti. I saw the discrimination they experienced as Black immigrants, and how they persisted even when the decks were stacked against them. They pushed education as the way up and out for my three sisters and me, and it proved prudent. My first job at 14 was as a walking tour guide with the youth organization MYTOWN, offering a people-centered history of Boston's neighborhoods. The late Mayor Menino appointed me to a committee to redesign the public schools' student assignment process. As a Ward Fellow, I also interned for former State Representative Marie St. Fleur. I am a graduate of Boston Public Schools, Columbia University, Harvard Law School, and Harvard Kennedy School of Government.

As a lawyer and advocate, I practiced before Boston Housing Court representing families facing eviction and foreclosure, worked to elect progressive prosecutors around the country, and worked on voting rights cases before the U.S. Supreme Court. I also served as the senior attorney on Senator Warren's presidential campaign and drafted agreements netting millions of dollars for first-generation homeowners to help close the racial homeownership and wealth gaps with the Massachusetts Affordable Housing Alliance (MAHA). I've spent my career trying to close gaps and make sure we are caring for our neighbors that have too often been historically excluded, especially Black and Latinx communities. As City Councilor At-Large, I look forward to fighting for affordable housing and homeownership, supporting our immigrant communities, improving funding and teacher diversity at our schools, and using all the tools at the city's disposal to address racial justice and equity.

During the Haitian refugee crisis, Boston came together to help. How can the community come together to support and help in these crises?

The country's attitude and policies toward the Haitian community have been disheartening to say the least. We bore witness to how the United States treats Haitian migrants when U.S. border patrol agents on horseback attacked Haitian migrants at the U.S.-Mexican border. Carrying on a Trump-era legacy, the U.S. government continues to deport Haitian migrants and block them from making asylum claims, ignoring international law.

But there have been glimmers of hope here in the Commonwealth. In August of 2021, Haitians and Haitian-Americans living in Boston gathered with allies to a crowd of nearly 200 denouncing the deportations and treatment of Haitian migrants. The Massachusetts legislature recently allocated $8 million to the Immigrant Family Services Institute, a Mattapan nonprofit organization that attends to the many needs of the Haitian migrants who have made it to Boston. Still, there is more to do. The community can help by supporting nonprofits providing legal assistance to migrants to obtain immigration status and Haitian-led organizations responding to emergency crises and routine needs of the Haitian community, such as IFSI, Association of Haitian Women in Boston, Haitian Community Partners, and others.

What is your vision for the future of Boston and what do you hope to achieve during your term?

My priorities include action on housing, climate justice, immigrant rights and civil rights. As the legislative arm of local government, City Council has the ability to pass ordinances, update the zoning code, and use the power of the bully pulpit to bring about change. The City Council also serves as checks and balances on the mayor's executive actions. As an at-large city councilor, I will be a voice for the people at City Hall, listening to what residents care about and helping them find solutions to their problems. My vision for the city is one where we truly look out for our neighbors, which means addressing the everyday constituent services issues and shaping policy to meet their needs.

You have been endorsed by many women political leaders, including Elizabeth Warren and Ayanna Pressley. Who is a woman politician you admire, and why do you think it is important to have women in city politics?

> "Women are close to the issues that matter most to working families and should therefore be centered in political and policy realms."

I admire the women who endorsed me, and many others, including former Congresswoman Shirley Chisholm and former State Representative Marie St. Fleur. Women are close to the issues that matter most to working families and should therefore be centered in political and policy realms. They see how city services do and don't work for families and prioritize addressing those issues. That's what we want from our political leaders. And that's what women do. I'm proud to be part of a City Council that is majority women and to be leading alongside Boston's first elected woman mayor of color.

Tamanna Raisinghani

On Shaping the Life You Want

You are originally from India, and currently a technologist based in Santa Barbara, California. Tell us about your journey and what made you the woman you are today.

I was born and raised in India, where I also completed my education and worked as a software developer for about three years before my marriage brought me to the U.S., which gave me access to new prospects in the literary and technological fields. In the beginning of my engineering career, I found the course material to be really dull. I came to see that engineering encompasses much more than just math and physics. My expectations weren't precisely met despite how much I loved these two subjects. And in order to restore some joy to my life, I began reading books on a variety of subjects and also began writing in my spare time. I never imagined that haphazard scribbling of my ideas and thoughts would lead to a new universe to discover, allowing me to better understand myself and advance as a person. It's simple to allow your duties as a mother, wife, daughter, sister, or friend to define you, but beneath those labels lies an individual who doesn't need to identify with these roles. Writing has helped me discover that person. In addition, I never expected that one day I would be writing for publications like *The Huffington Post*, *India Currents*, and *Thrive Global*.

You are a big believer in positive energy and showing up for life. Tell us more about your key values, how you live a happy and fulfilled life, and how you navigate challenges.

Life is bittersweet. It's not always possible to be upbeat under all circumstances. However, my idea is to show up for whatever life offers you without analyzing the circumstance in order to navigate the lows of life. Life will both astound and astonish us. What matters is how these experiences are shaping us. There is no secret to leading a content and happy life. No one can define it for us. It's very subjective and individualized.

Even if we conquer the world and achieve unparalleled prosperity, happiness may still elude us. As someone rightly said: "The mind is a wonderful servant, but a terrible master." Our biggest battle is not with the outside world but rather with our own mind. We can never lead a fulfilled and content life if we lose the internal battle with ourselves. So to live in harmony and peace, our relationship with ourselves has to be the top priority. When that is healthy, it reflects in every area of our lives. A healthy relationship with ourselves, with our family, friends, work and everything that we have translates into a life of happiness and fulfillment.

What is your advice for women who want to work in tech?

I just think that if women are interested in pursuing this field, they have access to everything they need to succeed. If there is anything holding them back, it's the perception that women shouldn't pursue this line of work. In my professional journey, I have had the privilege of collaborating with exceptional female programmers, and the team of developers I manage consists entirely of women. I entered the software development field after earning my engineering degree, not because I was particularly enthused about it, but rather because it was the only alternative that worked out and seemed the most promising given my background and qualifications. My early years were rife with uncertainty regarding my career decision but I'm pleased

> "I look forward to a future where we no longer label women in technology in such a manner because it has become the norm."

I held on to it. I found my interest and finally came to appreciate data and reporting technology. Your passion may not always serve as the sole determinant of your chosen profession. Sometimes all you need to make things work is patience and persistence. Subsequently, you can leverage the security and financial stability that accompanies a successful career to pursue your passion in your leisure time. More women should consider a career in technology, due to remote and hybrid work opportunities that businesses are now providing following the pandemic. That enables them to have a good work-life balance. I look forward to a future where we no longer label women in technology in such a manner because it has become the norm.

What is your next big dream?

I am really fortunate that life has given me more than I dreamt of. Fueled by my passions for reading and spirituality in particular, I am deeply intrigued to delve into these subjects extensively. I envision myself embarking on journeys to spiritual destinations such as India, Tibet, Bali, and beyond, with the intention of penning a book that explores this realm. Spirituality, in my opinion, can be a great savior in protecting our moral foundations in this day and age when everyone is concerned about the effects of AI on society.

Mridvika Raisinghani

Analyzing What Works At Work

You wrote about the sabbatical you took from your full-time job in order to find your 'why,' which led to you discovering the lack of equity for women in the workplace and the eventual founding of Sama. Why did this issue in particular drive you to action?

I have always worked at purpose-driven organizations who have created equitable access to quality education or helped unlock professional potential. In this decade of my life, I was looking for the North Star that would give me meaning and purpose. I took a short sabbatical of three months to figure out how I wanted to spend the next 5-7 years of my life, which is when I also launched a podcast called *Just an Ordinary Mom.* It was a creative pursuit when I started because I wanted to learn how to create content, learn how to interview people on a podcast and I just found a space that I was really passionate about: motherhood and the penalty it brings

along with it. So I began my journey of talking to amazing women who chose to become mothers and chose to continue working, despite all odds. As I started listening to these brilliant women, and started reading literature as a part of my research, I was left shell-shocked to realize that India's female Labour Participation Rate matched war-torn Yemen's, and India ranked 140 out of 156 countries when it came to women in the workforce. What was even worse was that only 9% of urban women in India were gainfully employed. If 91% of urban women in India, who I believe are relatively blessed because of access to quality education and exposure to opportunities, are neither in jobs nor are they seeking jobs, it feels like a huge waste of India's potential.

What made me even more passionate to find a solution to this problem was my own lived experience as an ambitious urban woman who also happens to be a mother. Being a mother to twin boys and continuing to build a career at startups had already given me perspective about my career and opened my eyes to the struggle of millions of women in India, walking the very thin line between career, caregiving, and identity. Since the problem is so huge, gains of a few percentage points to improve women's workforce participation will result in decades-worth of progress. This is what gave me the conviction and motivation to build Sama, whose objective is to help organizations build equitable workplaces for all.

Sama means equal. One of the ways you are working toward building equality in the

workplace is by creating an algorithm that tracks patterns in women's lives to predict their risk of falling out of the workplace. How does this work, and why it is important for companies to have access to this tool?

At Sama, we are building a predictive modeling tool that processes a complex dataset consisting of women's goals and aspirations, their skills and competencies, strength of their support systems, growth and mentorship opportunities received, flexible and safe working conditions at the workplace to find meaningful patterns that will predict their risk level (high/med/low) of falling off from the workforce. Insights generated by the tool will be used by organizations to create personalized interventions (via AI matching) to prevent women's drop-off. The tool will also provide benchmarked insights for companies in the same industry and sector. Organizations are increasingly realizing that diversity is not just a nice-to-have thing; it has a direct impact on the top line and bottom line. A McKinsey report cited that organizations with gender diverse leadership teams are 25% more profitable relative to those who are not. For organizations to be able to build gender diverse teams and support women to have long-tenured careers at their organizations, they need interventions that are rooted in objective data.

Implementing programs and solutions that are prioritized based on what women want within their organizations is going to be a better investment from the perspective of time, effort and their money. Sama's hope is to help organizations retain as many women as they possibly can within the workforce so that women don't have to choose between their life and their ambitions.

> "Sama's hope is to help organizations retain as many women as they possibly can within the workforce so that women don't have to choose between their life and their ambitions."

One of your ventures before Sama is the podcast Just an Ordinary Mom, in which you tell stories of everyday Indian women and their identities. Have there been any stories or women that particularly struck you, and how did the podcast inspire you to start Sama?

Women are always juggling professional goals, societal expectations, and the responsibilities of families and communities. One cannot stress enough how important it is for women to see other women succeed and progress in life. The podcast is a step in that direction to bring stories of mothers to life and help them find support and solidarity in familiar stories. I started this podcast with a sheer passion for creating a safe space for mothers working outside of their homes to share their life journeys, tactical ways of finding more time in the day, their frustrations and disappointments both personal and professional, their struggles to keep up with conflicting priorities on their time, and to tell that quiet mother in the room who is hanging by the thread before she breaks that she is not alone.

Ritu Kapur

In the Heart of the High Himalayas

How did your passion for the Himalayas begin?

I went to Mt. Kailash in 2018 after I had dreamt about it for eight years. That trip to the high Himalayas in Tibet was so incredible in so many ways that I relived it for months after getting back home to Boston. There is something about the energy of the Himalayas that leaves you mesmerized and in awe of such divine Nature.

I had gone there with a friend, and soon after we got back, we started scheming about a trip back to the Himalayas. We considered going to the Annapurna Base Camp (ABC) or the Everest Base Camp (EBC). We did a lot of research on the routes, watched many videos, and read on the topic. Both of us made up our minds very soon about doing EBC. It took us a few months to break it to our families that

we were going to do this – but the decision had been made!

How did you prepare yourself, and what were some challenges you faced?

I have never been an avid athlete, but I had prepared myself for the trip to Mt. Kailash. It was a 12-day trip, with nine days to go from Kathmandu to Lukla and then to trek from Lukla to the base camp, increasing the altitude from 9,000 feet in Lukla to 18,000 feet at the base camp with a steady climb every day. I had never done a multi-day hike before, and at this high an altitude. Thousands of young and fit people do it every year, but for someone like me, it was daunting.

I created a strict fitness regime for myself, working out for 3-5 hours every day with a focus on aerobics, weight training, and yoga. I would do stairs for 1-3 hours 2-3 times per week with a 10-pound backpack. The first time I did it, my legs were so sore for five days that I could barely walk, but I was able to continue my yoga practice for deep stretches. The second time I did it, I was able to recover quickly and was able to continue my workouts the next day.

There is no way to train for this high altitude other than slow acclimatization, so the only thing that is in your hands is getting your body ready for the grueling conditions. You need to be able to recover after a full day of hiking and then do it all over again the next day while the living conditions may not be the best. The food, sleeping, and toileting conditions can be tough, but you go with an attitude to tackle it as it comes.

Mount Everest in Nepal is the tallest mountain on Earth, 29,000 feet above sea level. The base camp is located at 18,000 feet – higher than most mountains in the U.S. with the exception of Mount Denali in Alaska. It is at this base camp that people who aspire to climb to the top of Everest put their tents for weeks or months to acclimatize and wait for the perfect weather window.

> "As they say, your mental strength is way more important than your physical strength on the mountains; in my case as well, it was mostly my willpower that allowed me to push myself to do this trek."

For me, going to the base camp was more than I could dream of. I wanted to experience this journey as a physical challenge but also as a spiritual journey in the high Himalayas. I wanted to experience the energy of these mountains, and it was incredible. The sublime beauty and the grandeur of these mountain ranges is way beyond what any words can describe. This divine beauty has the potential for shifting the mountains of consciousness within oneself.

Can you talk about your diet while you prepared yourself physically for the trek?

I am a vegetarian, so I depend mostly on beans for protein. I do eat eggs, and include a lot of nuts in my diet as well. One thing that I had to figure out was to eat small but dense meals before my daily workouts. After all, you can't really eat Punjabi paranthas (I am a shuddh Punjabi) and then kick ass in the gym. I started using vegetable-based protein powders for the morning shakes, and that would allow me to work at the gym for a few hours and then have a healthy lunch at home. Taking care of your diet so precisely can be very time-consuming, but it is really important when you are pushing your body beyond its usual limitations.

You are also an avid practitioner of yoga. How do you feel yoga prepared you mentally and physically for the climb?

Although I have always been a healthy person, I have never been much into sports, so I think it was only because of yoga that someone like me could complete a trek like this at the age of 48. I have been teaching yoga for 12 years and have a daily personal practice. Yoga has not only helped me strengthen my physical body but also helped me mentally and spiritually. Yoga was very helpful for me to recover after long daily hikes during the months-long prep and during the 12-day trek. Although we were limited in how much weight we could carry, I kept a thin, lightweight yoga mat with me. I knew I would have to stretch at the end of the day to recover and sleep well. As they say, your mental strength is way more important than your physical strength on the mountains; in my case as well, it was mostly my willpower that allowed me to push myself to do this trek. I used pranayama to increase my breath capacity and chanting to focus my mind every day during the trek.

Anusha Ramachandran

Carving Out a Niche on Wall Street

On three hours of restless sleep and multiple cups of coffee, I nervously walked onto the trading floor. I was greeted by a sea of dual monitor workstations, mounted television screens blaring CNBC, and energy so intense that it enveloped me immediately. Ironically, despite the nervousness, this view calmed me. This was my first day on Wall Street and I was ready. More than ready.

I had just been accepted to a sales and trading analyst program at a major investment bank, and the move to New York City was exhilarating. It was everything that I had worked toward for four years during my undergraduate program. I was a confident 21-year-old, but I have to admit that being in the midst of seasoned experience was unnerving. Over the course of the training week I

interacted with many people: senior portfolio managers and research analysts who would calmly grill CEOs on their financial statements, as well as traders who could read stock charts and make predictions on the direction of the market. It was all so new and yet so familiar. Years later, I am still learning as the markets never sleep and continue to echo the broader sentiments of a changing world.

Over the course of my career, I have had the privilege of being trained by folks who were not only subject matter experts, but also emphasized softer skills. These lessons continue to keep me honest and grounded. Discipline, a strong work ethic, the mindset to be flexible and the willingness to roll up your sleeves have given me the ability to drink from a fire hose and swim to the finish line. Additionally, a few important pieces of advice have stuck:

Get right back up: If there is one thing to be said about the markets, it is that it keeps you humble. You can spend countless hours researching a company, tearing the financials apart, and come to an informed, intelligent decision, but one unexpected mishap and your thesis falls apart. While it is disheartening when that happens, your faith behind your analysis and due diligence should propel you ahead. So, dust yourself off and march on. And of course, continue learning to try to minimize such occurrences.

Do it for the right reasons: Yes, there is glamor and glitz in the industry, but at the end of the day, you are spending a lot of hours working. Working to get it right! Working to make an impression! Working to win a client! The stress is real and the work never ends, so make sure you enjoy it.

Raise your hand and volunteer to take on opportunities that others may pass on: I was given the opportunity to trade Asian markets because I was OK with working nights. At that juncture in life, I had a husband and two little kids who had not yet started kindergarten. We all adjusted to allow me to take on this opportunity, and it ended up being a steppingstone that has enriched my career.

> "You can spend countless hours researching a company, tearing the financials apart, and come to an informed, intelligent decision, but one unexpected mishap and your thesis falls apart."

Be a lifelong student: Being part of a constantly evolving and dynamic industry has encouraged me to read extensively and continue to expand my knowledge base. This is why despite already having multiple academic degrees, I successfully completed an Executive MBA at MIT to further my knowledge and upskill in the industry.

Shyla Shrinath

Finding – and Promoting – Work-Life Balance

You are a physician at Atrius Health in Boston. What inspired your interest in healthcare? How did you know you wanted to be a doctor?

I grew up in Bangalore, India, an only child but in a large family always surrounded by people. My dad's brother was a doctor and was the most revered man in our family. I adored him, so I wanted to emulate him. My mother wanted to be a doctor when she was younger, but was not allowed to go to medical school since she came from a very traditional family. I think subconsciously, I wanted to fulfill her desires.

I was also a very dreamy child with my nose always buried in books. Idealistic by nature,

the thought of helping people always appealed to me. Biology as a subject always interested me, and since I got tracked into the sciences once I finished 10th grade (in India one chooses the track after 10th grade and enters medical school after 12th grade) and got the marks required to get into medical school, it all sort of fell into place.

I don't think I really thought much about being a doctor in the true sense of the word until I came to the U.S., after I got married and started my residency. My residency program at St Vincent's Hospital in Worcester, Massachusetts was a very nurturing program, and I truly fell in love with medicine during my years there, despite the fact that I had a two-month-old child when I started internship and barely saw him or slept much through that first year. Fortunately, I had a very supportive husband, and my parents came from India to help me out for the first few months.

What do you like most about being a primary care physician? What is your advice to young women who want to become PCP doctors?

I love being a PCP because my interest in medicine is broad, and internal medicine speaks to this. I also love listening to people tell me their stories; it gives me great satisfaction to try and help my patients by either figuring out what may be going on physically or otherwise with them, or just listening to them and being there for them in their times of need. It's also nice to see my patients come back to see me year after year and see how much progress they have made in their lives. Though being a PCP may have its challenges, I can genuinely say I am never bored because I am on my feet and thinking through problems and solving (or trying to solve) them multiple times in a day.

Medicine is as much an art as science, and I love the art of practicing medicine as much as I love the science of it. I am a nerd who truly loves all things medical. I will happily read books and articles about medicine and follow my fellow physicians on med Twitter with great interest.

Some of your interest areas include endocrinology and women's health. What is your top tip to women for staying healthy and managing their health?

My top tip for women regarding their health is to really set aside some time for themselves on a regular basis. This is particularly so for women who are mothers because motherhood can be all-consuming, and in the process of being a good mother, partner, and/or employee, women forget to take care of themselves. They should make sure to set aside time to exercise and for fun activities, whether with family or friends or by themselves just to relax and de-stress.

I always tell my patients – men and women – that it's important to be healthy and not to focus on weight alone. I really think that being able to go for a brisk walk or run up a flight of steps without getting out of breath is far more important than getting to an ideal weight that you've set for yourself. The latter can feel impossible, while the former is not.

> "I always tell my patients – men and women – that it's important to be healthy and not to focus on weight alone."

Sleep is very important and is the thing we seem to sacrifice the most. Eating a plant-forward diet and not depriving oneself but eating in moderation can help with staying healthy and fit. In these days of remote work, I also tell my patients that they need to move around as much as possible and use a standing desk for work, rather than sit all day.

The life of a doctor is certainly busy. How do you find your work-life balance?

I had both my children while in residency, my son before I started internship and my daughter at the end of my third year as I finished my MD program. I have always worked part time (usually four days a week) and I try to not let my day off be my day to just do chores. I read a lot, and belong to several book clubs. I also love music, especially retro Bollywood, and any time I'm stressed I just play my old Hindi songs and they are an instant pick-me-up. Prior to Covid, I volunteered at a health clinic at Rosie's Place and Women's Lunch Place in Boston, and I hope to start that up again very soon.

Vishakha Darbha

Making a Difference Through Journalism

You are an associate producer at The New York Times, and have had quite a career in the media industry. Tell us your story. How did you find your passion for storytelling and creating content?

When I was nine, I was asked to write a fantasy story for a creative writing assignment. After reading my story about an ice queen and her human friend, my teacher scribbled a note in the margins, "You have a gift. Don't give up on it." While I don't remember a word of that story, that note remains in my memory. Her words inspired me enough to decide right then that I wanted to be a storyteller, and five years later, when I began high school, I decided journalism would be my medium to tell stories.

Now, almost fifteen years later, I'm glad I stuck to that dream. I have changed mediums multiple times – from writing to video to graphics and now audio – but at the core of my passion lies the need to tell a good story.

How do you find inspiration for the content you create? What are the qualities that make a good story or video resonate with the audience?

I don't think there is one answer for what inspires my pitches. A lot of my work is related to the news, so I derive some inspiration from consuming media on various news websites, including social media. A big part of my current job requires me to pick up on the big stories that have national and international consequences, and work on subjects inspired by those topics. For example, the coronavirus pandemic inspired a range of stories, from ICU delirium to vaccine mandates.

I also get inspired by conversations I have with people around me. You're curious about how much flying contributes to climate change? Well, so am I. Then I read up and see if there's a surprising element to something people know to be general knowledge. And somehow, there almost always is.

You have put together some amazing pieces, particularly The Power of Comedy During Quarantine. At The Times, you are focused on a series, The Argument, and their podcast series, Sway. Tell us about these projects. What is your favorite project you have worked on thus far?

I feel like I have lived many different lives. When I started out in journalism, I was covering politics and breaking news. Then I shifted to environmental stories, and now I'd say I work on more general interest, genre-spanning work.

Comedy in Quarantine came about as a combined project between me and a former colleague, now good friend and established filmmaker. The pandemic had just taken hold in the U.S., and we had all shifted to working from home. A part of the struggle was figuring out how to tell stories via video when you weren't sure if it was safe to leave the house. The only example we had was China, where people had already experienced lockdown. So we started reading up about how they were coping, and stumbled across the comedian featured in the documentary. In many ways, that's how a lot of my stories pan out. I have an itch about something I read, or experienced, and I just want to know more.

Currently, my main focus is producing *The Argument*, which is a debate show with a host and two other guests, usually with opposing viewpoints. I was pulled onto the show to revamp it, and now it's gone from a podcast about U.S. politics to pretty much any topic under the sun. Humans are highly opinionated, so that makes this a really entertaining and interesting show to work on.

"I also get inspired by conversations I have with people around me. You're curious about how much flying contributes to climate change? Well, so am I. Then I read up and see if there's a surprising element to something people know to be general knowledge. And somehow, there almost always is."

I've learned so much about the world and how people think.

The best thing about my job is the fact that I turn into a researcher for every project I am on. For example, I know a lot about lead pipe poisoning in the Midwest, as well as why Americans love stories about serial killers. It's also been quite a journey, moving from one medium to another, which makes it harder to answer the second part of this question. I have many favorites, but if I really had to choose, I'd say the documentary on ICU delirium, as difficult as it was to work on, was also highly informative, collaborative, and some of my best work during a very stressful time.

What is your next big dream?

I want to direct a film! I want to write a book! I want to run a documentary series – video or audio!

I have a lot of big dreams for my career. The way I look at it, 14-year-old me had a big dream that she worked toward, so I don't see why I should stop dreaming at 28.

I think everyone, particularly women, should dream big and dream bold. Not everything is achievable, as most of us realize along the way. But the way I look at it, at least when you look back at your life, you can't say you didn't give it your best shot.

Nesha Abiraj

Compelled to Help Strangers the World Over

I have been a lawyer for over a decade, licensed to practice in Trinidad and Tobago. I am also a permanent resident of the United States. In 2016, following the media coverage of the Syrian humanitarian crisis, the more I read, the more I wanted to learn. Perhaps it was fate that I came across an article from *The Huffington Post* which contained a link to Amnesty International's course on the rights of refugees. Upon successful completion of that course, it changed my life. I knew I had to do more if I wanted to help those who were suffering as a result of atrocities they never asked for and not of their own making.

I still remember the images of a man wheeling his dead wife, crying out for help, and the sounds of children saying goodbye to the world. I had no connection to any person affected, and I was not looking for fame. Rather, I felt a sense of duty to do something to alleviate their suffering, strictly from a place of empathy and duty from one human being to the other. I could not just continue to

sit and watch the news coverage. In that moment, I knew I needed to do better.

It took me eight years to develop a solid and lucrative law practice, and here I was so moved that I was ready to give it all up to pursue my postgraduate studies in international human rights law. While working toward my master of laws (LLM), I was fortunate to be chosen to participate in the Northwestern University's Access to Justice Project. The project was focused on infectious disease law and policy. It involved investigating barriers faced by the most vulnerable communities in accessing healthcare, for tuberculosis treatment in India, which has the largest tuberculosis burden in the world.

My commitment to human rights was reinforced during this project. Following a focus group discussion with women and children who were survivors of tuberculosis, I learned the depth of human compassion, courage, the power of listening, allowing others to be heard and empowering them in the process. While I do speak some Hindi and can understand it on a basic to moderate level, even through a translator, these women who had faced ostracism from their own family members and friends connected with me in a way I could never have imagined. Following the discussion, I went to these women to thank them for their courage in sharing their painful accounts with us. In that moment, just the gesture of a handshake literally erupted into hugs all around because these women who had been stigmatized, discriminated against, said they felt heard, understood and accepted, for the first time in a long time.

Upon completion of the trip and returning to the U.S., I became very ill, and had to be admitted to urgent care to be treated for food poisoning and dehydration. Despite the illness, I finished my assigned report truly motivated that justice and reform could come. Knowing that today those very women and children are now empowering others to break the barriers of shame and stigma down to enable others in their community to get accurate diagnostic testing and treatment made it all worth it. I knew in my heart and head that every bit of this work was fulfilling. This was no longer just something I wanted to study, but a life commitment to help others get justice in the best way I could. Often we think we need to take some sort of massive global action to create positive change, but the reality is that every voice that dares to speak out against injustice counts. We are all capable of bringing about positive change; you do not need to be a lawyer or an activist to do that. You can simply be you.

Upon completion of my master's, I became the first female of Trinidadian origins to be awarded the Schuette fellowship in Global Health and Human Rights. My placement for the fellowship was with Human Rights Watch

(HRW), which had newly incorporated its health policy in the Women's Rights Division, and enabled me to gain an in-depth understanding of the intersection between these two rights regimes.

My research was focused on ending early forced and child marriage in the state of Massachusetts and combating its linkages to human trafficking, sexual assault, modern slavery, female genital mutilation/cutting and domestic violence.

> "Often we think we need to take some sort of massive global action to create positive change, but the reality is that every voice that dares to speak out against injustice counts. We are all capable of bringing about positive change; you do not need to be a lawyer or an activist to do that. You can simply be you."

Even after completing the fellowship, I continued to work on this issue, as only two U.S. States had ended child marriage. I became a member of UNICEF Unite and advocated in my individual capacity and on behalf of UNICEF USA to end child marriage in other states, which came to fruition in May 2020 when Pennsylvania and Minnesota became the third and fourth U.S. states to end child marriage. Forty-six states have yet to pass laws to end child marriage. Personally, I have had no difficulty working with men in these campaigns; my only thought is that we need more male allies and survivors to speak out and join us. I also think human rights issues tend to be less polarizing, and provide an inclusive platform for both men and women to work together in important ways.

Aditi Soni

Making a Positive Impact

You are an inspiring woman in business and a community leader. Tell us more about the lessons you learned in your personal and professional journey.

My personal and professional journey has been driven by a passion for making a positive impact in business and community. As the leader of the Program Management Office at Aurion Biotech, I contribute to restoring vision for corneal endothelial disease. Collaboration has been a key lesson for me. Working with diverse teams is crucial to drive progress and develop innovative solutions for curing diseases. Witnessing the transformative impact of collective expertise, I've learned that collaboration with passionate individuals and organizations amplifies our efforts and brings about positive change.

You are the president of the United India Association and the VP of Saheli Board. Share with us about your journey and some of your community work. What are some of the achievements here that you are most proud of?

As the president of the United India Association of New England (UIANE) and the vice president of Saheli, I am actively involved in community work. In my role at UIANE, I have led initiatives to promote cultural awareness and community engagement. At Saheli, our focus is on empowering South Asian women through fundraising, women's empowerment programs, and supporting our staff. I am proud of the progress we have made in promoting gender equality and creating opportunities for personal and professional growth. I encourage all women to pursue their dreams, embrace continuous learning, and making a positive impact in their respective fields.

You recently completed your EMBA (Executive Master of Business) from MIT Sloan – congrats on this huge accomplishment! What made you decide to study further while you had a great career in pharma? And what is your advice to women looking to get their EMBA?

Despite managing professional responsibilities and community engagements, I successfully completed my EMBA from MIT Sloan. I pursued further education alongside my thriving pharmaceutical career due to my commitment to personal growth and excellence. The values of MIT Sloan, embodied in "Mens et Manus" (Mind and Hand), deeply resonated with me. The EMBA program provided a transformative learning experience, enhancing leadership skills, business acumen, and a global perspective. Engaging with talented professionals, esteemed faculty, and real-world challenges was invaluable. To women aspiring for an EMBA, I encourage you to pursue dreams, embrace continuous learning, and make a positive impact. Invest in education, leverage resources, and approach studies with dedication. Your unique talents can drive innovation and inspire others.

You are certainly a busy woman. How do you relax and unwind – what is your favorite hobby?

Despite my busy schedule with career and community commitments, finding time to relax and recharge is essential. I prioritize spending quality time with family, friends, and indulging in my favorite hobby of traveling. These moments of connection and exploration bring immense joy and rejuvenation to my life. Traveling allows me to broaden my horizons, experience diverse cultures, and gain fresh perspectives. Immersing myself in new environments, trying different cuisines, and exploring breathtaking landscapes fuel my sense of adventure, creativity, and provide valuable moments of relaxation and reflection.

What is your next big dream?

My next big dream is to make a meaningful difference in patients' lives. I'm committed to driving innovation, advancing life-saving treatments, and championing diversity. I envision an inclusive and sustainable world where equal opportunities empower all underrepresented groups to thrive and contribute their unique talents. Through advocacy, mentorship, and collaboration, I strive to inspire others to embrace their dreams and create a positive impact globally.

> "I'm committed to driving innovation, advancing life-saving treatments, and championing diversity. I envision an inclusive and sustainable world where equal opportunities empower all underrepresented groups to thrive and contribute their unique talents."

Bobbie Carlton

Public Speaking, "Innovation Women," and Using Humor to Tell Your Story

What inspired you to pursue the world of entrepreneurship, PR, & marketing, and what were some challenges or interesting experiences you faced along the way?

I began my career on the media side, writing for newspapers and working in radio news before realizing "Hmm, the PR people always seem to have all the answers" and switching sides. I worked in agencies and in-house before being enticed into the startup world where I was able to officially expand my purview to all things marketing.

Then the economy fell off a cliff in 2008 and I was out of work with a stay-at-home spouse,

two kids, a mortgage and little in the way of savings. It was a forgone conclusion that I would hang out a shingle and start offering PR and marketing services as Carlton PR & Marketing. But social media was peeking over the horizon and I was intrigued. I created Mass Innovation Nights to have a place to experiment. The monthly new product showcases were a great way to demonstrate what was possible with social media and help out local startups. During these events, I noticed a disturbing trend – the people onstage looked the same – male and pale, and often the same male and pale speakers and panelists. I started helping some event managers diversify their speaking slates but quickly realized this could become a full-time job (and I already had two!). I crowdfunded the money to develop a platform to connect event managers and speakers, and Innovation Women was born.

You are the Founder of Mass Innovation Nights (MIN), a social media powered new product showcase that has launched more than 1,500 new products which have received a combined $4 billion in funding. What inspired you to launch this venture, and what was the need you saw? How do you seek to empower women entrepreneurs?

Originally, Mass Innovation Nights were the result of my curiosity around social media and my position as a board member for the Charles River Museum of Industry & Innovation. By filling the museum with members of the high-tech community, I was seeking to construct a bridge between the past and the present while I built myself a sandbox in which to learn about social media and how it worked as a serious marketing tool.

Mass Innovation Nights aren't just for female entrepreneurs – they are for everyone. We do hold annual female founder events and were a part of the group that helped launch Boston's annual week for women entrepreneurs – WEBos Week. In addition, our "all new products" approach includes products not seen at other local product showcases which helps diversify our platform – both launchers and audience.

You are also known for your humorous approach, and your "Let's Make Something Happen" approach. Why is humor and personal voice/connection essential to every startup and every woman's story?

The business world (and many people in it) tend to take themselves WAY too seriously. I work at the crossroads of the creative and innovative industries. Humor is an important part of both. Innovation Nights have to be entertaining – it's business networking, a new product showcase AND a party. We try to

guide the companies to telling their story versus talking about the deep techy details that only people in their industry might know or care about. Successful businesspeople can tell a good story. It helps them gain media coverage and social media share of voice and expand their reach without spending a ton on advertising. When you talk about your company's origin story or a-ha moment, see what lines get a laugh. What part of the story gets your audience to perk up and where in the story do you lose people?

> "Successful businesspeople can tell a good story. When you talk about your company's origin story or ah ha moment, see what lines get a laugh."

What is your next big dream?

The pandemic has created a new level of challenges for women and other underrepresented groups. Women, especially women of color, are more likely to have been laid off or furloughed, stalling careers and jeopardizing financial security. Meanwhile, according to a recent survey from McKinsey & Company and LeanIn.org, more than one in four women are considering downshifting their careers or leaving the workforce completely due to stress and burnout. Progress we had been making could be erased. The fight isn't over – far from it. I want to bring together the platforms I have created and the ones I have purchased to establish a path to equal visibility and leadership opportunities for women and other underrepresented groups.

Eshani Shah

How Parents Can Set the Best Example

A healthy relationship between separated parents leaves a very positive impact. Honest, straightforward co-parenting is the best way to raise a contented child; children should never have to choose between parents. For an only child, this can become challenging. But my family dynamics made a profound impact on who I am today.

My parents' marriage was a love marriage, which always comes with higher expectations. You have already put your partner on a pedestal and believe that they are your soulmate or your dream partner. When these presumptions start shattering, it becomes difficult to save a relationship. Giving time to each other, shouldering responsibilities equally or respecting each other's ambitions are some of the key elements of a happy marriage; when these somehow started

diminishing from their marriage, they mutually decided to part ways.

I was 11 and a bit young to understand what was going on, but a decision was made to put me in boarding school. I went to a boarding school in Panchgani, the most memorable time of my life. My parents used to visit but never came together. I was 13 when they officially divorced. I was a very mature child at 13, so they did not fight for custody but gave me a choice of who I would stay with. I chose to stay with my dad primarily because it was an environment I grew up in. My mom eventually remarried. I came back to Mumbai when I was 16 after graduating from high school. Whenever I visited during vacations, both my parents always presented a unified front, spending some quality time together with me. Even my stepfather joined at times. My transitions spending time with both my parents were peaceful. The time at boarding school helped to build my high-spirited personality, which has helped me all my life.

My mother was fiercely independent and worked very hard to fulfill her dreams. Divorce in the 1970s was very uncommon and most of my maternal family, including my grandmother, broke ties with her. She was heartbroken, but with her resilience, continued her journey of theater. By then, she had taken a job with a bank and was multitasking. She never let her personal struggles influence me. My stepfather passed away when I was 19 and it was devastating. As now she was alone all over again, I started staying with her. In all those years, what I learnt from her is to be independent. She taught me that emotional dependency and financial dependency can lead to disappointments. This holds true for partners, friends, family and children. She had excellent taste in clothes and jewelry and was always very presentable. She was a good singer, dancer and an artist and always the life of a party. I think I have inherited most of her traits.

After I came to Mumbai, I stayed with my father, but he was as busy as I had seen him growing up. I was then going to college and busy with my life. It was around then that my stepmother, Induben, used to visit. Dad first introduced her as a friend. But whenever she visited, she cooked for us and did errands for my dad. I told my father that if he feels that she is the right life partner for him, I am with him. That's when they got married and my stepmother became a bigger part of my life. I did not need much parenting at that point, so she became more of a friend. She was very lovable and took such good care of my dad. Her struggles were similar to my mom's, due to my father's lifestyle, but she took it in her stride. She gave up her ambitions and became a homemaker. Starting in the 1980s, my father had become a household name with his column "Duniya ne Undha Chasma" in a Gujarati magazine called *Chitralekha*, and my stepmother became his PR. With all his popularity, he was shy and a bit of an introvert, but my stepmother responded to his fans and made them feel special. Her

> "Honest, straightforward co-parenting is the best way to raise a content child."

reverence for my father is what kept her going.

When I got married, both my mothers did my "Kanyadan" (gave me away). They were a team from the start. I came to the U.S. in 1984 and my relationship with both of my moms became long distance. Despite this, they were unified in looking after my needs. Whenever either visited, there would be goodies from both of them. This tradition continued after my twins were born. It looked like God had created a miracle so they each had a bundle of joy they could pamper. My son was attached to my stepmother and my daughter enjoyed the attention from my mother. This camaraderie, unity, and selfless teamwork was and is uncommon amongst divorced couples. Because I did not have to make any difficult choices and there was so much harmony in the relationship with both of them, I did not grow up with any emotional baggage.

Even after achieving celebrity status, my father was not abashed about his divorce and supported my mother through thick and thin till her last days. Their solidarity gave me a lot of peace of mind. These days, divorces are common, and custody cases can get nasty, creating a negative impact on the child. Fighting parents are not an uncommon sight for children, and if things just don't work out, then I think a seamless separation that allows the child a guilt-free upbringing is the key. I was blessed that I did not have to choose and balance my affections.

Swati Elavia

Making Food Science Delicious

You are the founder of Monsoon Kitchen and have had an exciting career in the food industry working with companies like General Mills. What inspired your interest in food and food science?

My mom was a teacher of home economics and a wonderful cook, so I grew up in a home filled with good food. While both my parents were very mindful about their food, they were also superstitious about when and what to eat, as most folks in India are. Being a student of chemistry, I started questioning why I couldn't have eggs in the summer or ice cream in the winter. When I didn't get reasonable answers, I researched and interviewed history professors and then wrote a paper called "Food Superstitions – Facts or Fallacy." I received an A for that paper, and

that is how the resolve to learn more about food science and nutrition came about.

You have worked in food science in the corporate sector at General Mills, Betty Crocker, and more. How did that experience translate to your experience as a food entrepreneur?

I was lucky to have learned from one of the best food companies in America. At General Mills, my experience was multifaceted since I worked with every division including researchers in academia, regulators, marketing, and legal departments. That experience continues to help me make sound decisions in my own business every day.

Why and how did you decide to start your own business in 2003? What are some of the products you retail, and how do you accommodate them to different palates?

In 1999, we relocated from Minneapolis to Boston because of my husband's job. Since there was no food company of General Mills' caliber in Boston, I decided to start my own business. And, since I was a decent Indian cook, I figured that was the best route to take. We started our business selling to institutions, which provided us data on top sellers, as well as favorite flavors and products of our chef customers. Feedback from the chefs was invaluable in designing new products and reworking our old products. We took our top sellers in food service and introduced them to retail market. We highly recommend you check out our three varieties of samosas with delicious tamarind chutney, basmati rice bowls, and fresh meals in the grab-and-go deli section.

You have won the Small Businessperson of the Year Award in a predominantly male-dominated industry, and your products are now carried in 1,800 college campuses and the nationwide grocery retail chain Stop & Shop. What are your top tips for women who might want to follow a similar path?

While it was an honor and a humble experience to go to Washington, D.C. to accept the Small Businessperson of the Year Award for Massachusetts, it was even more heartening to see so many other women win the same award in their respective states. Better yet, most of those women were in the food industry as well. From my experiences learning from other women leaders, I have a few tips to share. Ask yourself if you would like to work for someone like you, and it will put a lot of your actions in perspective. Don't be afraid to do the hardest thing because if it were easy everyone would do it. Don't be afraid to ask questions or make mistakes, and always remember that not everyone will be happy with your decisions so try to be fair and trust your instinct. My favorite quote for all women is by Eleanor Roosevelt: "A woman is like a teabag. You never know how strong it is until it's in hot water." I hope with this I can inspire at least one future leader.

> "Ask yourself if you would like to work for someone like you, and it will put a lot of your actions in perspective."

What is your long-term dream with your business?

We still have a lot of "wood to chop," as the saying goes. I want to make Monsoon Kitchens a favorite Indian food brand for America.

Pratibha Shah

Applying Ayurvedic Practices into Your Daily Life

Please tell us about your journey into Ayurveda. What inspired you to pursue this career path?

It is quite a story. In fact, I started believing in destiny after this. I had wanted to study architecture, but through a fluke of timing I missed out on taking the entrance exams. My dad had always wanted me to become a doctor or teacher. One day he came home and said "There is an Ayurveda college in the main city area. Would you consider joining that?" I went, got selected and in my first year itself, I got so intrigued and fascinated with Ayurveda that I decided this is what I wanted to pursue in my life.

What have you have done to propagate Ayurveda outside of India?

While doing my MD from the National Institute of Ayurveda, Jaipur, I took a UPSC (Union Public Service Commission) National Exam and was fortunate to be one of the 12 selected from all over India. I subsequently joined CGHS as a First Class gazetted officer, even before completing my MD. When I left India to come to the U.S. in 2004, I was serving as a chief medical officer, in what is now AYUSH Ministry.

After coming here, I was on a dependent visa for a short while. Then I resigned from AYUSH, took my GRE and got admission in MPH international health, at BU School of Public Health. All through my MPH program, I centered almost all my projects and assignments on Ayurveda. Upon completing MPH, I was immediately invited to join an integrative practice. Somewhere along the line, I founded two 501(c)(3) nonprofits, one national and the other now international. I also became a senior faculty at two leading Ayurveda schools. I have also been involved in many local as well as international Ayurveda projects, including being part of a six-member team that initiated World Ayurveda Day in 2018. One big milestone has been to get Ayurveda Day Proclamation every year for the past three years, from two local city mayors. As of today, I consult, teach, preach, live, and breathe Ayurveda. Ayurveda is not just my profession, it is my passion and my very life.

Can you tell us briefly what the Ayurvedic approach to health is?

Ayurveda, which is one of the world's most ancient continuously practiced systems of health and life, has the most beautiful and complete definition of health. It includes mental, emotional and social well-being in addition to physical health. If I could define Ayurveda in three words, it would be prevention (tools for primary prevention from diseases), promotion (building upon the baseline of health and well-being), and personalization (of health and well-being protocols and therapeutic protocols). As I often like to say, Ayurveda is the complete user manual of the game of life, where all guidelines and resources to live a wholesome life and reaching one's full potential can be found.

"As I often like to say, Ayurveda is the complete user manual of the game of life, where all guidelines and resources to live a wholesome life and reaching one's full potential can be found."

How does Ayurveda look at food and nutrition?

As per Ayurvedic principles, food is that which should nourish us and equally importantly, do us no harm. Ayurvedic approach to dietetics is quite vast and scientific. A few key Ayurvedic guidelines for optimal nutrition would be to eat food that is fresh, real, clean-sourced, whole, seasonal, preferably local, UNALTERED and aligned with one's unique body type.

Please share a few easy and effective tips from Ayurveda perspective for general health and well-being.

The three pillars of health as stated in Ayurveda are food, sleep and discipline. If one can pay attention to these three, one can go through life with optimal health and well-being. Additionally, pay attention to your metabolism – appetite, digestion, assimilation as well as elimination. Ayurveda has emphatically stated that most diseases arise from breakdown of gut health. It is fascinating to see modern medical science discovering the same.

What is your long-term professional dream?

I have been fortunate to be doing what I absolutely love, most of my life. I would like to continue to be able to spread the joy of healing through Ayurveda throughout the world. It is my dream to see more client-centric integrative models of care and a shift to health and wellness in our healthcare, rather than just a disease care model. Something that I do want to accomplish soon is to start writing simple and easy handbooks on Ayurveda for the common people.

Snehalata Kadam

A Passion for Physics

As a physicist, you have worked at Caltech and are currently an assistant professor at WPI. What inspired you to go into physics? Were you always passionate about science?

Since my preteens, my fascination for the world around me captivated my interest in science. I would question what made my voice so similar to my mom's but my physical features so similar to my father's. Delving deeper into the essence of questions like this sparked my passion for science.

I am a problem solver, learner and educator and have always believed in interdisciplinary cross- connections. The ecosystem of science bears no glass ceilings or walls, and allows the individual to thrive and prosper within its architecture. Mother Nature enables us to appreciate its breadth and beauty through its diversity. This diversity is enabled by the amalgamation of biological and physical sciences. As my career progressed, having an open mind allowed me to pivot toward the field of physics. I started appreciating that these subjects are silos, but that science is seamless. No boundaries! The biological sciences greatly rely on the physical sciences, and our living systems rely completely on natural laws. This process of thinking made me a biophysicist.

Physics is a field that women do not often go into. There have been a lot of initiatives initially regarding women in STEM though. What is your advice to young women who may be interested in science and physics?

In my day-to-day interactions with students, I convey one strong message: nothing is impossible if you put your heart and soul in it. When I started my scientific career at Caltech, a photo from the 1927 Solvay Conference blew me away. In physics, Solvay is one of the most prestigious conferences in the field. Dubbed the "most intelligent picture of the century," there was only one woman (Marie Curie) in the frame. If you fast forward to the 2017 conference, there were only a handful of women in attendance. That's my motivation! We do not have to wait for another hundred years to see equality. My advice to young learners is not to start with the mindset that physics is hard. It's the core of our natural being, and it's a gateway to understanding the world around us. The resources are ample these days; make yourself comfortable from the very beginning. There are so many instances in which we use physics in our day-to-day lives. To this end, one of the projects I developed was "Yoga Meets Physics." I worked with eight high school girls during the summer and taught Newtonian laws through simple yoga poses.

How do you aim to guide your female students and other young women interested in becoming physicists or pursuing STEM careers?

"Start early" is what has been proven through education research, so my aim is to engage with high school students and first-year undergraduates. At my university, there are 50% women who start off with their undergrad education. By the time they reach their third year, most female students have moved away from physics. I want to change that. I recently developed an idea to encourage first and second year physics students to participate in Physics LAWS (Physics-Learners and Achievers Women Students) Competition. This idea was awarded a grant by the Women's Impact Network (WIN). This is one of the several ways to motivate and guide women to pursue a career in physics.

What is your next big dream?

My big dream is to become a champion for women's education. I want to lead female students by example, and foster an environment where women should never question themselves. We tend to underestimate ourselves a lot, and I aspire to break that trend. Our lack of confidence in our abilities causes us to lose opportunities, and I wish to stop that. Women are very adept with the art of time management and are excellent multitaskers. We are compassionate. My father's faith in my abilities made me go abroad for my higher studies, and believe in myself. I am supported by an excellent family that encourages me to keep going. I want to create that belief and trust in female students to pave the best path for success in their careers and lives. I want to create an environment for women in which the mentality is always "I can."

> "My advice to young learners is not to start with the mindset that physics is hard. It's the core of our natural being, and it's a gateway to understanding the world around us."

Mariya Taher

One Woman's Fight to End Gender-Based Violence

I was born in the U.S. after my parents migrated here from India in the 1970s. At the age of seven, when my family went back to visit relatives, I underwent female genital cutting (FGC), also known as female genital mutilation, or as it is called in the Bohra community I grew up in, Khatna. Khatna was normalized for me as something every girl underwent. I didn't question it until I reached high school, and I recall a friend becoming angry and stating that we had undergone female genital mutilation. That was when I made the connection that Khatna was a form of gender-based violence.

I tried to learn more about the issue for educational purposes and to understand how the community I grew up in could continue such a practice. However, as I did research, I could barely find any information about it occurring to U.S.-born women, nor any supporting evidence that it happened in India; all I found was that FGC occurred in Africa and amongst African diaspora communities. I realized that my story was not part of the global conversation on FGC. In fact, only in the last few years has the United Nations recognized FGC as a global issue affecting women and girls of all different races, religions, economic statuses, etc.

I realized I wanted to work in gender-based violence (GBV) and went to graduate school for my master's of social work. I learned more about other forms of GBV, such as domestic violence and sexual assault, and I started making connections to FGC. For instance, sexual assault is a learned behavior just like domestic violence is for children who grew up in families where they witness it. Research shows these children often grow up perpetuating those cycles of abuse by becoming abusers themselves or survivors. FGC continues because one generation learns it and perpetuates it to the next generation.

In time I decided for my MSW thesis, since no data existed about FGC occurring in the Bohra community in the U.S., I would conduct an exploratory study to obtain the information. That was the beginning of my story in this field – because I felt left out of the global picture of girls who underwent it, I wanted to fill that gap in knowledge.

Today, we do have more data. Globally, FGC affects over 200 million girls and women, with many more at risk of undergoing the harmful practice each year. Within the United States, the Centers for Disease Control and Prevention reports that the number of women and girls affected by FGC is half a million. Both the global and the U.S. statistics are based on data collected by UNICEF in about 32 countries within Africa and the Middle East. The U.S. figure is extrapolated from the global figure. These numbers leave out anyone who lives outside of those 32 countries. Additionally, these figures do not recognize that the U.S. and Europe have a history of using medically "necessary" clitordectomies to repress female sexuality (until the 1950s, clitordectomies were used to treat conditions such as hysteria, mental illness, lesbianism). There is a stereotype that FGC doesn't happen here, or that only "outsiders" bring it to this country.

"FGC continued because no one spoke up about it, and challenges, such as fear of excommunication or social stigma from within the community, caused people to be silent about it and continue it."

To further fill this gap and decrease that sense of "othering," I went on to write about my experience and what I had learned from my MSW thesis. That led me to connect to the four other women who would become cofounders with me in establishing our organization, Sahiyo. Sahiyo is the Bohra Gujarati word for "saheliyo," or friends, and reflects our organization's mission to engage in dialogue with the community to find a collective solution toward ending female genital cutting.

One of the first things that Sahiyo did in 2016 was to conduct a larger study to gather some basis of understanding of what Khatna was and how prevalent it was in the global Bohra community. Over 385 women took part in our study. One major finding of the study was that 80% had undergone FGC, confirming it was prevalent in the community. We also found that the majority of participants stated that they did not want FGC to continue (81%). What our data showed was that the community was experiencing what we call "pluralistic ignorance," a social psychology term that refers to the idea that "no one wants to believe, but everyone thinks everyone believes." In other words, FGC continued because no one spoke up about it, and challenges, such as fear of excommunication or social stigma from within the community, caused people to be silent and continue it.

What we recognized was that FGC was a social norm, and we would need to reframe the idea that FGC was a way to be culturally accepted into the community, to show instead that it's a harmful practice that should be discarded. To do so, we had to help build a critical mass of voices speaking out against FGC. Our storytelling programs come in many different ways through blogs, social media, picture campaigns, and in-person events. This initial research informs many of our organization's projects and we see our education and awareness programs based on a theory of change – that storytelling can create the critical mass needed to inspire societal change.

Monika Rawal

Charging Through the Ever-Expanding Media Landscape

You are senior entertainment editor at Hindustan Times. What inspired you to become the woman you are today?

It may sound surprising, but I had never planned a career in the media industry. After completing my schooling in 2003, I was preparing for BBA (bachelor of business administration) entrance exams. At that time, mass communication was becoming quite popular. At Delhi University, a degree in journalism honors was provided in just five colleges. I applied to a few of them, and luckily, got selected in the first one only on the basis of an entrance exam and an interview.

That's how my journey started. The excitement I felt during the process of cracking my journalism exam somehow just

convinced me, *This is it!* Two decades later, looking back, I can proudly say it was the right choice, and it remains the best decision of my life. The person I am today is due to my never-give-up attitude. Each time I was stonewalled by circumstances or pulled down by competition, it pushed me further to make things happen and excel in that area. Having switched a few jobs in the 17 years of my career, I can undoubtedly say that each of them has contributed significantly to mold me into a learned professional, a confident leader, and most importantly, a better person. My inspiration has always come from within rather than seeking it from the outside.

The media landscape is changing all over the world, with the rise of over-the-top (OTT) platforms, social media trends, etc. What are you most excited about when you think about the future of media?

I feel these are the glorious times where boundaries have blurred between mediums. It gives the creators many more options to showcase their content. Similarly, being a multimedia journalist makes all the difference. With the explosion of social media in the last decade and the ever-expanding reach of OTT platforms and internet in remote areas, I see the reach of media expanding in a huge way. And that shall redefine the way news will be consumed over the years. This widespread reach of the internet shall also help us reach more people with our stories, as people have an easy and immediate access to news and entertainment on their phones. This exponential rise of OTT platforms has enabled us to see some of the best cinema in the world, something which would never have been possible otherwise. It has also empowered many people to come up with their stories.

In your role, you have had the opportunity to interview some of Bollywood's biggest celebrities. What are some of your proudest moments as a journalist?

I would say all of them. Starting from my first ever on-stage interview with cricketer Yuvraj Singh in front of a packed auditorium of 400 people, to interviewing actor Tapsee Pannu and filmmakers Anubhav Sinha and Madhur Bhandakar with a live audience, I relive them all. I especially cherish my freewheeling and insightful conversations with Anupam Kher, Akshay Kumar and Anil Kapoor. An interview with the legendary Amitabh Bachchan, Kamal Haasan will always remain special, and so will interacting with Pan-India star Ram Charan and multiple conversations with the supremely talented Raveena Tandon.

To do justice in this job, it's important to control the fan inside while meeting a celebrity. It's paramount to mark clear demarcations for oneself when interviewing a celebrity to ensure an unbiased view and conversation. Of course, I appreciate and am deeply inspired by some artists and their onscreen work, but I have always maintained a certain neutrality while interviewing them for the readers. I often tell aspiring entertainment journalists to not be starstruck with the glitz, and instead to stay true to the job at hand. My mantra is never end the interview until you get your desired headline, and prioritize a great story over the rest of the things.

Growing up, you also dealt with a rare skin condition. How did that impact who you are today? And what is your advice to other young women in similar situations?

The skin condition is what has made me into the woman I am today. There were times when I had grave moments of self-doubt, but with time, I accepted my freckles as a part of me, and that was all I needed. I own my flaws, and in a strange way, they empower me. I do wear makeup and also use filters on social media, but that's not to please others or to fit any beauty norm; it's because it makes me happy, which then translates into my confidence and strength while putting myself out there. My advice to anyone out there dealing with any kind of body issues or struggling because of their physical appearance would be to forget what others would think. Just be yourself and thank the almighty for giving you this life. There's so much to explore, discover, achieve, celebrate and be grateful for. Never ever compare yourself with others. You are unique and this is your journey, so start penning it now.

> "My mantra is never end the interview until you get your desired headline, and prioritize a great story over the rest of the things."

Samia Chandraker

How a Harvard-Educated Immigration Lawyer Confronts Screen Blindness

You are a lawyer specializing in immigration law and healthcare, and running your own firm, SamiaLaw. What is the most rewarding part of the work you do?

I founded SamiaLaw over 20 years ago, building on my previous experience in civil liberties and public interest law in the U.K. Last year, my transition to partnership allowed me to step back from day-to-day operations and do more of what I love: counseling clients, problem-solving, advocating for immigrants, and mentoring. As consulting partner, I offer my two decades of experience to get through tricky consultations, assist with the most difficult cases, mentor younger attorneys and interns, and inspire staff and clients to challenge unfair immigration practices.

You have also overcome adversity with strength and resilience in your own life – being diagnosed with "screen blindness." Tell us about this. What exactly is this

condition, and how did you push through it? How did you stay positive during this experience, and what did the recovery look like?

It happened after a busy year of being buried in my computer late into every night. In 2017, I had developed a rare unknown vision disorder – severe sensitivity to artificial light. At the same time, I had no problems with sunlight or natural light. The consequences were debilitating. I could not tolerate viewing computer or phone screens, even for a few seconds. Wearing sunglasses did not alleviate the problem and sometimes made it worse. I could not go to stores flooded with glaring fluorescent light, and even standing next to a monitor, waiting to make a copayment at the doctor's office, was agonizing.

I was thrust into living out a digital nonexistence in the 21st century. A year of pursuing medical treatment led to little relief. Institutions I visited included the Massachusetts Eye & Ear Infirmary, The Carroll Center for the Blind, the Irlen Institute, and the Boston Foundation for Sight.

With change, in order to survive, you have to adapt. And that's how my frustration ended. It was either sink or swim, and it had to be swim. Gradually, I found my way out of the ubiquitous fog of screens. I rearranged my life and my business: technology would have to work around me, and not the other way around. I stopped convincing myself that this was impossible, or that was unattainable. It wasn't easy; it took innovation and persistence. I shifted my business from sole owner to partnership, giving me a new opportunity to do more of what I was good at, and hired an intern to be my vision assistant. I resumed writing and connected with my writing group: handwriting, reading pieces out loud, and oral discussion do not require computers. I was back in business, and I also had my life back.

My awareness of the world around me shifted from digital to analog. I reconnected with humans in a way that my digital consumption would not have permitted earlier. There was a real and physical community that I was becoming central to, keeping its members connected outside the digital universe: neighbors, businesses, friends, family, and clients. In the process, I had created the space I needed to heal and improve. I had found the silver lining in that dark digital cloud. (Very recently, a leading eye specialist has identified inflammation in the nerves of my cornea by studying images taken by a revolutionary new corneal confocal microscope. His investigations are ongoing and may lead to treatment.)

> "I rearranged my life and my business: technology would have to work around me, and not the other way around. I stopped convincing myself that this was impossible, or that was unattainable. It wasn't easy; it took innovation and persistence."

As a woman running her own law firm, and a graduate of Harvard Law School, what is your advice to other women lawyers?

Over the last two decades, I have mentored many law school graduates transitioning as interns or entering as fresh associates in my office. There are a few things I always encourage. Firstly, if you don't know how to do something, don't give up too easily – ask. Even if you are a solo practitioner, you can seek out those with expertise and empathy, and ask. There are often designated volunteer mentors within bar associations and professional organizations – that is a good place to start looking for the right help. Remember – ask! Secondly, don't be afraid to think creatively. Be bold about doing something unconventional. For example, sometimes the solution isn't a legal one, it's a social or practical measure that provides the resolution. Don't lose sight of the real goal: it isn't always applying the law, it's helping your client. Thirdly, another thing I see younger attorneys do is fall into the trap of telling clients that the law says you can't do this, and you can't do that and you can't do the other. Shift your perception of your role – tell the client what you can do for them, and never tell a client "there's nothing we can do," because there is always something.

Sangeeta Bahadur

Author and Ambassador On Discovering the Best Way to See the World

What inspired you to go into foreign service, and what has that journey been like as a woman?

Would you believe that my first choice of career when I was at university was that of an air-hostess?! A born rebel, I had already disappointed my parents by turning down their suggestions to become a doctor, engineer or lawyer, opting to pursue English literature instead. I was now stubbornly refusing to even consider the civil services as an option, for no other reason than that half my family – including my father – was a part of that glorified clan! Besides, who wanted to be stuck for life in a dim and dusty government office in some dreary town in the vast hinterland of India, when I could be flying around the globe, staying in fancy hotels, buying designer clothes and dating handsome pilots? You see, by then I'd read both *Coffee,*

Tea or Me? and *English, August.* You can't really blame a 20-something for being far more dazzled by the lifestyle described in the former than in the latter!

Unfortunately, my parents had different ideas. They were convinced that I'd either gone nuts – a strong possibility, in their opinion – or was simply bent on cutting off my nose to spite my face, an even stronger possibility in view of my wild-child proclivities. Our war of words soon escalated into a war of silence. We hadn't been speaking to each other for a week when my father's best friend from college, now my late father-in-law, came for a brief stay with us. After calming us all down, he had the good sense to ask me WHY? With a master's degree almost under my belt, didn't I think I was a tad over-qualified for the job of a stewardess?

I told him that I was opting not for a job but for the life of a global gypsy. "In that case," he pointed out, "Why not join the Indian Foreign Service instead and travel in style?"

I must admit that I'd never even heard of this golden arrow in the government's quiver. So I had an epiphany right there and then and renounced my dream of handing out dinner trays in the sky. As the then-foreign secretary said rather bemusedly when I told him this story during our first interaction, "Well, it seems some airline's loss was our gain!" That was over three decades ago, and the journey that followed has been phenomenal. I have lived and served in six countries and twinkle-toed my way to at least another 40 for work and pleasure, a far higher tally, I suspect, than I may have notched up as an air-hostess. My gypsy genes are more than satisfied. In between, I found the time to marry, bring up two lovely daughters, make friends around the world, do a lot of interesting work and charm interlocutors as a woman-diplomat! I have loved being both, and have found my femininity to be mostly an advantage. The only grouse I have is that, unlike my male counterparts, I don't have a wife to take care of my home, my children and my dinner parties! The dual obligations have been tough, but challenges are what keep us going.

You are also the author of the Kaal Trilogy, full of amazing and powerful stories. What was the inspiration behind these books, and what is it like being both an author and in foreign service, two very different worlds?

For me, writing has always been an absolute joy, flowing from the love of books and great stories inculcated in me by my father at a very early age. I wrote a number of stories and novels through my school and college days, which were eagerly devoured by my friends and teachers, but since I had no idea how to get them published, they remained confined to the notebooks in which I lovingly scribed them by hand. All romances, incidentally – and the reason why I never sought my parents' help regarding publication. They approved of my writing but did not approve of the genre, which they described as "trash literature." I chose to continue my rebellion rather than change my genre, content to bask in the glory of the admiration that came my way from fellow students. It was only much later in life that I discovered the genre that resonated with me so deeply that I decided not just to write such books but to also get them published if I could. That genre was speculative fiction, which lent wings to my imagination and allowed it to soar.

> "Surprisingly, I have found the two worlds I straddle – diplomacy and writing – to be rather symbiotic."

That was how the *Kaal Trilogy* was born, along with an entire universe that contains the world where the action takes place, and a dazzlingly original superhero called Arihant – a divine weapon created for the impossible task of killing an immortal God. Besides telling a rip-roaring action-adventure tale, I also wanted to give the reader a glimpse into the bottomless treasure-trove of Indian spiritual traditions in a fun and interesting way. Surprisingly, I have found the two worlds I straddle – diplomacy and writing – to be rather symbiotic. Language and imagination play a big role in both, for example, as do the ability to connect the dots to form a bigger picture and the skill to resolve dichotomies and encourage a happy outcome. The difference is, of course, that a diplomat necessarily has to be a people person, spending a great deal of time making and maintaining helpful contacts, while an author's job is a lonely one, confined to her intimate and intense relationship with her computer screen. In my case, the transition has always been rather effortless, because I am basically an extrovert who finds her periods of creative isolation refreshing and energizing. So the symbiosis is complete!

Sangeeta Pradhan

Demonstrating the Power of Good Nutrition

It was November 2008. I was charged with presenting a convincing argument to my audience on how impactful medical nutrition therapy, AKA nutrition counseling, can be in preventing, managing, and reversing the course of chronic disease. I felt approximately 70 pairs of eyes staring intently at me. They were the eyes of seasoned doctors, and a few residents. I had been speaking in public most of my life, but this was the first time I was presenting to such a large audience of doctors, and I was all but a bundle of nerves.

As I stepped up to the podium, my throat was parched, and I could feel the adrenaline coursing through my veins as excitement and nervousness vied with each other. My first few sentences are a blur, but as I presented my case, my love of nutrition took over. I felt myself visibly relaxing; my faith in the power of food as medicine energized me to present a compelling case for the MDs. To my utter surprise, I was able to summon all my persuasive power to convince them why food is the most powerful weapon in our ammunition against disease.

That was a teachable moment in my life, a moment that taught me that the faith of one's conviction overrides all fear and apprehension.

This has been the story of my life, and though the audience might change, the message does not! It is the message that we can leverage the power of food to heal both body and mind. It is about helping people summon inner strengths they did not know existed and channeling them to change their eating behaviors. Historically, food as a therapeutic agent has been largely ignored, despite the age-old advice of Hippocrates. Drug companies perpetrate the belief that their so-called blockbuster drugs are the answer to every chronic disease afflicting mankind. However, as the science of nutrition evolves and emerges into the spotlight, the scientific community is finally acknowledging how powerful a role this innocuous entity called food plays in modulating the course of disease. Given this, I am so grateful to be in a position where I can influence the nation's food choices and set my patients on the path to good health and happiness. What could be more rewarding than that?

I grew up in Mumbai, in a middle-class Maharashtrian family. As I look back at my childhood, the most profound impression it has left on me is what a remarkably joyful childhood I had. The oldest grandchild on both sides of the family, I was doted on by my parents, grandparents, aunts, and uncles alike. Today I am positive that that kind of loving, nurturing, and supportive environment instilled in me a sense of confidence and shaped my desire to in turn help others attain their health-related goals.

When I was very young, I wanted to become a doctor, but changed my mind in a hurry when a phlebotomy class in college so unnerved me that my hand literally shook as I drew blood from my unfortunate, unsuspecting patient. As an undergrad, majoring in microbiology, I almost became a microbiologist myself, except somewhere along the way it dawned upon me that people were far more fascinating than microbes. My passion for the sciences,

food, and cuisines coupled with my innate interest in people to lead me to a career in the science of nutrition.

My motto is if you do what you love, you will love what you do. Whatever you do in life, attack it with passion and a sense of purpose and the effort will pay untold dividends. My blog is a humble attempt on my part to help readers demystify nutrition and just tell it like it is. My vision is to bring Hippocrates' vision to life and convey a simple but powerful message. Food can be the most potent arrow in your quiver against disease, or it can be a slow and insidious toxin that brings on disease. The choice is yours! It is not about eating less, but eating right and your journey to good health begins right now with your next meal.

> "Food can be the most potent arrow in your quiver against disease, or it can be a slow and insidious toxin that brings on disease."

Sue and Kat of Makan Malaysia

Introducing Malaysian Food to the Masses

What inspired you to launch your Malaysian catering business and food blog in the U.K.? What was the need you saw?

Makan started because we were hungry for more. Specifically, more Malaysian food. When we first moved to the U.K. around 12 years ago, we struggled to find places to truly satisfy our Malaysian food cravings (on a student budget) so we were "forced" into the kitchen and learned how to cook the food we missed from home ourselves. After being in the corporate world for a few years, we both found ourselves feeling unfulfilled and looking for something to do that we were really passionate about, so we turned to our one true love – FOOD! We wanted to share our love of Malaysian food with as many people as possible and use the unique flavors of Malaysian cuisine to blow the minds of those who hadn't tried it before. We are still working hard to make Malaysian food in the U.K. a high street regular, right alongside the

likes of Italian, Indian or Thai. The U.K. needs more of a Malaysian food presence!

How do you find inspiration for your recipes? And how would you describe Malaysian cuisine? What are some Malaysian dishes everyone must know?

Bloody. Delicious. Those really are the best words to describe Malaysian food – if you know, you know! For inspiration we always listen to our bellies and are led by the personal cravings we have for the food that we grew up eating. The new dishes we create are often our own personal trip down memory lane, we just hope that everyone who eats our food gets a taste of those warm fuzzy feelings that helped create it.

The nonnegotiable Malaysian dishes everyone should know about and try at least once in their life (there isn't any going back once you do!) are:

Nasi Lemak: Malaysia's national dish that consists of coconut rice, egg, cucumber, ikan bilis (fried anchovies), peanuts and sambal (a Malaysian chili sauce). It usually comes wrapped up in a banana leaf that doubles up as a plate and we would eat this at any time of the day!

Char Kuey Teow: Wok fried fresh rice noodles is the queen of Malaysian street food! It's a simple noodle dish but the flavor from the hot wok over a big old fire and the fresh ingredients make it truly unique and addictive!

Marmite Chicken: Not a lot of people seem to know about this one, and those that hear the name are often quite wary, but, unlike actual marmite, we have yet to find someone that doesn't love this! It's deep fried chicken in a sweet and savory sticky glaze. And it is gorgeous!

What is your next big dream?

We are already surrounded by a lot of strong female business owners within our community but would love to see more female leads in the rather male dominated field of food, at an international level, too. We have always believed in community over competition, and having more open platforms for female food entrepreneurs would be an amazing tool for helping other women businesses out – somewhere we can all share the struggles and the rewards. Because a lot of our business is based on social media and is very personable, we've often found ourselves caught in the trap of having to be bright and shiny even when we're really not, just because it seems like that's what we're supposed to do and that's

> "We wanted to share our love of Malaysian food with as many people as possible and use the unique flavors of Malaysian cuisine to blow the minds of those who hadn't tried it before."

what people like to see when they're buying food. But the reality is that it's really bloody hard at times and we do have meltdowns and lose our minds a little bit, and it's important that we share this and other female food entrepreneurs know that's normal and it's OK. It's a hard business to be in and having people around us to support us through the darker times has really kept us going.

Aside from this, we want to take over the world with our badass Malaysian food and events!

Quratul Ain Bakhteari

Putting Refugee Outreach First

You say that you have the activism of your mother and the wisdom of your father. Was there a specific moment from your childhood or any moment with them that made you who you are today?

I was married, at the age of 16, to a very decent, educated man, but his family was traditional. My husband was a very successful professional at 21 and I was a mother to three amazing boys. I had just moved in 1971, designed and constructed my own home with five bedrooms, lounges and a great living room when war broke out between India and Pakistan, a conflict on what was then East Pakistan. I was in my own little world; me, my children, my husband, the cars, the domestic helpers and other luxuries such as clothes, jewelry, shopping, hairdressers and friends. Slowly, I started seeing refugees, mostly women with their babies and little children, pouring into our neighborhood in very poor overall condition.

I found my extravagant ways of living in deep contradiction with this new reality around me. I started meeting the refugees and organizing support for them.

As a mother and a housewife whose only world was her children and home, these stories made me realize that I could not live with these contradictions. I stopped all expenditures on my home. I gave shelter to the family of a widow who lost her husband and two sons. We all lived together as a family and my children grew up in a refugee camp-like experience. As guests would come to meet them, we heard a lot of the horrible stories of the war of 1971.

This life-changing experience inspired me to visit refugee camps. I dedicated my time to the refugees in their settlements and helped build their homes and communities. I joined the university's program for a master's in social work and got involved with community practices in the refugee settlements in the form of community rehabilitation. This shift of my involvement outside my home domain created problems. I was no longer the same efficient and full-time available housewife and mom who only cared for her three children. My vision of motherhood had gone beyond personal boundaries.

It was a tough choice. I had to continue what I was engaged in. Leaving one's home and children is a brutal decision for a mother. When I returned after my Ph.D., we all came back together as a family. My sons had grown and my husband understood my path. I was a mother, but also a professional in community development, committed to making changes in the lives of women and men trapped in the circle of decaying lives. I was hired by several international programs as a consultant. My husband and children held me in great respect and acknowledgment. Finally, we had a real relationship as a family with meaning for their existence.

What are the challenges you faced as you opened 2,200 schools in Pakistan?

In 1992, I was asked by the government of Balochistan to be their adviser for promoting girls' education in the province, a five-year project funded by The World Bank. I was very happy to take this challenge, as I had no knowledge of the deep, rugged, tribal, dry and arid mountainous and plain deserts of Balochistan. With its largest land area just the size of France, and its poor, isolated population being less than 5% of Pakistan in 1990, not many professionals wanted to work in Balochistan on a long-term basis at the time.

The most resistance I saw was when I wanted to convince the government to hire only teachers from rural areas. With very intensive lobbying and arguments, we finally readjusted the policy, on the condition that within three years of their appointment, the new teachers would complete tenth grade, and go for

teacher training. This methodology helped create 2,200 girls' rural primary schools, under the leadership of 3,000 rural women as teachers, who enrolled more than 200,000 girls for the first time in the history of the country.

Your advice to women growing up in poor, oppressed communities and families? How can they become empowered?

Women in challenging situations must learn and practice inner emotional strength. They must not be ashamed of anything they have done or what people say against them. They must focus on developing their intellect and becoming economically independent. Being of service to others and contributing to the process of social change is the best route to empowerment.

> "Women in challenging situations must learn and practice inner emotional strength. They must not be ashamed of anything they have done or what people say against them."

Can motherhood stand in the way of a woman who wants to advocate for change?

Motherhood should not be considered an obstruction to working for social change. The one major lesson of my life is that a woman must not take motherhood as a limitation or restricting factor in her abilities to grow and nurture her intellectual, spiritual and emotional growth and development. A strong, active, socially, educationally and politically engaged mother is a great pride, and these abilities assist her in raising her family as well. All change has to start from within the family before it can move outward to communities and then globally.

Jaishri Kapoor

Making Artists' Dreams Come True

You are based in New York City and are a high-profile female patron of the arts, supporting amazing organizations such as the Metropolitan Opera and the Newport Jazz Festival. Tell us your story. What inspires you about the arts?

Music and dance motivated me as a child, and they galvanize me as an adult. As a little girl, I loved staging dance performances with my friends. I was a shy speaker; dance let me connect with people in ways words didn't. I dreamed of being a professional dancer. When a famed Bollywood actress and Bharatnatyam dancer invited me to stay and train with her, I was on my way to my dream!

But this dream remained just that, because it just didn't fit the cultural norms and expectations of a woman. My mother was a professional classical singer, and had seen how difficult it was. So I retreated, and went on to a life as a banker and homemaker. But I

quietly kept my childhood passion. I stayed involved as a spectator. I married someone who introduced me to opera and jazz. I followed my children into electronic music and modern dance.

Each of these experiences connected me in unexpected ways with new people and cultures. They reminded me of what had energized me as a child. They also showed me how many performers face the social pressure that prevented me from staying on stage. So I have committed myself to bringing others the joy I sensed as a child. And helping performers – especially women – do what I never got to do.

Tell us more about your work and support in the art space. You were influential in the Met's revival of the Philip Glass opera Satyagraha, which is based on the life of Mahatma Gandhi, and oversaw the staging of A Bridge Together in Newport. What were some of the most rewarding experiences you have had? How do you find your inspiration when you take on a new project?

I try to use these arts to build my own little bridge – from my childhood in India to my life in America. I grew up in a traditional South Indian family but lived in different places around the world. I trained in Bharatnatyam and ballet. I grew up with ragas with my mother, all kinds of music with my husband – from rock and soul to ghazals and qawwalis. And my kids have led me to Latin and African artists.

So most of my projects combine these art forms, and reinterpret them for an American audience. My husband and I helped revive *Satyagraha* at the Metropolitan Opera. We presented a fusion of Bharatnatyam and jazz at the Newport Jazz Festival. I'm working on using electronic music to revive the classics. Every one of these brings me closer to America and deepens my bond with India.

> "I have committed myself to bringing others the joy I sensed as a child. And helping performers – especially women – do what I never got to do."

Why do you believe it is important to support emerging artists, particularly women of color?

It has taken me many years to see what held me – and indeed my mother – back from the performing arts. It has taken a lot of soul-searching and confidence to face the social pressure that molded me. I think these pressures and expectations still exist for many women and even men who want to be performers – especially for those of color and/or from traditional societies. I try to do my little part to help these artists find a platform to express their art, find their own path to fulfillment, and in the process, share the joy with their audiences.

What is your next big dream?

I may not have realized my dream of dancing and singing on stage. But in my own quiet way I have made my artistic dreams come to life. I hope to continue helping every girl find the courage and voice to fulfill her artistic dream.

Geeta Vallecha

Empowering Women to Be Their Best Selves Through Yoga

What inspired your personal journey with yoga? What inspired you to want to teach yoga to others?

Growing up in India, I had exposure to *yoga* and *ayurveda* as a holistic way of life. Folks around me practiced *Sanatana Dharma,* and I was introduced to *pranayama* (breathwork) and *dhyana* (meditation) during my teenage years. Later, I started my journey with shallow goals such as finding fitness through asana (yoga poses). Little did I know that I was embarking on a journey that would give me a renewed sense of identity, connected deeply within myself. *Asanas* are very helpful, but there is deeper meaning to yoga: union of mind, body and soul. I found that meaning by combining internal and external practices. There are

many ways to fill our cups. One way is by sharing what you love, be it food or experiences. Sharing is an act of love that forms deeper meaningful connections with others and with oneself. To me, it is equivalent to offering flowers to God when worshiping. I chose to offer my practice to people as a form of reverence.

What are some good positions for beginners to learn? What is the best time of day to do yoga?

The best time for yoga is early in the morning, so one can establish and operate from a tranquil state of mind throughout the day. If morning is not possible, then any time is better than not practicing at all.

For beginners, it is more important to start gently and learn the fundamentals of overall practice including awareness of breath and actions within poses. This will help develop mind-body awareness, proper alignment and a distinction between (healthy) discomfort and (troublesome) pain.

Do you have a favorite position, or type of yoga?

I have practiced a variety of asana practices from Ashtanga, Iyengar, shivananda, power yoga etc. and I like them all. All yoga practices have a few things in common: they strengthen and purify the nervous system and quiet the mind, so it doesn't matter what style

168

is chosen for practice. One should choose a style that suits them and they are able to commit to and sustain.

The formula that works for me is asana practice, followed by pranayama and dhyana. All of this is incomplete without studying ancient texts on yoga and self-contemplation.

How do you define women's empowerment, and how do you seek to empower other women through yoga?

"A woman is empowered when she accepts all parts of herself, does things that line up with her values, and becomes an equal partner in decision-making for the society."

A woman is empowered when she accepts all parts of herself, does things that line up with her values, and becomes an equal partner in decision-making for the society. Through practice, yoga literally strengthens the mind and body, and a key benefit is profound self-acceptance, which some women especially need. As I have deepened my practice, not only have I experienced the benefits, but I have inspired others to achieve better physical and mental states. I hope to inspire everyone around me by introducing this deeply empowering practice.

What is your next big dream?

My dream is that yoga reaches everyone without losing its real purpose: self-inquiry, balance in life and the pursuit of equality, happiness and oneness, besides health and fitness.

Various upheavals in the world – violence, segregation, and discrimination – could be resolved (at least in part) if everyone practiced the key principles of yoga. Centuries-old Indian philosophical texts teach concepts such as self-acceptance, healthy boundaries, right action and creation of harmonious society while celebrating differences. This dream can come true if yoga is offered as a holistic approach and not just actions performed on the mat. My hope and dream is that everyone who practices yoga is also interested in the philosophy and roots of yoga, and not just asana practice, which is primarily physical. I am continuously learning, so I can offer authentic information and curate courses that educate yoga students about inner practices that are equally strengthening as external practices, therefore creating a superior (overall) yoga experience. I hope by advocating true yoga principles, we also address cultural appropriation and superficial training in yoga.

McKenzie Elliott

A Career in Computer Gaming

You have had an exciting career as a product manager in the tech industry. What inspired you to be the woman you are today?

I expected college to be a breeze, but Georgia Tech was tough. Despite the difficult classes, I found solace in joining campus organizations. Greek life gave me the opportunity to serve as my chapter's president and, subsequently, the Collegiate Panhellenic Council president – two formative experiences that built the soft skills needed to be professionally successful, particularly as a product manager (though I didn't know it at the time).

With a degree in CS and graphic design, my classmates were recruiting to be developers, which was a problem because I had never been the strongest dev in the room. Facing major imposter syndrome, I applied to none of the big tech companies upon graduation and got lucky that a Microsoft recruiter reached

out on LinkedIn for a consulting role. I took the role and this decision is what changed the course of my career.

Through consulting at Microsoft, I discovered that program and product managers existed – roles that fit people like me with technical backgrounds who excelled in soft skills. I found a new team on the engineering side of Microsoft that took a chance on me and soon became a TPM working on GamePass Ultimate before following a mentor to the PlayFab team where I built backend services for Xbox titles.

The keys to my journey thus far have been building strong foundations through leadership experience in college, seizing every opportunity presented to me, and developing relationships with leaders I admired in my jobs and organizations.

You are in the gaming tech industry, having worked for XBOX at Microsoft. What has your experience been like as a woman in the gaming industry, which is traditionally more male-dominated?

When I tell people I work in gaming, the response I get most often is, "Do you even game?" There is this fallacy that a "gamer" is someone who plays shooting games on a console for hours a day. Though this demographic exists, the reality is the definition of a gamer is far more broadly reaching. If you play crossword puzzles on your phone or Tetris on your computer, you are a gamer. The existing "gamer" stereotype contributes to the lack of women we see working in the space as well as the lack of feminine interests represented in games on the market. Women are reluctant to consider gaming as a valid career path and, in turn, classically feminine interests are missing from the games that studios are building because there are not women in the space to push for that subject matter. It's a chicken-or-the-egg problem.

You are also passionate about fashion tech and have worked with multiple startups. Tell us more about your passions here.

I always loved playing dress-up as a kid but, in particular, computer games got me hooked on fashion. When these games did not grow up with me, my passion translated into physical clothing. Getting dressed became my favorite way to start my day.

> "The existing 'gamer' stereotype contributes to both the lack of women we see working in the space as well as the lack of feminine interests represented in games on the market."

After a ski trip, I took a gander at building my own physical goods startup called Blubird, a company reimagining the function of travel ski-bags. Although Blubird was not successful, I discovered a passion for startup.

I moved to New York City from Seattle to get closer to fashion and startups. Here I was able to take advantage of a strong Launch House community (a startup incubator I joined in May 2021) to build a strong network. Since moving here, I've organized fashion-focused happy hours, consulted on the intersection of fashion and gaming, and have built branding and launch strategy for up-and-coming startups in the digital fashion space!

What is your next big dream?

My dream is for games to inspire all people to discover their passions in the same way fashion games inspired me growing up. On top of this, the act of play is good for your brain, so when we limit adult games to a specific set of content (in this case, typically masculine interests), we are losing out on a part of the population that could benefit from playing games both through discovering new passions or through improving mental health. Gaming should be for everyone!

Alanna Flax-Clark

Creating Change Through the Lens of Disability

Photo by Kristin Lee Photography

You are a public speaker, para equestrian, and disability inclusion advocate. Tell us more about your journey, and how it shaped who you are today.

I acquired my disability when I got sick while I was working as a special education teacher. I then had to decide if I could go back to teaching in the classroom. Ultimately, I decided I would not return due to accessibility and safety reasons. I wasn't sure what I would do at first, or what I would be good at besides teaching. It took some time to realize that education and teaching are incorporated into many things, and don't have to take place in the traditional classroom setting.

I've done a number of things, but they all come back to my passion for education and

devotion to inclusion. I always was an ally to people with disabilities, but once I was thrown into the situation myself, it created a stronger desire to bring about more awareness.

While teaching kids with disabilities, I never imagined that I would have a disability myself. You never plan for it to happen. It's not always easy, but I would never take it back. It's changed me as a person and the way I view the world.

You were the first seated model and the first disabled model ever in Fashion Institute of Technology Future of Fashion runway show. You were amazing in that show! Tell us more about this. What did that moment feel like?

I was honored to be the first seated model and the first disabled model ever in the Fashion Institute of Technology's Future of Fashion runway show presented by Macy's. I wore a fabulous design by Sonia Yanes and had fun working and getting to know her throughout the design process as I was able to provide my feedback on what worked or didn't work as a wheelchair user.

Disabled representation in the fashion industry has been practically nonexistent until recently. Despite the fact we comprise the third-largest segment in America according to the federal Office of Disability Employment Policy, disabled people are largely excluded from contemporary fashion design. However, we are now at a moment where form and function have been amplified and the value of the world's largest minority is playing a significant role in true culture change. The realization is that through creativity and design, fashion can be accessible across the gamut of human variability.

Being a part of the Future of Fashion runway show spoke to the transformative power of clothing. Fashion and style are not concepts exclusive to able-bodied communities; everyone deserves the chance to express themselves through their clothing and feel confident about their appearance. Adaptive fashion ultimately is not about a trend, but rather a real necessity that every brand should be aware of, just as they recognize different shaped bodies such as plus size, petite, or maternity.

> "Fashion and style are not concepts exclusive to able-bodied communities; everyone deserves the chance to express themselves through their clothing and feel confident about their appearance."

Tell us more about your work as a disability inclusion advocate. What do you hope to change or inspire for women living with disabilities?

It's important for all people with disabilities to be productive members of society. Disabled people need to know that they can hold a job and be supported in the workplace. It is actually advantageous for a business to promote equity, tolerance, and management of disability in the workplace. A 2018 study by Accenture and Disability:IN reported that companies embracing practices that support and encourage individuals with disabilities in the workplace saw their bottom line improve. Strong DEI practices were associated with a 28% increase in revenue, double the net income, and a 30% boost in economic profit margin, compared with their peer companies that scored lower on DEI practices. So, there's no reason that employers shouldn't promote these practices for their employees!

It's also important to remember that since the passage of the ADA in 1990, employers have to make sure that they do not discriminate against job candidates or employees on the basis of an individual's disability. Interestingly, a study by the Job Accommodation Network (JAN) shows that accommodations in the workplace provide consistent employer benefits over time with minimal costs. The study found that providing accommodations to individuals in the workplace resulted in such benefits as retaining valuable employees, improving productivity and morale, reducing workers' compensation and training costs, and improving company diversity. Most employers in the study (59%) reported that the accommodations they provided had zero cost, and when accommodations did involve costs, the amount typically was only $500, so not very much in the scheme of things. People with disabilities have higher unemployment rates than people without disabilities. One reason for this is a common misconception that disabled people can't contribute to the workplace, but with the proper training, support, and accommodations, disabled people can absolutely thrive in any workplace.

Java Joshi

On Building an Art Community for All Ages

You were originally teaching weekly classes, and now have created an entire arts academy. What inspired you to pursue this? What was the need you saw?

Little did I know when I started teaching a few students (mostly friends and neighbors' kids) at my home, that teaching and spreading the love for art would grow into an entire arts academy. There were multiple factors that contributed to and inspired the growth and formation of Academy of Creative Arts, which started with just me teaching art. It has since grown to 30 different art forms that are all taught under one roof at our Academy.

Most of us South Asian parents focus on academics that mainly deal with left brain development. Our entire generation has grown up being forced to either become a doctor or

an engineer. Even today, most parents are pushing kids to focus on English, math, science and robotics, all good disciplines, but what makes kids more successful is the right balance between left brain and right brain development. EQ is valued much higher than IQ in today's world and unfortunately, there are very limited options if you want your kids to engage in activities that focus on right brain development.

Having two kids of my own that were in Lexington elementary and middle schools at that time, I myself was having a hard time getting creative and performing art education for my kids. My husband and I were both fortunate to have parents who allowed and encouraged us to explore the world of arts, and that defined and made us what we are today. We are all greedy parents who want the best for our kids. We got frustrated when we could not find high-quality creative and performing art programs that we wanted for our kids. As they say, necessity is the mother of invention. We basically took it upon ourselves to create a platform that can bring passionate artists/teachers and parents together. So what started as a quest for our own kids became a mission to do it for all the parents and kids in our community, so that the next generation has access to programs that are focused on creative and performing arts education.

Why do you think arts education is important for kids?

Arts education is critical for the success and well-being of our kids. The creative process involved in art education enhances and strengthens critical thinking skills for kids. Visually learning through drawing, sculpting, and painting develops visual-spatial skills. This teaches kids how to interpret and use visual information. Art stimulates the imagination. Art opens the heart and mind to possibilities and fuels the imagination. Art makes you more observant. Art enhances problem-solving skills. Art boosts self-esteem and provides a sense of accomplishment. Art reduces stress. What parents don't often realize is that art education complements and strengthens the learning ability in kids. It helps with focus and imagination, which are critical elements no matter what subject the kid is learning. Art not only helps kids, but it also helps as adults and in life, as art in any form can give people emotions that lift up their moods and help them to lead a happier life.

"Art stimulates the imagination. Art opens the heart and mind to possibilities and fuels the imagination. Art makes you more observant. Art enhances problem-solving skills. Art boosts self-esteem and provides a sense of accomplishment. Art reduces stress."

What is the most rewarding part of your job?

When you see the eyes of parents and grandparents light up at the creations and/or performances from their kids or grandkids, there is no better feeling of gratification. Art brings people close to God. We have had parents and grandparents come to us, thanking us for creating a platform that allowed their kids to get access to learning dyeing and traditional art forms. We have seen their eyes wet with tears of joy at seeing their little ones use their creativity to express and create something of their own. It's those blessings from our community of students and parents that makes it most rewarding and keeps us going. When we started the Academy, we said, "If we can create one artist or can impact one student to make them a better and more considerate human being, our purpose of life will be served." We feel fortunate to have created a positive impact now on hundreds of students from three to 73 years who have been a part of the Academy family. One of the most shocking moments for us was when we heard that a family moved from New Hampshire to Massachusetts so they could be closer to the Academy – not because one of the parents changed jobs or anything, but simply because their daughter loved to be at the Academy so much. What could be more rewarding than knowing that our Academy is a consideration in our students' and parents' life decisions? We feel so blessed to be able to promote the proliferation of our arts and cultural education for our next generation.

Pratima Penumarthy

Lessons Learned As a Caregiver

You worked so hard to have your elderly parents come and stay with you in Boston. Unfortunately, your mom was diagnosed with terminal cancer in 2019. How did that impact your family?

After my mother was diagnosed with colon and aggressive gall bladder cancer in January 2019, I had to set up a PET scan and biopsy to confirm her diagnosis, but I did tell my mom that this was basically just a formality. Obviously, I was absolutely devastated about this news. The cancer is unfortunately inoperable, and I didn't know how long she had left, but I knew we were talking months rather than years. Because mom was 77 years old and was weak, her oncologist didn't want her undergoing chemotherapies, and she too resisted. Understanding the potential changes in the way we relate to our specific family members did help us take steps to grow healthy, mutually supportive relationships during this challenging time. Of course, it

added responsibilities that became sometimes overwhelming and even led to resentment. Even though I sometimes felt saddened, and even frustrated, I always wanted her to be emotionally stronger, and she actually was really calm and showed amazing strength at every moment in her journey.

How did you and your family handle such a tough situation? Did you have any support?

Mom's diagnosis changed the whole dynamic of our family. As an only child who took on most of the parenting responsibilities, initially I didn't have anyone around me to speak to who would understand my situation. I couldn't share my fears much with my dad, as he is a post-stroke patient and could get too emotional. I held back how I was feeling for fear that seeing me upset or scared would make my mother feel worse. But I was very fortunate to have an insightful spouse and children who simply listened and asked questions and seemed genuinely interested and concerned about what I had to say. My biggest support system was and is my family. I joined many support groups, which gave me more ideas for getting more resources for mom. A cancer diagnosis can feel like swimming in an endless stream of appointments and treatments. I made sure to spend time outside of these to create some good memories as a family. We as a family planned to spend time together, even if that meant just watching a movie at home.

What were some of the important life lessons that you learned in this time frame?

While my mother fought cancer bravely, I fought fear. In the end, cancer changed my entire outlook on life and my relationship with her. The biggest lesson I learned from this is to be active and assertive. When someone we truly love and care about is very sick, everyone in the family should take an active and assertive role in their care. I was once told that if you're lucky, at some point in your life, the parental roles get reversed and the children begin to care for their parents as their parents once did for them. That shift started a bit quicker for me with my mom's illness. Since I was young, my parents had always advocated for me. When the roles were reversed, I made it a point to do the same for them.

I strongly believe that if you are not happy with the level of care your loved ones are getting, you need to speak up. I made sure that the hospital staff or hospice staff were meeting all her needs. I asked many questions. While I was in the hospital with her, I never let a doctor, nurse, or technician do anything to my mother without them first explaining it to me. Though I don't speak medical jargon, I always requested the explanation in understandable terms and made sure that it was my job to advocate for my mother to ensure that she got the best care. I'm so proud of my mother and all that she and her cancer taught me – life lessons of love, strength, gratitude, and humility. Big moments in your life teach you life lessons.

> "The truth is, caregiving doesn't have to be a one-person- all-or-nothing role, and getting help is not failing; sometimes it's the most sensible thing to do."

What is your advice for people who are in a similar situation?

Caring for someone in our lives is ongoing, and the situation has the potential to change rapidly. Even young, healthy people can sometimes find themselves in situations they could never have imagined. Without a plan, the result can be real chaos. It is very important to try to recognize the powerful emotions at play and handle the situation as sensitively as possible. We as caretakers need to build a team. The truth is, caregiving doesn't have to be a one-person all-or-nothing role, and getting help is not failing; sometimes it's the most sensible thing to do. One should ask to share the load with family and friends. Offer tasks they feel comfortable with, and regularly share details of your loved one's ongoing needs to get everyone on board. Another option is to bring in professional caregivers who can develop a personal relationship with the person you care for. Professional caregivers don't have to replace your own care – they can simply add an extra pair of hands and work as part of your team. Online support networks can also be a lifesaver, especially if one doesn't have friends or family members who can relate. Thanks to the development of modern technology, caregiving communities are always just a few clicks away. I would tell everyone in a similar situation that I faced, that do not ever be afraid to ask for help and try not to beat yourself up if you think things have gone wrong. You should remember that you are doing an incredible thing for someone else.

Veena Rao

NRI Pulse Founder Shares Her Vision for South Asian News Outlets

You are based in Atlanta and are the editor/publisher at NRI Pulse Media Inc. You have been a writer/journalist for many years. What excites you about the media world?

I am a newspaper journalist by profession. Before I moved to the U.S., I worked for several years on the news desk of Indian Express, one of the largest circulated Indian newspapers. When my family moved to the U.S., I continued working for South Asian publications. In the summer of 2006, a friend suggested that I launch a newspaper. Holding a newspaper of my own in my hands seemed like an exciting idea! What I did not know back then was the nurturing the baby would

need – the sweat, toil, and disappointments that would be part of the journey.

But I believe in persistence. We survived by keeping our overheads low and providing content not found elsewhere. Stories about men and women in our community and their activities form a large chunk of our coverage, and this ensured that our copies were picked up month after month.

The Limca Book of Records (the Indian version of the Guinness Book of Records) recognized me in 2010 as the first Indian woman to edit and publish a newspaper outside India. This honor has validated my efforts at running a quality publication. I think I am a newshound by nature. My enthusiasm for news has not dimmed in 16 years. I wake up every morning raring to go – gathering news, writing or editing reports, attending events, and planning the future of NRI Pulse. And I am excited to lead what could possibly be the only all-women-run South Asian news publication in the country. Our team is as passionate as I am about bringing news to people as it happens.

You've written many pieces, and been a part of many stories. Is there a particular article or project you are most proud of?

The articles are too many to list, but I am most proud of stories that have made a difference in somebody's life, or illuminated an issue. In the past year, I have interviewed an Indian American woman who was swindled of her savings by a cyber romance swindler, and wanted to tell her story so others could be alerted. I have raised awareness of the story of a physician and mother of small kids who was sentenced to 63 months in prison for a crime she says she did not commit. My team has worked on in-depth stories that shine a light on racism and discrimination. We have interviewed political candidates to enable the community to make informed decisions about whom to vote for. The list gets longer every year.

What is your mission with NRI Pulse? Why do you think is it important to have a South Asian media house? What was the need you saw?

I launched NRI Pulse because the community did not have a news publication back then. The market was full of feature magazines, but no publication that focused on news. Every community needs a news publication to help it grow stronger and widen its outlook; to provide a platform for its people to share their stories, concerns and

> "Women of color represent less than 8% of U.S. print newsroom staff. I look forward to seeing more diversity and inclusion in newsrooms."

aspirations. We work hard at raising awareness on issues that affect us all, while also acting as a bridge between the South Asian and mainstream American communities.

What is one thing you would like to see change for women in the media/journalism space?

Women of color represent less than 8% of U.S. print newsroom staff. I look forward to seeing more diversity and inclusion in newsrooms.

What's next for you?

My team and I are committed to serving our community in better ways for many more years. I also have a second career as a novelist. My debut novel, *Purple Lotus,* which was released two years ago, is still going strong. I am working on my second novel which is set in small-town Georgia. I write about immigrant women finding themselves in America because I am an immigrant woman who found herself in America.

Ramila Thakkar

A Lifelong Commitment to Community Service

Where did you grow up, and how did you start your exciting life's journey?

My journey from the rolling Khasi and Jaintia hills of Meghalaya to the rich cultural metropolis of Boston has been nothing short of a fairy tale. I grew up in Shillong, a small hill station, where one never saw a beggar on the streets. The Khasis are the matrilineal society where children receive their mother's last name, husbands move into their wives' homes, and the youngest daughter inherits the ancestral property. I grew up in a society where women were cherished, respected, and empowered; the birth of a girl child was celebrated with aplomb and the arrival of a son was met with, "Better luck next time."

My educational journey began with St. Joseph's and ended with St. Mary's College, where I graduated with B.A. honors in economics and political science. I migrated to the U.S. in 1972, after my marriage and having lived in Mumbai for one year. I landed in New York in awe and petrified of the city, bustling with people, skyscrapers that blocked sunshine on the streets. After six months in New York we moved to Boston, our home for the last four decades.

You are a community leader. Tell us about your service journey.

As a child, an indelible mark was made by my parents, and the community service seed was planted early on. In 1984, I joined Shishu Bharati, the Indian Cultural School in Burlington, with a twofold purpose: one, to teach, and the other to learn Gujarati culture.

After serving Shishu Bharati for ten years, in 1994 I joined Gujarati Association of New England (referred as Gurjar) as a secretary, later holding other positions. In 2019, after 25 years of continuous service, I retired from the Executive Committee and volunteered to help the Gurjar Constitution Committee, for a mammoth task undertaken to update and amend the 44-year-old constitution. I have been recently elected as a trustee of the newly established Gurjar Board of Trustees. In my Gurjar journey, I am most grateful to three outstanding individuals for the support: Bipin Parekh, Eshani Shah and Deval Kamdar. What Gurjar gave me for my Gujarati cultural growth is a tremendous gift, since I had very little exposure to it in childhood.

Gurjar is one of the oldest nonprofit cultural organizations in the New England area. It was formed in 1977 primarily to celebrate the Gujarati Raas Garba during Navratri. Gurjar has evolved with the demands of the changing times. During my first presidency in 1996 I initiated a cookbook project with recipes submitted by the members. During my second presidency in the year 2018-2019, as Gurjar was celebrating its 40th anniversary, so many first-time-ever events were planned: the first Casino Night fundraiser followed by the Heritage Fest on the Lowell promenade, Supermom competitions, where three generations of women could showcase their talent on the same platform. The highlight was the New England Choice Award, bestowed upon Gurjar as the best nonprofit organization in New England. I believe my biggest contributions to Gurjar are my strong communication and organizational skills, discipline, and punctuality. I can be a tough taskmaster; the word commitment is a sacred mantra to me.

> "I grew up in a society where women were cherished, respected, and empowered; the birth of a girl child was celebrated with aplomb and the arrival of a son was met with, 'Better luck next time.'"

In June 2019 as I stepped down from the Gurjar EC board, Dr. Manju Sheth invited to me to join the Saheli Advisory Board (Saheli, which means a girlfriend, is a domestic violence support group.) I am currently the vice chair of this board. This group is very close to my heart. The plight of women and children affected by domestic violence is truly gut-wrenching. I hope to make some difference in their lives. In 2018, I was nominated for Woman of the Year and I was in the top 20. That was the biggest confidence booster of my life.

What are your top three tips to the next generation of young professionals?

1. Hone your communication skills. Often your verbal presentation becomes more important than narrating your achievements and academia. Hard work and good ethics speed up the ascent.

2. Never sweat the small stuff; pettiness exhausts the energies. If you wish to soar with eagles, don't let the turkeys (negative people) pull you down.

3. Be humble and apologize if you have erred. Arrogance and attitude have brought the might to their knees. Life's oxygen is family and friends. Always be grateful for them.

What is your next big dream?

I believe there's a lot more to do. I would like to get involved with the youth of this generation. I truly admire their belief and vision that anything is possible. My motivation comes from my forever-curious mind and the positive people that surround me. My dream is to someday cross the finishing line with 50 years of community service.

Saira Hussain

Promoting Integrative Health As a Way of Life

What inspired your passion for healthy living and wellness? What inspired you to pursue an integrative medicine fellowship at the University of Arizona?

I have always been extremely passionate about healthy living, since my grandparents emphasized a very clean and healthy lifestyle. They grew their own vegetables, made their own fertilizer, had incredible discipline about healthy eating, and valued good quality sleep. Due to all of these traits (and a dose of good luck), they lived very long and healthy lives. I can't recall them ever getting admitted to the hospital, or even going to the doctor. Moreover, they never suffered any chronic diseases nor took any pills throughout their life. They really exemplified values that I wanted to practice throughout my own life. Fast forward twenty years, when I made the switch from working at the hospital to working at a nursing home. It was a deeply disturbing experience, and I was horrified by the poor quality of life and poor conditions that most patients were living in! Most of them were suffering from at least five different chronic diseases, resulting in them taking a plethora of different medicines, each with a terribly long line of side effects. It affected me very deeply and made me question what I knew about my profession. I felt like a glorified drug dealer who was prescribing different medications for my patients and without even really improving their quality of life.

What inspired you to pursue a career as a doctor?

I have been practicing medicine for the past twenty-five years. I completed my primary care residency from Brown University, and rather than doing a fellowship or owning my own practice, I decided to work as a hospitalist. This is due to the flexibility that shift work gave, and that I needed because of my dynamic family commitments: three kids and a husband, and multiple fellowships. My job as a hospitalist allowed me to spend time raising and nurturing my three children, an act that I deeply valued and emphasized.

Once my kids all left for university and I became an empty nester, I decided to quit my job and enroll in the integrative medicine fellowship at the University of Arizona. It has completely changed my outlook on medicine, and fills me with excitement and passion about the potential future of it. I have been learning about nutrition, healthy lifestyle, exercise, and mental health.

The key to this fellowship is the emphasis upon all aspects of your being: mind, body, and soul. The focus is not on treating the diseases, but rather on preventative care. We want to address the root of the problem, not just slap a Band-Aid on the horrific diseases people suffer every day. Preventing many diseases lies within healthy eating, meditation, good quality of sleep, maintaining a low-stress environment and staying active.

> "We want to address the root of the problem, not just slap a Band-Aid on the horrific diseases people suffer every day. Preventing many diseases lies within healthy eating, meditation, good quality of sleep, maintaining a low-stress environment and staying active."

Always remember: your body is a temple, and filling it with positive energy and habits will allow you to become a better and healthier version of yourself. I wish you the best of luck with your journey. It is truly up to you whether you want to take the initiative and kickstart a healthy lifestyle that will significantly benefit you now and down the road.

Menka Hariani

An Introvert's Journey to Harvard

Why is women's empowerment important to you?

I see a lot of women giving up on their dreams after getting married or having kids. I often hear them saying that they don't have time to fuel their passion. I am a workaholic who works for over 14 hours a day, but when I'm with my daughter, I make sure that we spend some quality time together. Apart from the long work hours and fruitful family time, I do take out some time for my passions too. That "me" time is what keeps me going! I do things that truly make me happy, whether it is a long walk at the beach, 30 minutes of meditation at home in the morning, or literally jumping off a plane (skydiving!). By sharing my story, I would like to inspire women who want to be both a great leader at work and a fully engaged parent at home. I would like to show them that a woman can have it all.

You describe yourself as shy and introverted. How did you overcome your shyness and put yourself out there, at Harvard and at work?

One of my main goals at Harvard was to create a solid network group but it wasn't very easy for an introvert like me. During the very early stages I realized that if I was to grow professionally, I would have to get out of my comfort zone and start striking up conversations with other students and professors. Engaging in any conversations with my professors was tough because I was coming back to school after 12 years. I had very little confidence and the technology had evolved so much that I was very afraid to speak up or share my thoughts on any of the advanced topics that were being discussed in the class. To overcome this problem, I started reading a lot. I made sure that I was fully equipped with knowledge and was completely prepared to talk about the topics that were to be discussed in class. Once I saw that my ideas were appreciated and recognized in class, I grew more confident.

Another very important lesson that I learned was that there is no right or wrong answer. It was all about sharing different perspectives. And with this lesson, I no longer had the fear of being judged and I started to open up more, even with the students.

The biggest change occurred when I started a part-time job assisting a professor for one of the most demanding courses at Harvard. Most of my students are CEOs or CTOs of big companies. Having a 1:1 project discussion with them on an everyday basis really helped me professionally and personally. In my personal life, I'm still an introvert and like to keep my circle small, but at work, I'm known to be a talkative, bold and courageous woman who is not afraid to speak her mind.

What is your advice to introverted students?

I would encourage all students to get out of their comfort zone and try engaging in conversations with people of diverse backgrounds and cultures. As most jobs these days require collaboration with the cross-functional teams, I don't think there's any escape for people hiding behind their cubicles.

Tell us about how you got to Harvard. What were the challenges you faced along the way and while there?

In 2013, I lost my job when my visa status changed. It was very frustrating to sit at home and do nothing. Finally, I decided to pursue advanced studies and make use of my time here in the U.S., which is known to be the land of opportunities. After the decision was made, the biggest roadblock was where we would get the funding for my education. Having a young daughter, it was tough to not think about her future and to invest thousands of dollars on my studies while I already had a master's degree from India. There was a lot of money at stake! But we decided to take that risk with the hope that we would get our

reward soon and that I would find a well-deserving job when I had a work permit. Enrolling into this degree program at Harvard was just the beginning of my journey. During my first semester, I got hit hard by reality when I "failed" and got a C in my course. The education system and the academic culture both are entirely different from what I had experienced back in India. And because it was Harvard, scoring an 84% meant nothing; the passing grade was 96%. But I didn't lose hope, and enrolled for two more courses in the next semester. By creating a continuous feedback loop with the professors, I kept track of my grades and maintained my standing in the class. As time passed, the courses got more demanding, as did my daughter at home! They both needed equal attention. And by this time, the societal pressure also increased. People started asking me how long would this go on. Being an empath, it wasn't easy to not listen to those harsh words and criticism, but I didn't lose focus on my goal and kept going. With all my hard work and dedication, I was able to ace nine out of 11 courses toward my degree and made it to the dean's academic list. I was not only rewarded as the best project manager twice but the business proposals that I wrote were also selected as one of the best in the class. Harvard has been a life-changing experience for me, an experience that was totally worth all the hustle and something that I wouldn't trade off for anything else. It's the best thing that happened to me.

> "I do things that truly make me happy, whether it is a long walk at the beach, 30 minutes of meditation at home in the morning, or literally jumping off a plane (skydiving!). By sharing my story, I would like to inspire women who want to be both a great leader at work and a fully engaged parent at home."

Gunjan Kuthiala

A Writer by Heart, A Producer by Destiny

You are the founder/CEO of NRILIFE Productions and owner/head of Jobgini.com. A writer by heart and producer by destiny, what inspired your passion for creativity?

Creativity is ingrained within all people whose right brain is active, and it was my soul calling from an early age. I have been a writer and storyteller since childhood. An artist usually starts showing their natural traits very early on. But I have been in the corporate HR/talent acquisition sector for 19 years now, and the universe conspired for me to pursue my soul calling with two initial missions. The first was to create a production house that gives opportunities solely and purely on the basis of production. It came from a series of experiences, especially when a top casting director in India asked me if I was available

for compromise or not. I wondered: if they had the audacity to ask a strong and settled mom of two like me, what other small-town needy individuals go through. Secondly, for most creativity seekers among NRIs, it's not feasible to quit their financial, social, and family commitments and explore Mumbai or LA. Hence, the intent is to bring authentic filmmaking within the vicinity of our neighborhood since we have great shooting locations, integrity, talent, money, and more here. All we need is the right production ecosystem. I had the belief and dream, and then the universe started connecting many angels to support the mission. I always say NRILIFE Productions is not just a company but a community of crazy passionate creativity seekers working together to create films.

Tell us more about your work at NRILIFE Productions. What types of stories do you like to tell, and what need did you see?

So far, we have two films at Amazon Prime: *Encrypted* and *NRI Wives*. We have also produced a few ads and music videos, with more film projects in the pipeline. Stories I want to tell are preferably real-life inspired stories of NRIs. Every life is a story. I personally love touching taboo subjects with beautiful messages woven within them, stories that are entertaining and super engaging, unique in some ways, thought-provoking, yet inspiring. I would prefer creating anthology stories but don't want to limit us either.

You are also a managing partner at Jobgini. With the current challenges in the job market, what are your top tips for women in finding a job that excites them?

Job hunting is a job, so when hunting for your dream job, don't just limit yourself to applying for a few jobs. Post your resumé on top-tier job boards, as 60%-70% of jobs don't get posted, but resumés are sourced for those via recruiters. Moreover, career fairs and LinkedIn are great ways to connect with talent acquisition professionals. Lastly, people don't hire people because of their mandatory skills, but when they resonate with them, when they feel the click with them. Go into an interview with your "authenticity hat" on along with professional attire as that will automatically make you confident and humanly resonating. I also give a Triple E formula for public speaking/interviews, which is to remind yourself of Energy, Enthusiasm and Eye contact.

> "Just believe that your dreams are given to you by the universe for a reason, and if you know the A and Z, start taking baby steps."

You are working on multiple amazing initiatives. How do you balance your time between projects?

Well, I am a very average next-door mom full of flaws and can be lazy at times, but if I can do it, so can you! Moreover, women are born with multitasking genes. Just believe that your dreams are given to you by the universe for a reason, and if you know the A and Z, start taking baby steps. The whole world full of wisdom around you will guide you, and gradually, you will learn to maintain balance.

What is your next big dream?

Honestly, my biggest dream is to contribute to millions of souls' dreams through both my babies: Jobgini and NRILIFE Productions. Creating ecosystems is my profession and my Ikigai, and I feel that the universe blesses us with specific strengths and weaknesses for an explicit calling or purpose, like a piece of a puzzle.

Ushma Roy

Finding Ways to Help Those Who Need It Most

Giving back is so important for you. Who inspired you to do that?

I was born and brought up in Kolkata. My father was a renowned doctor and my mother was a housewife. Both of them were very well connected to social organizations. The culture of helping others was embedded into our thought process from our childhood. I was introduced to social work when I was in school. We were told to collect vegetables and newspapers from our buildings and give them to Shishu Kalyan, an organization run by Mother Teresa.

I came to Mumbai in 1986 and got married into a lovely family. Unfortunately, I had a tough few years with my health. I have had three miscarriages, three IVF treatments and two knee replacements at a very young age, which led me to depression. My family, especially my husband, played a very important role in supporting me and getting me out of it.

You have been associated with Lion's Club in Juhu for a long time, and are very active with the Lion Ladies specifically. Share some work done by this work for the community and your role and contributions. What excites you most about Lions Club?

My father-in-law was an active member and he played an instrumental role in introducing us to Lions Club of Juhu. At the start I was a very passive member, but in 2017-2018, when my brother-in-law became the president of Lions Club of Juhu, he encouraged me to became Lion Lady auxiliary chairperson and after that there was no looking back. I feel that it was the best thing that happened to me, I became an extrovert, gained self-confidence and realized that giving back to society brought me immense happiness. In 2019 I became chairperson of the Speech and Hearing Impaired Committee. We organized a Navratri celebration with children who could not hear or speak but still danced. In 2020 I became chairperson of women empowerment. In 2023 I became joint chairperson of October service week.

You were instrumental in executing the Women Who Win shoe project, whereby we donated shoes to women in Mumbai. Please share that experience.

In collaboration with Women Who Win and Lions Club of Juhu, we conducted a very big shoe project where we provided 700 pairs of shoes to women and children who were working barefoot in villages. We also did another project in collaboration with Rotary Club in Kolkata where we distributed shoes to rickshaw and handcart pullers. Many women

> "I became an extrovert, gained self-confidence and realized that giving back to society brought me immense happiness."

in this community have to work in the fields during heavy monsoon seasons and are working barefoot, putting themselves at a higher risk of foot infections. We are excited to help these communities be safe and healthy.

Shalini Singh

An Insider's Scoop on Dating Apps

What inspired you to launch your dating app andwemet?

The thought behind launching *andwemet* came from listening to unpleasant and frustrating online matchmaking experiences shared by family and friends. These experiences were crystallized after conducting an extensive survey with single, urban Indians and by participating in social experiments to gauge the situation and to define the gap. The analysis of results led us to a single outcome, "lack of trust," which in turn led to disengagement. Addressing this became the cornerstone on which our platform stands.

In the wake of the pandemic and associated lockdowns, what do you think the dating scene will look like now?

To be honest, finding a partner during lockdown was no different than when life was normal, other than the fact that face-to-face meetings were replaced with video calls. The lockdown I believe worked in favor of those seeking love who could not invest more for want of time: the lockdown gave them the time to be introspective and invest in searching for their prospective partner. I personally believe that the dating scene did not go through a major shift during the lockdown; therefore, expect no major changes in the days to come, either.

The above being said, for the majority of singles, the thought of searching for a compatible companion keeps cropping up from time to time. Your search ends when you meet someone by chance or are introduced by family, friends, or on online platforms. My advice here would be that if you are seeking love online, look for a platform that you can trust.

On your site, you emphasize the quality and background of your clients. For those using more open dating apps with less "vetting" and free sign-ups, what are your strategies? How do you recommend using a dating app and making sure you are finding the right people, and the most honest people?

It's a tough one, as each individual is unique and has their own flavor and needs. If you are one of those who seeks a committed relationship, your first challenge would be to identify and filter individuals. There is a plethora of information out there suggesting that 40%-50% of profiles on dating platforms are fake. Once you wade through this challenge, each of us has our own way of interacting and building connections. If I had to give any advice, it would be to just be yourself.

You wrote a piece on how to know when you are ready for a relationship. As life becomes busier and work-life balance becomes harder to achieve, how do you think people will know they are ready? What types of sacrifices should people be willing to make, and which ones should they not make in relationships?

How does one know they are ready for a relationship? Well, there is no set formula for this. You can ask why you seek to be in a relationship and what it is that you can bring to it. If coming out of a failed relationship is the driver, please be introspective and be sure that you have moved forward emotionally from the past relationship. In all honesty, relationships are extremely personal. As for the sacrifices that you talk about, I would address it by saying that every long-lasting relationship is a TRAP (Trust, Respect, Acceptance and Patience) and couples have their own thresholds.

> "The analysis of results led us to a single outcome, "lack of trust," which in turn led to disengagement. Addressing this became the cornerstone on which our platform stands."

What are the most common dating pitfalls you see, and how does this vary among age groups/cultures?

Dispassionately thinking dating is defined by emotions and not logic happens across age groups and cultures. If we consider this, we can see that initial decisions may be made based on emotions and the initial euphoria, and that this may cloud judgment. Therefore, it is important to be introspective before diving completely in, and I must admit that it is easier said than done. We aim to help people make an informed decision through our app.

What are some common glitches you see in mass market dating algorithms, and how have you worked to mitigate this for your clients?

I see technology as an enabler that certainly helps with factors for some users, but I think that is where it stops. Technology that works on data and gauging personality traits through only data is yet to reach maturity, though it may never truly achieve this, as this is about understanding the human mind and emotions to help give "perfect" matches. I believe that for technology to aid a successful relationship, you need unstated information, which is difficult to convert into actionable data. For us, the technology is being used around approaches that help our members to make an informed decision.

Vyjayanti Chhabra

Bringing Indian Fashion to the U.S.

The Chhabra name has become synonymous with bridalwear in Delhi, India. You are the founder of Chhabra Bridal in Cambridge, Massachusetts, introducing the various Chhabra women's clothing designs to the Boston area. What inspired you to pursue the Indian fashion business?

My journey into the Indian fashion business started with my arranged marriage into a large textile manufacturing and trading Chhabra family in Delhi. Coming from a salaried job environment, I was thrust into fashion all around me. My inspiration to delve into Indian fashion came from my father-in-law, who established the Chhabra women's

clothing businesses in Delhi after India's partition in 1947. In the six weeks I was in Delhi before I had to migrate to Boston to join my husband, he showed me around numerous Chhabra retail, wholesale, and manufacturing establishments. I was in awe, and my father-in-law mentored me every step of the way.

My father-in-law's destiny of migrating to Delhi and establishing the Chhabra brand in Indian women's clothing inspired me to take that dream across the oceans on my migration to Boston to accompany my husband's engineering job at MIT. Coming to Cambridge was an eye-opening experience for me, with just a couple of Indian grocery stores and a couple of Indian restaurants. The Indian-American community traveled to Queens in New York City or Toronto for their clothing and other ethnic needs.

There was a huge opportunity, but it took a long time and a couple of turns for my dream to materialize. Importing Indian wedding clothing from my Chhabra family was the easy part, and I started part-time from home. Our first-generation community was used to traveling to India for their clothing needs, but that changed with the coming of the second generation. I did not have any daughters, and my next inspiration came from my two daughters-in-law. They helped me in designing and styling to the needs of Indian-Americans born here, and for the mainstream American community that started participating in Indian weddings and galas as guests and through intercultural weddings.

My older daughter-in-law opened a boutique called Shelley Chhabra Indian Bridal in 2007. In 2010, Shelley spun off her boutique within the Chhabra family, and it is being operated now by me. I chose Cambridge as the location for my boutique to be near all the campuses, as well as for easy accessibility for young people, and that is where I migrated from India.

What are some of your favorite Indian clothes styles? And what are some trends you are seeing in modern Indian clothes?

The beauty of Indian clothing is its diversity and its dynamism. Indian ethnic clothing styles are in a constant state of flux, ever-evolving and returning to the same traditional styles. The most traditional Indian clothing style is the saree. It is the one style that is typical Indian, and for a long time many Americans who came to our boutique thought that all Indian clothing is called a saree. But that has quickly changed as awareness of Indian ethnic clothing is more prevalent these days in the local society. Lately, sarees are getting pre-stitched to make them easier to wear for the uninitiated. The Lehenga/Choli/Dupatta is the most formal style in Indian attire, and it is the style of

> "The beauty of Indian clothing is its diversity and its dynamism. Indian ethnic clothing styles are in a constant state of flux, ever-evolving and returning to the same traditional styles."

choice for most brides who buy from us. This style has a long history, and like the evergreen saree, it has been the most popular style in Indian weddings. Most of the lehengas that we sell are paired with a crop top. The third popular style for us is the Salwar/Kameez, which is also known to many customers as a Punjabi. I guess because it is very popular with Punjabi women in India. Other styles that are not too popular these days include Anarkalis, the Moghul era fashion that became popular for a few years but is not in vogue now; gowns, which are Indianized Western wedding gowns; and fusion outfits. One recent trend in Indian fashion designs is the sharara suits. This outfit takes the kameez from the salwar/kameez and pairs it with a sharara which are pants that look like a skirt when worn.

What is your next big dream?

My next big dream is to be able to evolve our boutique to meet the needs of families getting married in the Boston area with availability of more wedding-related services and for ample customization of outfits. My aim is to make Chhabra Bridal Wear the boutique to go to for Indian clothing in the Boston area.

Priya Gupta Israni, Lavina Datwani, and Urvashi Mishra

Empowering the Victims of Sex Trafficking

Tell us about your nonprofit: its mission, impact and reach. How do you help the victims of sex trafficking and raise awareness to prevent others from becoming victims?

Priya: I am the president of TAARA (Trafficking Awareness, Advocacy and Rehabilitation Advancement), formerly named IHC FOR HER, which is dedicated to the empowerment of survivors of sexual trafficking through education and vocational training, and keeping our youth safe by promoting awareness of the issue. The sex trafficking industry is a 150 billion dollar industry and ever growing. It's a terrifying realization that it can potentially impact any and all parents regardless of their geographical location. It's a global issue and the access to our children via social media has greatly exacerbated this problem.

Sex trafficking is taking place in every single state of the United States. At-risk people come from all walks of life, irrespective of age, gender, ethnicity, immigration or socio-economic statuses. It isn't just girls who are vulnerable...so many boys and members of the LGBTQ community were being trafficked that we decided to rebrand ourselves to take on a gender-neutral, global identity. Predators go where our children go, so it is no surprise that there are many lurking on social media sites with access to our unknowing children. It is of paramount importance that we inform our youth on the dangers lurking on these platforms and what resources are available to them if they should need help.

TAARA hosts awareness initiatives at local high schools and self-defense technique training to keep our youth safe through our R.A.I.S.E. (Real Action Inspiring Self Empowerment) program. We are also working with Covenant House NJ to provide spoken English lessons and job placement for survivors here. In India, our first batch of 78 survivors from shelter homes in Boisar and Delhi and a center in West Bengal graduated from our Empowerment Program in May 2023. The survivors enrolled were taught basic literacy and numeracy skills along with financial and computer literacy (Excel, Word, etc.). Once the foundational course was completed, based on their aptitude and desire, they took on a vocational course of their choosing. Some graduates chose to pursue positions such as sales clerk, secretary, tailor, entrepreneur, etc. Almost all have been employed with the few remaining to secure employment imminently.

We are so proud of their resilience, ambition, and determination to build a brighter future. TAARA continues to follow their journey and provide financial assistance until they are truly financially independent. If they chose to open a small business, we provided them with the seed money for the endeavor. TAARA's efforts are supported by generous donors. For $1600 or $6/day, we are able to provide the Empowerment Program to a survivor which will change her/his life forever.

How did you start working on this cause, and what have you learned in your work?

Lavina: I serve on the board of TAARA TAARA was born during the Covid-19 pandemic because it became heartbreakingly apparent to the board of India Heritage Center (IHC) that when everything else shut down to minimize the spread of the virus, sexual trafficking, pornography and exploitation rose exponentially. After months of deliberation, the fully-volunteer team at IHC decided to pivot our mission from collecting, preserving and highlighting stories of the journey of Indian immigrants to the United States, to empowering survivors of sex trafficking. I was personally drawn to this cause after learning of the cruelty being endured by children younger than my own

every day. If they are fortunate enough to be rescued, most were taken when they were so young that they don't have adequate skills to gain employment and become financially independent. Many return to a life of prostitution because that is their only means for survival. While there are several organizations which support education for underprivileged children, the survivors of sex trafficking are often overlooked. I wanted to be part of a movement to give them a second chance at life and the gift of choice.

Tell us how others can get involved with TAARA.

Urvashi: As a member of the Board of Directors at TAARA, my role encompasses overseeing both the Empowerment and Awareness programs. Currently, we are actively seeking to host outreach events in numerous high schools across the tri-state area, as well as community centers, town halls, and religious establishments. The purpose of these events is to educate the broader community about the warning signs of trafficking and how to safeguard themselves and others. We are looking for volunteers to assist during these events and help spread the word about our cause. If you are passionate about making a difference and possess skills or time to contribute, we warmly welcome you to get involved with TAARA. Please reach out to us by emailing info@taara.org, as we would be delighted to hear from you and explore how your unique abilities can support our mission.

> "While there are several organizations which support education for underprivileged children, the survivors of sex trafficking are often overlooked."

Leyre Pedrazuela

A Life In Pastry

You are a renowned pastry chef in the U.K., currently the head of pastry for Wonderland restaurants group. What inspired you to get into baking?

I have always loved baking and getting my hands into the kitchen. I haven't got a memory of when it all started. I used to love baking or cooking at home with my mum when I was a kid. When it was time to choose what to study, I never felt like doing anything else – I just wanted to become a professional pastry chef, and so I did.

Do you remember the first dish you ever baked? How would you describe that feeling when you finish baking a pastry?

I used to have a kids' magazine at the age of three, and I remember I loved to make the recipes inside with my mum. I was so little, but these were my first memories in the kitchen. I think I still have some of these recipes hidden at home!

You were a finalist in The Great British Bake Off: The Professionals. What was that experience like? What were some exciting moments you had on the show? What did you learn about yourself as a pastry chef?

It was one of the toughest experiences I have ever had. I spent several months training and taking pastry courses to improve my skills. During the competition, everything went very fast. I feel so happy for taking part in a challenge like this, and to come in second place was amazing.

It was a week when I had the flu, and I was so ill with a very high temperature. On the filming days, I wouldn't talk to anyone to keep my energy. I would spend the little breaks between challenges and the judging breaks drinking hot teas and sleeping. Then I would just push myself to the limit to complete the challenge. It was so hard, and I have never felt so ill and weak in my life, but we did it! We won the challenge that week! I was like dying, and everyone was so proud and amazed with me, even myself. I still cannot believe I did it, and I think I learned how strong we can be when we are focused and we have something to fight for.

Which pastry are you most proud of from the Bake-Off?

I couldn't choose. I'm really proud of most of the things I produced; I put so much love and passion and thought into it. If I had to choose only one, I would probably say the reinvented apple tart tatin. It was a ring of puff pastry, filled with a salted caramel and mascarpone cream, then topped with a caramelized apple spiral and decorated with a green apple spherification, a calvados Chantilly quenelle and apple blossom flowers. It was delicious!

What is your top tip for every baker?

Every baker and pastry chef is different. Do not compare yourself with anyone else, find your own style, believe in yourself, and don't let anyone tell you what you are capable of or not. If you follow your dreams and you fight and work to gain a little achievement every day, you will see the result with time. We all have started in the same position, knowing nothing, so we all have had to learn before we made it right. Little steps every day are what will allow you to grow your skills. It does not matter how long it takes as long as you never stop trying.

> "When it was time to choose what to study, I never felt like doing anything else – I just wanted to become a professional pastry chef, and so I did."

What is your next big dream?

I am constantly dreaming. To be the best I can be every day and to become a renowned pastry chef is my dream. To be rewarded for all the hard work, time and passion I put in every day. Every day I fight and get up to be closer to what I want to be and to achieve.

I am also writing my very first book. It is about quality patisserie recipes also adapted to gluten free and vegan versions, where I not only give recipes, but also explain every ingredient used in the pastry kitchen, and explain how to convert a traditional recipe into a vegan or gluten free recipe, as well as the difference between good quality and low quality ingredients and the importance of high quality ingredients to our health.

I really would love it to be sold worldwide, and for it to be able to help many people, amateurs and professionals alike, to understand patisserie in a different way and to value the artisanal work many talented pastry chefs do around the world.

Neelam Wali

Making Strides for Women's Empowerment

You are the president of Saheli and have led the organization in many important initiatives. What achievements are you most proud of?

Saheli has been part of my life for the last 20 plus years. I have served as a volunteer, an advisory committee chair and now Saheli board president. As the community has expanded, so has our capacity to serve them. Though I have nearly 35 years under my belt as a small business owner, overseeing the workings of a nonprofit organization required me to learn new skills. We serve the public and because of that, there are many regulations that need to be carefully observed. This takes strategy and vision

along with a great deal of heart and soul. Our vision was to maintain the connection of our volunteers, advocates, and social workers to our community members in need. We want to continue to invest in our team so that they can do their valuable and courageous work. We have experienced tremendous growth in our capacity to serve as well in our physical footprint. We are able to serve many types of South Asian and Middle Eastern clients. We can support clients with housing by providing rental assistance. We have in-house mental health counselors and family lawyers. We started offering scholarships in 2019 for clients pursuing continuing education.

How would you like to see Saheli grow in the future?

Despite many gains, South Asian women continue to confront limitations that prevent them from participating in and contributing to their households and society. Saheli is actively working on outreach in areas including engaging South Asians in the foster care system, offering education in gender-based and domestic violence, advocating for laws that help and empower women, and encouraging women to take on leadership roles and participate in decision-making processes by making them understand their financial health.

What does female empowerment mean to you?

Female empowerment to me means achieving the independence required to overcome any struggles which may arise; to learn from and teach one another to stand on your own two feet; and to use your voice to express yourself and in turn empower those around you to speak up for themselves. For centuries, social norms and expectations have held women back, limiting their potential.

How do we foster a culture in which women are treated with respect and dignity and given the freedom to decide for themselves?

When given the chance, society prospers from women's successes and builds healthy societies. In South Asian and Arabic families where patriarchal structures dominate family relationships, females are prevented from reaching their full potential, no matter how educated the female is.

> "When given the chance, society prospers from women's successes and builds healthy societies."

What inspired your passion for women's causes?

Growing up, I was surrounded by strong women. My mother, Jaya, and my Aunt Ratna were my first role models. Though my mother was educated only up to fifth or sixth standard, she is savvier about world affairs and human relationships than anyone I know. At 96 years old, she is still a voracious reader of Hindi and Sanskrit, committed to keeping her mind busy and engaged with the world. My aunt was an educator and a step ahead of those in her generation. She ran her household of three daughters with efficiency and love. I continue to be inspired by my own wonderful daughters, who have proven to me and to the world that when women are given full freedom and resources, they can excel and lead their own lives. I am also fortunate to have an ally and a partner who understands my vision and passion for Saheli's causes. I believe that no one can decide your path but you. It might take a little longer to get there, but the destination is within your control.

Revathy Ramakrishna

Helping the Visually Impaired to Navigate Their World

Vision-Aid is a truly remarkable organization. Tell us about Vision-Aid's mission, and your journey as the co-founder.

Vision-Aid's mission is to enable, educate and empower the visually impaired to live with independence and dignity. India is home to the largest number of blind and visually impaired persons in the world. Despite the many miracles of modern medicine, millions live with incurable vision conditions. Vision-Aid believes that what cannot be cured has to be endured, and aims to serve the population of visually impaired persons through a set of well-designed interventions. Our vision is to create a network of resource centers for the visually impaired, which all offer a comprehensive range of services including assistive devices, rehabilitation, a broad range of training programs, and counseling. Our

mission is to help the visually impaired reach their highest potential.

Vision-Aid started as a small project in 2004 in Visakhapatnam, India, and has grown by leaps and bounds, thanks to the tireless efforts of its largely volunteer team and the generosity of its supporters. We run resource centers in 12 locations in India in partnership with many reputed organizations including Aravind Eye Care, L.V. Prasad Eye Institute, Sankara Nethralaya, Shroff Charitable Eye Hospital, Community Eye Care Foundation and several others. Vision-Aid also works with several blind schools and community-based organizations and helps them to build capacity. The partnership model helps to effectively scale up the program, reaching thousands of visually impaired children and adults, many of whom come from under-privileged backgrounds.

Who are Vision Aid's founders? Who are some of the key people involved?

The founders are Ramakrishna M. Raju (Ram Raju) and Revathy Ramakrishna. Mr. Puran Dang is the chairman emeritus of Vision-Aid. Mr. Lalit Sudan serves as the president of the organization and Mrs. Veena Handa is the vice-chair. In addition, over 30 distinguished community leaders are part of the leadership team. Vision-Aid's ownership rests with the board of directors who are elected every year. All board members and officers serve in a voluntary capacity, so that the funds raised can be put to use directly in the programs benefiting the visually impaired.

How was Vision-Aid born? What was the need you saw?

The idea of Vision-Aid was born because the founders had direct personal experience of visual impairment and the immense challenges it poses. Ramakrishna Raju started losing his vision at the age of seven, as he was afflicted by optic nerve atrophy, a condition which he inherited from his grandfather who was also visually impaired. So, while the vision impairment was a setback, he discovered that with proper support, including assistive devices, training and an accessible environment, these hurdles could be mitigated or even overcome to a great extent. The close and personal experiences with vision impairment got Ram and Revathy thinking about what they could do to give back and make the world a more inclusive place for people suffering from terminal vision conditions, since where there is accessibility, there is no disability.

The Vision-Aid model is to enable, educate and empower. How do you seek to bring this mission to life for the community?

"Our vision is to create a network of resource centers for the visually impaired, which all offer a comprehensive range of services including assistive devices, rehabilitation, a broad range of training programs, and counseling. Our mission is to help the visually impaired reach their highest potential."

The services in the Vision-Aid model fall into three categories: enable, educate, and empower. Programs which enable persons with low vision offer a comprehensive low vision evaluation for infants, children, and adults, and provide them with optical and electronic magnification devices. Depending on their needs, patients who are blind are provided with training, such as orientation and mobility, which teaches navigation techniques that help them to walk and move around safely. Additionally, the centers provide skills trainings such as computer applications, mobile technologies, Braille training, spoken English, and advanced courses such as digital accessibility testing, Python programming, and more.

Roopa Modha

Pulling Success from Adversity

Photo by Dr. Poonam Modha

You are truly a multi-faceted woman. What inspired you to be the woman you are today?

I strongly believe each one of us has a spark within us that requires us to believe in ourselves in order to truly blaze a trail ahead. We need to use moments – both good and bad – as fuel to help that spark turn into an eternal flame of positivity and success.

For me, the road hasn't always been easy or straightforward to blaze my way in life, but I remained determined and driven that I will make it. As a child, I had gotten a major sports injury in my right hand from playing hockey in gym class that turned into chronic pain. A hockey stick had hit my right hand

little finger's growth plate, fusing it and trapping my nerve. The pain was such that I could see only half my visual field and used to be paralyzed in the mornings from it as pain had extended up my arm, down my back, to my right knee. I could barely attend school due to the severe pain. I even had to give up my dream of doing my arangetram (Indian dance graduation) with my sister.

However, in the evenings sometimes the pain would lessen, so I began to take college classes at night to gain enough credits to graduate in time with my class. While my family and all my classmates were my strength and pillars of support, many teachers and even the principal were not. In fact, I had even been told by the principal that I would never make anything of myself. That moment is what turned the spark inside me into a fire within. I realized that the only way one can achieve anything is to trust in oneself to discover inner worth. It doesn't matter if others don't believe in you.

I persevered by believing in myself and recognized that hard work can really open any door for you, even if others think they have blocked access for you. It is also this moment that made me realize I will never let any girl think she cannot make it and will light a way for others. I made it my goal to help other girls rise up and succeed even if no one else believed in them. When someone believes in you, it can change your life. I am blessed with parents and a sister who never doubted me and who always fuel my dreams with their constant faith in my talents.

Thankfully, the pain went away as I stopped growing, and I was able to achieve in many fields. After high school, I went on to get three degrees – AS Honors in computer programming; BS Honors in health: science, society, and policy from Brandeis University, doctorate in jurisprudence (JD) from UConn Law, and two additional certificates in tax law and intellectual property law, and was a commencement speaker at all three graduations. I wanted to push myself so I always took the hardest classes.

Not only are you a lawyer, but also a TV host and pageant competitor. Tell us more about your creative pursuits.

While in law school, I fell into the world of media and entertainment and have had the privilege to emcee and host for channels like Zee TV, TV Asia, Awesome ITV, and IBC Tamil. I have written over 3,000 articles for magazines, newspapers, and blogs around the world. It was during that time when I entered pageants and went on to get many titles (highest title is international). Although many individuals assume pageantry is for the superficial (I am guilty to have thought that before doing them myself), in fact, pageants draw incredibly driven women who are championing legitimate causes into their mix. Pageants allowed me to connect with like-minded women and brilliant individuals I am proud to have as sash sisters.

My parents have always taught my sister and me that whenever we succeed, we need to remember to help the less fortunate who may not have access to the opportunities we have had. As my parents' families are from Gandhi's birthplace, they truly imbibed his philosophy of being the change you wish to see. I have used my voice to speak up for and focus on getting girls quality education. Even while in high school, I helped raise funds to build schools in poor communities abroad. I have been lucky that I was able to help many girls around the world achieve their dreams through my work for initiatives like Girl Rising and Indian Dreams Foundation, both of which I am an ambassador of. For IDF, for example, a social media campaign I spearheaded helped them raise $10,000 in three days. These funds were used to cover full education costs for life for over 30 girls in India.

> "I realized that the only way one can achieve anything is to trust in oneself to discover inner worth. It doesn't matter if others don't believe in you."

The person I am, therefore, is really a reflection of the winding journey I have had and the strength and support given to me by my parents and sister. Through my struggles, I learned to live in the moment and appreciate each day. I also realized to never have fear of failure, and – at the very least – to always attempt to achieve any goal. Take those first steps, regardless of what others may think, and if you can bring others with you on your journey to help them rise too, do so! We all have our own destiny and path, so lighting the way for others won't dim your own light.

Jharna Madan

Preserving Our Cultural Heritage for the Greater Good

You are an inspiring woman and actively involved in the local community. Tell us about lessons you learned in your personal and professional journey.

My personal and professional journey has been transformative, teaching me invaluable lessons about the power of community and the profound significance of giving back. Through my experiences, I have come to understand that by fostering connections among individuals, preserving our rich cultural heritage, and actively working toward social causes, we have the ability to create a lasting and meaningful impact on society as a whole.

I am profoundly grateful for the opportunities I have been given to contribute to both the Indian diaspora community and my local community in New England. These experiences have shaped me into the person I am today, instilling in me a deep sense of

purpose and a strong commitment to making a positive difference in the lives of others. Throughout my journey, I have witnessed firsthand how the power of community can transcend boundaries and unite people from diverse backgrounds. Whether it is through my involvement in Hindi Manch, where I have influenced and touched the lives of over 10,000 NRIs, or through organizing cultural events that have provided a platform for more than 500 children to embrace their Hindi heritage, I have witnessed the incredible impact that community building can have.

Moreover, my journey has shown me that preserving our cultural heritage is of utmost importance. By promoting and celebrating the Hindi language and culture, I have had the privilege of witnessing young adults across New England grow up with a strong sense of identity and pride in their roots. These individuals now carry their traditions and culture openly and with unwavering pride, contributing to the vibrant tapestry of our society.

In addition to my involvement with Hindi Manch, I have been fortunate to contribute to myriad other organizations and initiatives that are dear to my heart. From my role as a volunteer and creator of IndiArt for Ekal Vidyalaya, where I have engaged the next generation in the importance of making a difference, to co-founding Sew We Care and Care For Janitors during the challenging times of the pandemic, where we provided essential support to those in need, these experiences have reinforced my belief in the power of collective action and community-driven initiatives.

In my professional capacity as an interior designer and project manager, I have found fulfillment in shaping the spaces we inhabit. By creating functional, efficient, and aesthetically pleasing workspaces, I contribute to the growth and development of my local community in New England. Collaborating with a diverse range of professionals, I witness firsthand the transformative impact our work has on the productivity, satisfaction, and overall well-being of those who utilize these spaces. The tangible results of my efforts

serve as a reminder of the influence we have in shaping the environments that shape us.

"Collaborating with a diverse range of professionals, I witness firsthand the transformative impact our work has on the productivity, satisfaction, and overall well-being of those who utilize these spaces. The tangible results of my efforts serve as a reminder of the influence we have in shaping the environments that shape us."

In conclusion, my personal and professional journey has reinforced the understanding that the power of community, the preservation of cultural heritage, and the pursuit of social causes can leave an indelible mark on society. I am humbled and grateful for the opportunities I have had to contribute to the Indian diaspora community and my local community in New England. With unwavering dedication, I am committed to continuing my efforts to create a more connected, inclusive, and vibrant society for all.

Nikki Barnes

Driving Change in Public Education

You're a visionary leader with a passion for public education. So tell us more about this journey and what inspired you.

I am inspired by my mother and my ancestors. They are truly my inspiration. I am a descendant of enslaved Africans from Chapel Hill, Durham, North Carolina, and Norfolk, Virginia. My mother and father attended segregated schools and learned from used textbooks that were discarded by the white schools. They always knew education was key and that you had to fight for it. I was blessed to have really powerful black female elementary school teachers, and I loved school. I knew early on that I wanted to be a teacher. And I also knew early on that integration did not fix everything. I knew that, even after the march in Washington, we still had the same segregation and racism living within our school buildings. But I had hope. I had a vision for how schools could look from the young age of 18 years old. And so I went to college to teach. I came back to my hometown as a teacher. I taught for about 12 years. And in those 12 years, I've really worked to be a great teacher, a warm and demanding teacher who integrated what was in my heart and in my mind. And in those years, I learned that teaching is rocket science and brain surgery at the same time on someone's hopes and dreams, and that it is one of the most complex, multi-dimensional bodies of work that anyone can engage in.

I then realized I wanted to lead other teachers, and I found my way to a KIPP school, a charter school that was mission driven, which spoke to my sense of justice that I gained from my parents. And now I find myself in one of the most historical states in our country in Massachusetts, leading KIPP Academy to ensure that our children have what they need to be on a path to a fulfilling life. And all of that goes all the way back to my ancestors and to my mother and the lesson they taught me that knowledge is power. I knew that. KIPP actually stands for the Knowledge is Power Program. And my mom's words still inspire me today.

What are some of the key lessons you've had regarding how education can empower young women in particular? And is there anything that schools and families can do to really empower young women to pursue things like STEM?

Education is historically a female-led space. Years ago, the norm was that the majority of teachers were female, and the principal or superintendent in general was a man. And of course, we do now have female principals, superintendents, and academic leaders. But I do want to point out that public education has historically been a female-led and female-driven career path. I don't think we as a country have ever done education fully right. Education has never really been given what it should be, the understanding and the respect, even to this day. So what I've learned is that education is education, but it's also political. There is no education without politics. And so the role that women have played is that we've had to hold almost a double consciousness that we often talk about in terms of being people of color. Women have had to be smart, strong, demure, strategic and becoming. We've had to do all that. And I've learned that women are powerful and wise, and we probably should be running more organizations, more countries, by the way because we are some of the most powerful people I know. One of the first things we do at KIPP is we have a model of family engagement called co-authorship. And it means we share power with families because the family role in education is significant.

> "We ensure that they see STEM teachers who are women. We ensure that there are teachers and leaders that relate to them. We also honor the voice of the women in their families. We have lots of town halls to encourage collaboration. Finally, we don't prescribe what it means to be a woman."

Could you elaborate on that? How does the family role influence education?

Families should have a voice and decision-making rights. And when families don't have the decision-making rights and they don't like the decision that we've made, we engage in conflict, we engage in disagreement. At KIPP, we see the disagreement as an example, or as proof that we are doing the right thing because we are not pacifying each other. We're not walking around an issue. We are addressing it head-on.

So bringing this back to the previous question, how do we get more girls into STEM? We have strong relationships with their families. We ensure that they see STEM teachers who are women. We ensure that there are teachers and leaders that relate to them. We also honor the voice of the women in their families. We have lots of town halls to encourage collaboration. Finally, we don't prescribe what it means to be a woman. We have women who wear pearls and a silk blouse and a blue jacket. We might have some women who are wearing sneakers and a button-down shirt. We don't prescribe what that looks like. We ensure that our young women have the opportunity to become whoever they want to become. And that they see various examples of women every day that they come to school. And when we walk in partnership with their parents, their parents have a voice. We engage in conflict in a constructive way. This is key to our approach.

Pratima Abichandani

Breaking Educational Barriers

What inspired your interest in finance? What inspired your interest in giving back to the community?

When I started at Harvard Business School (HBS), the popular career paths were investment banking and consulting. I interviewed with many of the prominent consulting and investment banking firms, but fortunately for me, I did not receive offers from any of them. That made me broaden my search, and I discovered the field of asset management. I loved that my performance was very numbers driven with little subjectivity. While I put in long hours and traveled a lot, I had a lot of control over my schedule, which proved to be extremely valuable once I had children. I have learned to be grateful for all the things in life I thought I wanted, but did not get.

As I invested a lot of time and energy in raising my own children, I realized that the educational aspirations of mothers in the country of my birth, for their children, were no different than the ones I had for my own children. My children and I have been winners of the birth and immigration lotteries and have had access to a great education. It behooves me to not let birth become destiny for the less fortunate children who lack access to basic education and vocational skills. Lack of basic reading and writing skills exposes children to predatory behaviors including crime and human trafficking. Malala Yousafzai very eloquently says, "There are many problems, but I think there is a solution to all these problems; it's just one, and it is education." I decided that helping educate young children was going to be my avenue for giving back to society. Pratham has improved learning for 75 million underprivileged children over the past 25 years, leveraging its organizational scale and breadth.

You have worked in the financial sector for many years after your MBA at Harvard. You also served as the executive in residence for Babson College Fund, a program where students are trained to invest a percentage of the endowment. What has been your experience as a woman in finance, and how do you seek to empower other women interested in the field?

When I started at Fidelity after HBS, it was a very testosterone-driven environment. I was one of very few women in the Equity Research Department and the only non-white woman. I never focused on that, and instead concentrated on putting in my best effort, confident in the fact that the numbers could speak for themselves. Most of my male colleagues had pictures of their kids or artwork from their kids in their offices, but I never displayed any personal items because I wanted to minimize the attention on myself as a woman, and let the emphasis remain on my work. Many more women now work in fund management, and I am thrilled to see them successfully manage their professional and personal lives.

I mentor students at the Babson College Fund (BCF) by reviewing their stock research and helping them get their stock ideas into the portion of the endowment they manage. I love analyzing companies and looking for stock ideas, and the enthusiasm that the students bring is a great combination for helping them become better stock pickers. When I started as an executive in residence at BCF about nine years ago, I was the only woman along with half a dozen men, and I am happy to report that we have more women who serve as an executive in residence at BCF. I often have young women reach out to me from either BCF or HBS to discuss careers in the investing field and am happy to chat with them.

As president of Pratham, your focus was on helping underprivileged kids in India. What was 2020 like for the organization? How did it change things, and what were some takeaways and challenges from this?

The year 2020 proved to be challenging, and Pratham stepped up to help children and youth who already experience education barriers. Volunteers and staff turned to a variety of mediums – Zoom, WhatsApp, text messages, even phone calls – offering daily lessons and supporting parents in home schooling. We shared learning activities through WhatsApp, SMS and more with children in 12,000 communities. We also partnered with 14 state governments and 200+ NGOs to share our vast repository of digital content. Our supporters in Boston and across the U.S. have been extremely generous and many have increased their giving to ensure that we are able to keep our organization on the ground in India intact, and education can continue to lift generations out of poverty. This season of giving, let a digital Indian learning village adopt you. Giving brings as much if not more happiness to the giver than the receiver.

> "Lack of basic reading and writing skills exposes children to predatory behaviors including crime and human trafficking. I decided that helping educate young children was going to be my avenue for giving back to society."

What is your next big dream?

I love what I do and I have already won the lottery of life. My dream is to be able to continue my journey of personal growth and use my potential in the best way possible to help myself, my family and society.

Ranjani Saigal

Reflections on Ekal USA's Efforts to Empower Rural Communities During Covid-19

You are the executive director of Ekal USA and the heart of the organization. Tell us about Ekal Vidyalaya's mission to make rural India literate, healthy, and Atmanirbhar (self-reliant), as well as about your personal journey with the organization.

Our mission is to bring literacy, health services, and economic prosperity to 100,000 rural villages in India and Nepal. We work in the places the world has forgotten: rural and tribal villages that otherwise lack viable access to education, basic amenities like nutritious food and reliably clean water, and living wages. Our first intervention was education. We are the largest educational nongovernmental organization in rural India, running single-teacher schools in 100,000 very remote rural villages. We also now are working in the areas of health and livelihoods.

The schools run at the low cost of $1/day. It takes just $365 to run a school in a village for a year. This is possible because every dollar given to Ekal is matched by over $8 in volunteer time. The success of Ekal is due to the dedication of its volunteers. The scale and depth of our work was recognized by the government of India with the Gandhi Peace Prize, the highest award given to nonprofit organizations in India.

My professional career was in educational technology. However, I have also been actively engaged in volunteering for a variety of social enterprises. When my children got off my payroll, I changed careers and joined Ekal as executive director. I was drawn to Ekal because it was focused on bringing education to the most underserved. Education is a cause that is very close to my heart. My father, who was a founding member of IIT Bombay and retired as dean of the institute, came from an Ekal-like school. With my career in education technology, I could also see the new opportunities that technology provides to bring quality education at scale. Since I joined Ekal, we have added digital literacy to Ekal which we provide using Ekal on Wheels, a mobile computer lab. I feel passionate about bringing development to the underserved rural remote areas, and Ekal is a great platform to deliver this service. We now have a presence in many countries, including Canada, the U.K., Australia, Thailand, and others.

Many nonprofit organizations have had to take on new projects and shift gears during Covid-19. What are some key programs that are implemented to achieve your mission and how has Ekal adapted these programs with Covid-19?

Ekal's mission is the holistic development of remote rural villages. Ekal has four main pillars: literacy, digital literacy, health, and livelihoods. We hire local youth and train them to be teachers at the Ekal Vidyalayas (schools). Our livelihoods section provides a variety of skills to the youth in the village and empowers them to become entrepreneurs or fill government or other jobs in the remote areas. Arogya powered through telemedicine brings health care to the last mile. Women empowerment is a central focus for Ekal. Most of our teachers are women who are well trained and are respected in the villages. We have nearly 80,000 women teachers. Our health care workers are also women and the services we provide keep women as a central focus. Our most important skill training is tailor training for women, which allows them to gain a good income while providing a much-needed service in the village.

During Covid, we played a critical role in keeping the villages safe. We trained our teachers and healthcare workers to provide information about the pandemic through wall writing and pamphlet distribution. They were given oximeters and thermometers to test the vitals of those that may have symptoms. We set up a telehealth lifeline to provide teleconsultations. Women trainees from the tailoring centers made masks and distributed them to frontline workers in the rural areas. Over 300,000 masks were distributed. We worked to combat vaccine hesitancy in the villages. Our schools were run in the open and we continued to engage the children.

What are some future goals and programs in the pipeline for Ekal? As executive director of Ekal USA, what is your dream for the future of the organization?

Use of technology to bring higher-quality education through our E-Shiksha initiative in the villages and to bring health services using telemedicine is our next big step forward. Vivek Sharma is working on launching GRANE – Gramothan Atma Nirbhar Ekal initiative, where we are creating value-added agricultural products like high-quality haldi and using the profits to not only provide higher value to the farmers for their produce but also use the profits to make Ekal itself self-sustaining. We plan to upgrade the skills at all our skill training centers to provide greater economic opportunities to the villagers.

"We work in the places the world has forgotten: rural and tribal villages that otherwise lack viable access to education, basic amenities like nutritious food and reliably clean water, and living wages."

Dolly Raja

Leading with Resilience

You were the president of United India Association (UIA) in Boston for 18 years. How did you get started in UIA and what are some of the accomplishments that you're most proud of?

I came to the U.S. in 1985 after I lost my husband to a heart attack. My older brother sponsored me. The Indian community had formed an organization under the banner of UIA and my brother was a member. I was nominated and elected as the president of UIA in 1987.

As the president of UIA for several years, I organized and upgraded the cultural functions such as Diwali, annual picnic, Holi celebrations and more and created collaborations with several other Indian organizations such IAGB and Saheli and provided support and help whenever required. I also became the vice-president and later the president of IAGB. For two consecutive years, we organized the Independence Day parades around Boston Common. The parades included decorative floats depicting parts of

Indian life in different regions; school bands; folk dances; etc.

You went through a major tragedy in life at a very young age. You worked hard and raised a family and also became a great community leader. How did you face the challenges and what is your message to those going through tough times in life?

There is no doubt that tragedy hit me at a very young age. I lost my spouse and was left with two young innocent children. Initially, I was unable to bring them with me to the U.S. and had to leave them behind at my parents' house. I at that time had one mission and that was to take care of my kids and raise them well. I worked at many jobs to support the family while studying at the same time. In the face of all these adversities, I could never forget the other people who were facing difficulties in their lives. I had the desire to reach out to those who had either suffered the same plight or had undergone hardships due to the loss of their loved ones. Nothing is easy in such circumstances and one faces numerous hurdles and oppositions from within the family and without as well.

When I came to the U.S., leaving behind my children, it always irked my mind: was that the right step I took? Could I have waited? It was heart-wrenching to see the innocent sad faces of my kids when I was about to board the plane. At that juncture and on many other occasions, I doubted my own decision. That has been a challenge.

My advice to people going through tough times:

- Do not lose heart; think of all the good time/life you had,
- Think of the people who still need you,
- Always have a positive attitude (difficult but doable),
- Do not show your weaknesses in public; people capitalize on them,
- Remember, when you cry, you cry alone but when you laugh, the world laughs with you.
- Have faith in yourself and in God.

Who is a woman in your life that you truly admire? How do you define women empowerment?

I grew up in Delhi and went to an all-girl's school. We were introduced to Mother Teresa, her work and dedication to society in Calcutta. I was very impressed with what she had done for poor and the downtrodden. She performed a very noble task. The woman I have always admired was my mother, Saraswati Devi Mathur. She was educated in Hindu culture and religion. Although married at the age of 12, she continued her studies and passed the F.A. examination, one of the highest degrees allowed for women during 1915-16 in a small village in Gwalior. Punctuality, detail, adaptability and consistency were some of her strong traits.

Women empowerment is respecting women; accepting women's viewpoints; economic independence; social upliftment; recognition, equality, self-awareness higher education; acknowledging and accepting equality between women and men. Women empowerment is misconstrued as being "belligerent" or "insulting men." That is not empowerment; that is simply being rude.

What is your next big dream?

My biggest dream is to provide an informal platform for women where girls, mothers, grandmothers or anyone can share their grief or a mistreatment or any misgivings without the fear of getting exposed. There are many women who are still verbally or mentally abused, degraded or put down. They have no venue to share their frustrations and have no guidance as to how to handle both men and other abusive women. My dream is to create a very informal, collaborative and cohesive ambience for these women who can contact and unload their frustrations.

> "Women's empowerment is: respecting women; accepting women's viewpoints; economic independence; social upliftment; recognition, equality, self-awareness higher education; acknowledging and accepting equality between women and men."

Manisha Jain

Creating a Village Through a Ripple Of Kindness

Tell us about how Sew We Care was born.

In March 2020, when people's lives came to a standstill, mine took flight in an unimaginable direction. The threat of an unknown virus brought forth severe anxiety and a feeling of helplessness…of not knowing any answers, of not being able to help or make a difference!

I came across a hospital's plea for homemade masks for their staff. I apprehensively stitched my first mask, and to my pleasant surprise, it fit my husband perfectly. It gave me a sense of purpose and satisfaction and I realized that this could be my contribution to survive the crisis facing healthcare heroes and all of us.

I put out a request on Facebook and Whatsapp, urging people to help me with any of the steps of mask making, whether it be procuring fabric, cutting, ironing, sewing, or delivering. I made an instructional video and began to spread the word. Soon, I had countless people join in, willing to help in any way they could. Having evolved in the Covid era, Sew We Care was a completely collaborative, yet socially distanced, process. Everything was facilitated via Whatsapp, like an assembly line spanning across households. Though it was my anxiety that spurred this project, it gained wings through the generosity of community members who kept joining our group, aptly named "Sew We Care" by my daughter. A simple act of kindness created a ripple in the community resulting in a village of selfless service!

You believe in selfless service. Tell us about your philosophy and passion to give back.

Being an educator at heart, I have always believed in creating a difference and making an impact. Teaching academically gifted students for almost two decades, my goal was always to inspire them to use the gift of their intellect toward serving society at large. Inspired by the African philosophy Ubuntu, I strongly believe that the world is interconnected and true happiness stems from putting others before self. "I am because we are. In seeking happiness for others, you will find it in yourself. Do the right thing, try to make it better, keep doing it till you make a difference in the lives of others." Each one of us has unique gifts and talents, and we need to constantly utilize them for the collective good of society, and that is how we build a caring community. Our best achievements happen only when we share ourselves with others and care for them.

You have founded and are involved with various philanthropic organizations like Sew We Care, Ekal, and American Red Cross. Tell us about your involvement /impact with them.

Sew We Care has woven a fabric that brought hope into a seemingly hopeless time. More than 150 volunteers and their families, from 33 different towns, stitched and donated close to 25,000 masks, scrub caps and other PPE to about 250 hospitals, senior centers, homeless shelters, etc. It was extremely gratifying when an NGO near Kolkata followed our video and model and made and donated 5,000 masks. Sew We Care recently sponsored blood drives for the American Red Cross – urging the Indian community to adopt a very powerful way to give back, yet uncommon among the Indian community. This compassionate village continues to serve selflessly through food and clothing drives, homelessness relief, etc.

> "Each one of us has unique gifts and talents, and we need to constantly utilize them for the collective good of society, and that is how we build a caring community. Our best achievements happen only when we share ourselves with others and care for them."

I have been involved in planning and execution of several virtual as well as in-person events that bring communities together and create an impact. Helping manage musical events for Palakurthi Foundation, Din Check, and Triveni School of Dance, chairing the Sangeet Vibhag for Hindi Manch, all help me utilize my creative and problem-solving talent for the common good. My most gratifying work has been for Ekal Vidyalaya – a movement very close to my heart, committed to bringing education and empowerment to rural India. I conceptualized and organized some of their recent fund-raising musical galas, "Dhadkan" and "It's The Time To Disco!" It was truly an honor for me to be of service to Ekal and help create a tribe of kindness!

What is your next big dream?

My dream is not anything well-defined but rather nebulous in nature. I hope I continue to have the courage to take small steps that can have a big impact on humanity. I hope my heart pulls me in the right direction and guides me forward on the path to selfless service. Above all, I hope and dream that we as a society focus not just on individual self-interests but hold ourselves accountable for the greater good of others.

Manisha Sinha

The Academic Pursuit of History

You are a historian currently in the role of Draper Chair in American History at the University of Connecticut. What inspired your interest in studying history?

My father is a historian and so are all my siblings. My mother was an Indian nationalist who only wore Khadi. History was the main topic of conversation at our family dinner table. I guess my interest in history was literally in my genes.

Who are three women in history that you believe every woman must know?

It's really difficult to choose just three, but if I had to I would choose Rani of Jhansi who fought against the British, Angelina Grimke (the American abolitionist feminist), and Frances Ellen Watkins Harper, the black abolitionist feminist and writer. I would also mention other pioneering feminists from around the world. Miraben in India, Mary Wollstonecraft in Britain, Olympe De Gouges in France, and Margert Fuller in the U.S.

What does a day in the life look like for you as a renowned historian and author? What is your advice to budding historians?

My days are consumed with teaching or writing, with meetings in between. My advice to budding historians is: Since history is mainly the stories we tell about the past and ourselves, choose to research and write about a subject you feel passionate about. You will be living with the topic you choose for a long time, so choose one that you care deeply about.

> "Since history is mainly the stories we tell about the past and ourselves, choose to research and write about a subject you feel passionate about."

What are some women's history topics you would like to explore deeper in your career?

I would love to write a history of feminism.

Who We Are

Women Who Win is a leading nonprofit media platform, with a mission to amplify voices of diverse women of all races, cultures, and backgrounds. We are a free and accessible platform, and is a minority women-owned 501(c)3 nonprofit company headquartered in Boston, Massachusetts. We have members in over 80 countries, have shared over 500 stories to date, and have built a community of over 30,000 women around the world. We were founded in June 2020, and this book is a celebration of our three-year anniversary. Thank you for celebrating with us!

We hope you enjoyed the stories in this book. We hope that our stories inspire you, and ignite conversations on diversity, inclusion, and equity. Whether you are just starting your career, launching a business, navigating a promotion, pursuing your education, or working on a new passion project, we hope you were able to connect and relate to the journeys of the women in this book.

We aspire to be a source of inspiration, motivation, empowerment, and enrichment for women around the world, and invite you to join us.

Become a "Woman Who Wins"

Find out more at www.womenwhowin100.com/get-involved

JOIN US

WOMENWHOWIN100.COM/GET-INVOLVED

Interested in sharing your story with us, or want to nominate a fellow woman?

www.womenwhowin100.com/nominate

MEET THE WOMEN WHO WIN BOARD OF ADVISORS

Ami Ambani

Rita Advani

Kathleen Walsh

Dr. Archana Srivastava

Sangeeta Moorjani

Kay Khan

Brenda Thompson Stuckey

Sonica Arya

Dr. Kavita Navani

Dr. Rollie Lai

Anusha Nanavati

Yoshika Sherring

Krupa Sheth

Dr. Dinesh Patel

Dr. Drumil Shah

David B. Alper

Words from Our Male Allies

"It has been both an honor and a pleasure to have been associated with the work of Women Who Win, and in particular Dr. Deepa Jhaveri. Dr. Jhaveri came to me initially as a podiatric colleague, looking to enlist our professional national organization, the American Podiatric Medical Association, to work with Women Who Win in order to provide footwear to people in poor countries. By providing proper shoes, foot coverings and patient information through literature, the goal of amputation prevention could be realized for people who might otherwise lose limb, and life.

Because of the relationship that Dr. Jhaveri and I have developed between WWW and APMA, we have also been able to provide public education materials for various events targeted to the Indian community. Again, this leads to WWW benefiting many people who might not otherwise have access to such important medical information.

Women Who Win has a mission to help get information and supplies to people who might otherwise not have access. Bringing them together with APMA has allowed me to witness exactly how much good WWW can do."

David B. Alper, DPM
Board of Trustees, American Podiatric Medical Association
Surgical Staff (Emeritus), Mount Auburn Hospital, Cambridge, Massachusetts

"The genius and strength of half of humanity has been stifled and chained for centuries. I commend the trailblazing women in this book, not only for their leadership but also for paving the way for the rise of women leaders. Empowering women is better for our society and humanity as a whole."

Bittu Sahgal
Editor Sanctuary Asia

"Historically, culturally, and otherwise, we all have known and experienced women in the form of caring mothers, wives, daughters, sisters, and friends. India's culture of heritage includes three respected goddesses: Lakshmi (wealth), Saraswathi (education), and Parvati (Shakti). All of them help us to value creation, to explore the world, and to make it better.

Unfortunately, women's unmanifested inner powers have been boxed up, like a bird in a cage. It is incumbent upon our society, via organizations, businesses, healthcare facilities, educational institutions, nonprofits or individuals, to unearth those inner hidden spirits existing in women to add value for society as well as inner fulfillment. The organization Women Who Win is making efforts to free that spirit by celebrating successful women and inspiring others."

Dinesh Patel, M.D.
Emeritus Chief of Arthroscopic Surgery
Massachusetts General Hospital

"As an advocate for diversity and gender equality, I wholeheartedly support Women Who Win and their mission. Their dedication to empowering women in various fields is commendable and aligns with the values I hold dear. Through my involvement as a male ally on their advisory board, I have witnessed firsthand the positive impact they make on women's lives and the broader community. Women Who Win is a force for positive change, fostering inclusivity and breaking down barriers. I am proud to be associated with this organization and will continue to champion their efforts in building a more equitable and prosperous society for all."

Dhrumil Shah, M.D.
Family Medicine Physician
Past President, Indian Medical Association of New England

Meet the "Women Who Win" Co-Founders

Shaleen Sheth

Passionate about media and technology, Shaleen Sheth oversees the website, content, and strategic partnerships for Women Who Win. Shaleen is based in Boston and works full time in e-commerce technology. She graduated Magna Cum Laude from Babson College. She is on the Young Professionals Leadership Council for Akshaya Patra, the world's largest mid-day meal program serving schools across India. She was appointed to Saheli Boston's Advisory Board, making her their youngest advisory board member. She was recognized by Massachusetts State Commission for Asian Americans & Pacific Islanders at their annual Unity Dinner, and received a leadership award from Akshaya Patra USA. She received a citation from the Massachusetts State Government for "Leadership in Women Empowerment." She was a finalist for their Digital Women for Good award. Shaleen was also featured on Boston Business Journal's BostInno 25 under 25 List for 2023, which highlights young technologists and nonprofit leaders making an impact in Boston. Shaleen believes Women Who Win provides the opportunity to share stories of women that haven't been heard before so they can inspire and resonate with the broader community.

Dr. Deepa Jhaveri

Born and raised in Mumbai, India, Dr. Deepa Jhaveri came to the States at a young age to pursue further studies. She was determined to study medicine and pursued her path with strength and grit through undergraduate studies at University of Maryland, College Park and onto Temple University in Philadelphia followed by residency at Plantation General Hospital. She is an experienced podiatrist in the Boston area and works at Boston Medical Center in Roslindale and serves on their Diversity, Equity and Inclusion Committee as well as Beth Israel Lahey Health and South Boston Community Health Center. Her accomplishments include being the President of the Indian Medical Association of New England (IMANE) [2023], an organization bringing South Asian physicians together. She has also been co-chair of the Indian Women Physicians Forum. She has been involved in local organizations such as Saheli and Akshaya Patra. Her upbringing in India and migration to the United State as a young girl, gives her a unique lens to view women empowerment across races and cultures. She is very passionate about bringing to light women; their stories, struggles and perspectives. She believes Women Who Win is a platform for empowered and like-minded women to strengthen their network and works to empower both her daughters through the inspirational women in the Women Who Win platform.

Dr. Manju Sheth

A physician with a passion for media, Dr. Manju Sheth is an internist at Harvard Vanguard/ Atrius Health. Dr. Sheth's accomplishments in the field of medicine include an appointment to the prestigious Patient Care Assessment Committee at Harvard Pilgrim Health Care Committee. She served as the President of the Indian Medical Association of New England in 2013 and was also the co-chair of Indian Women Physicians Forum. Dr. Sheth's medical training and practice across three continents gave her a unique perspective into issues that impact women across the globe. This is what led her to serve as the Chair for the Advisory Board at Saheli, an organization that supports South Asian victims of domestic violence. She also served on the Board of Asian Task Force Against Domestic Violence and as a trustee for Indian American Forum for Political Education. Dr. Sheth co-founded the annual New England Health Expo in 2013 to raise awareness around health and wellness related issues that are prevalent in the South Asian community. As co-founder of India New England Multimedia (INE), a nonprofit organization dedicated to empowering, entertaining, and educating the Boston community, Dr. Sheth created the annual New England Choice Awards (NECA) to recognize and celebrate the achievements of the Indian diaspora. Keynote speakers at this event include Dr Laurie Glimcher, CEO of Dana Farber; Congressman Joe Kennedy and Robert Kraft, owner of New England Patriots; amongst others. Dr. Sheth's passion for media led her to create the popular celebrity interview series, "Chai with Manju," an inspiring talk show and podcast sharing stories of South Asian leader with millions of viewers. The show recently celebrated its 10 year anniversary. Dr. Sheth has received numerous awards for her community service including being named India New England Woman of the Year (2011), featured as a "Notable Bostonian" in the Boston Globe, listed in the "150 Women of Influence" by YWCA Boston and named as one of the 50 most influential Indians in New England (2012).

Photo by Dyuti Majumdar

Women Who Win – In the Community

Acknowledgments

This book is the culmination of over three years of story-telling, collaboration, conversations, and creativity. The Women Who Win team would like to thank our dedicated community of supporters – family, friends, advisors, volunteers, mentors, well-wishers, partners, and more – for all of their tireless support and shared passion for Women Who Win!

In particular, we'd like to thank the following individuals:

Dipak Sheth, Vishal Gupta, Aanya Gupta, Myra Gupta, Kavita Navani Dharampuriya, Rajesh Dharampuriya, Sushil Tuli, Navjot Singh, Gouri Banerjee, Usha Vakil, Ushma Roy, Mayank Roy, Anand Chawlani, Ritu Chawlani, Upendra Mishra, Ramakrishna Penumarthy, Ajay Ghosh, Ankita Narula, Rachana Kulkarni, Jaishree Deshpande, Nancy West, Lucy Karis, Tamanna Raishinghani, Priyanka Dharampuriya, Khushee Nanavati, Naisha Roy, Victoria Harding, Gia Katwa, Dia Arora, Amisha Arora, Yasmin Padamese, Vaishali Gade, Ramila Thakkar, Anne Marie Flanagan, Anita Chitnis, Elyse Carmosino, and Sanjay Kudrimoti.

We are also indebted to several organizations who have supported our work, including:

Lions Club of Juhu, Rotary Club of Kolkata, IAGB, India Society of Worcester, Indian Medical Association of New England, Lokvani, the American Podiatric Medical Association, and Atrius Health.

Made in the USA
Columbia, SC
16 November 2024

e78e11c1-1be6-4906-8451-d1e5eec13688R02